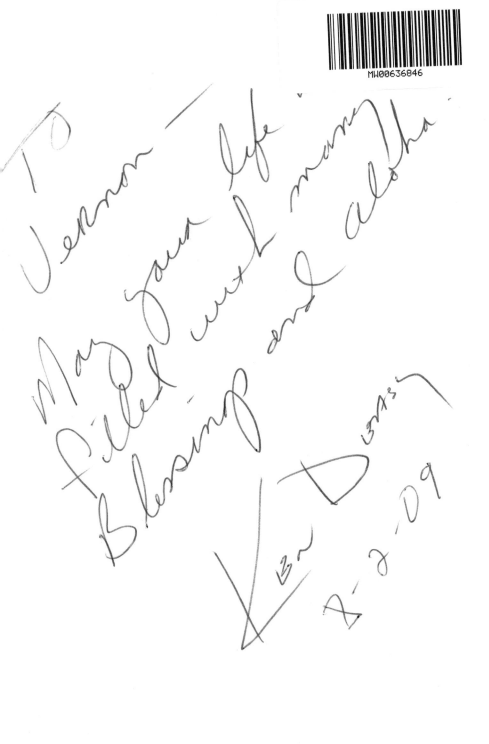

To
Vernon
May your life
filled with many
Blessings and aloha

Ken Dang
8-2-09

GET OFF THE CROSS

SOMEONE ELSE NEEDS THE WOOD

The Experiences of a Roamin' Catholic Priest

KEN DEASY

Dedicated to:
All of us . . .
and I mean all of us!
. . . the hungry poor and the hungry rich.

When people discover their own capacity to give life and hope to others, then they want to give more . . . the power of love rises up.

—Jean Vanier

CONTENTS

PREFACE

It was a buddy of mine who shared with me this awesome pearl of wisdom, reality, shock, and discovery. One day when I was complaining about life more than usual, he said, "When I was a boy moaning and groaning, my momma would say to me, 'Get off the cross, someone else needs the wood.'" So, as I focus on the harsh realities and disappointments of the past (all of which I not only survived but became a good person and man as a result of) I thank God daily for keeping me on course as I have grown to accept that I have not only been wounded (like everyone else) but have been fortunate to receive a distinct calling to become a healer of dreams, memories, and despairs as a result. I focus on those "little slices of heaven" that the Lord gives us to get us off living on the cross, especially those crosses that only we design and assign ourselves.

This writing began in 2002—it is now 2004. When I first began, man was I angry! I am not that person anymore. I am calm. I don't blame anyone for my problems. I am not beating up on mommy and daddy anymore. I am no longer STUCK! A struggle I am having already with writing this is trying not to write a personal journal. That presumes celebrity and an arrogance that I do not enjoy. In other words, you would not want to read this just because I am Ken Deasy. *Wow! I wouldn't want to read it especially because it is written by Ken Deasy!*

Hey! My name is Ken. Kenny Deasy. Betty's Kid. Kenneth H. Deasy. Father Ken. Father Kenneth Herbert Deasy. Padre Kenito. No big deal. Or maybe it is. . . . Everyone's journey IS a big deal. At least this is what I try to convince people of. So, I guess, even my stupid old journey can be a big deal. Trust me! I am not assuming that anyone wants to hear it! Believe it? But you did buy the bloody book, though!

1

Everyone's story is a big deal whether anyone wants to hear it or not. Right or wrong—it's your story. It is your personal book of scripture with your name right on it. The greatest and most exotic trip one can take is into one's own soul. One's past and present discoveries with it are truly a big deal. That is a big frigging deal. Some of the most fascinating journeys I have heard about are from people traveling—struggling from feeling "stuck" in life to being "rooted" in life. It is a major deal!

Upon reading this again, I should tear it up and throw it away. Not because I can't write—but because my perspectives have changed drastically since I began this thing. They will drastically change by the time you finish reading this. It's called "growth." It's called confession. I should rewrite this whole thing and change the title to *I Confess.* Please forgive my lackings. Please forgive my past sins, doubts, and underestimations of self, you and God. Please pray for hope in my future as I do promise to do for you. I will be writing simply about experiences and perceptions. Throughout, I realize that I am not always going to be gentle with my own self, world, church, and God. At the same time, in expressing my experiences I realize that I may not seem loyal or gentle with the Catholic Church which has been my life, my love, home, my family, my cross, my thorn and my salvation.

Please forgive me if this offensive. This is not my intent. I am loyal to my Catholic experience and the salvation it has afforded me. At the same time, I worry about "her." With love in my heart, I care about where she is going and being led.

"What's your name, who's your Daddy? Is he, rich like me?" Along my own personal journey, the way I have been named, and what I've been called is quite significant in itself.

Okay, it is about MY journey and ME. Okay, it's about OUR journey and me! One of the greatest "sins" I experience in myself and in our world is a growing individualism that blinds us to the common good. There is a growing sense of protecting our private property and not wanting to be aware about the neighbors next door. Our journey is not a solitary journey. It is in connection to each other—especially the stranger. But it's not about a solitary journey, though often times it has seemed that way. That *sucks!* It's about our journeys and us. *Yeah! You and I went to different schools together!* It's about a conviction that there is a journey of an "us" and about a hope "that the best of us is yet to come." *Right now I could use an "us" experience.* The only thing about me that is certain, as you will soon discover, is that I am all over the place. This is what happens when a guy is still taking as gospel truth that, as Aristotle taught *(Okay, again with the gospel truth!)* that the difference between a rational being (the human) and the irrational being (an animal) is our ability to wonder.

I wonder like hell oftentimes because it causes me torment. (*I'm Irish! We thrive on torment!*) I wonder like heaven because it is so freeing, liberating, and fulfilling. I am constantly "the wonderer" (not to be confused with being a "wanderer"). I am caught in that search for meaning, being, fulfillment, love, and wholeness. Call it "born again" if you like. How can we not be born again with every single day?! Man, have I made great mistakes along the way! But, I've also kicked some major butt. (Usually my own and my own underestimations!) I have been lost; I have been found. I have been downright exhausted; I have been renewed. I have been sure; I have been confused. I have been connected; I have been totally flipping around like a water hose left to go wildly out of control as the pressure runs through it. But, like a cat, I always land. And if you're really pursuing life to its fullest, and I mean fullest, we just can't avoid the TIMEX philosophy of life: *It takes a licking, but keeps on ticking!*

I always seem to land on my own two feet. Again, like the cat, I have nine lives. And I sure as heck have not used them up yet! I have a long way to go in getting liberated, unstuck, and being rooted—grounded in the "now" and awaiting *(dreading)* the "then" and the "yet to come."

I am also on an intimate journey with others, though I am sure, most don't understand this. I am not a solitary being living in my own world. As I change and as others change, it's the world that holds the other changes. So does the journey; so does my search. This writing will cover a lot of turf as any real journey does. I am not a writer, so, if this treatise is not up to the quality of a professed professional writer—good! I am not a scholar. I am still amazed at the amount of education that I have been blessed to have experienced in my priestly formation. The most I learned, though, in life has not been from books. I am a roamer! Like all of us, I hope to use my experiences in life as stepping stones to tomorrow. The "thens" of my life have certainly given cause and dignity to whatever today has in store for me "now." In other words, we all possess a slice of wisdom that we really should recognize. Wisdom is everything you've remembered after you've forgotten everything that you've learned.

My beliefs are rooted in my Roman Catholic tradition, though my personality is more about being a "roamin' Catholic priest" than "a Roman Catholic priest"! *A Roamin' Catholic Priest! It's got a nice suggestive note to it, huh? It is so true, though.* I'm roaming (and I know this may be perceived initially by you as admitting that I am "flaky"). I hope not! I pray not! I'm alive. I'm fresh. I'm smiling. I'm crazy! I'm searching. I'm wondering. I'm questioning. I'm moving. I'm looking. I'm risking. I'm asking questions. My humanness is my greatest gift to offer in a tradition that struggles with its own humanness. This is so stereotypically and realistically non-Roman of me. I am on a journey that, no matter how often I try to plot and plan it, there are many wonderful, dangerous and risky curves to it. Luckily, I have survived and grown with each challenge.

I tried using an outline to write the following pages. I just can't seem to stick to it as I would a term paper because of the many thoughts, feelings, angers, joys, passions, and depressions that arise in trying to express each stop, event, obstacle, road sign, discovery, and flat tire along the way. You will especially and vividly notice these side steps: back roads, short cuts, and detours off the road to relieve myself, indicated in *italics*. Good God! I just don't know any other way to do it.

What a great thing to be able to write and digest for myself and then share with you: Life connecting with life. Love connecting with love. Touch connecting with touch. The God-within connecting with the God-beyond, the God-among. A "human being" connected/disconnected with his trying to collaborate with his reality of a "human doing." I, personally, have the "human doing" thing down pat. And this is not bragging, but a confession. If anything, I want to be a human "being." I have been blessed with a wide scope of early life experiences that make me appear "lived" and very, very *human*. Being a bachelor all my life, I can cook. Having worked in restaurants during my early years, I enjoy parties when I actually know some of the people at them! Being a volunteer and professional special event fund-raiser for a while, I can throw a party! Because I have tried to escape from home, monasteries, and rectory living, I am an endurance athlete who loves to work out with weights (Gold's Gym in Venice, California), a water skier, a snow skier, a mountain-bike rider, a swimmer, a body surfer, and a guy who loves to run along the beach about six miles, three days a week—I have run four Los Angeles marathons.

I wasn't born a priest and I wasn't born in a manger. My experiences that I use as a priest: I am an auctioneer, a former professional fund-raiser, a former short order cook (since thirteen years of age), a former armored truck driver, a former high school teacher, a former supervisor of the gift shop in Terminal Seven at the Los Angeles International Airport, and a former circulation supervisor at a newspaper in Glendale (i.e., I supervised paperboys). These experiences contribute to my drive to be a preacher (minus the demand for its listeners to be bowing and scraping) intimately in touch with his audience—a teacher who not only knows his stuff but can sell it and motivate—and who oftentimes wanted just to stay in bed. I am a good shopper. I also have been a great thief. One dear lady in Santa Monica calls me Robin Hood. In all, and not above all, I am a priest.

On the "human being level" I am very sensitive. I am very gentle. I struggle with having a good concept of myself. (I am Irish.) Though I often see only the dirt on the window, I basically still see the glass as half full even when it appears to be totally empty. Like most men, I don't know how to say "What about me?" And when I lose my temper, it's exactly because of this lack of admission and the constant curse that comes with being a man—we're never enough. It is hard for me to be objective because I am a right-brain man in a left-brain world. This really comes to a head in being a pastor where you are supposed to be the compassionate Jesus and the businessman Ted Turner at the same time.

When I was a high school instructor, I would have the kids write their names on the back of their papers. Why? Because if I saw the name I could not be objective enough to give them the grade they earned. If I knew the paper was written by a kid who I thought was the son of Satan, I would be influenced not to be fair. If the kid was Mr. Straight A, I would be influenced to continue the same momentum. I usually do okay with this until someone or something that I deem as being a greater power than I is allowed by me (unfortunately) to shake it up. Surprisingly, I am more tormented with my inadequacies than contributions. Pride.

At the same time, I preach and strongly believe IF GOD IS FOR US WHO CAN BE AGAINST US?! From my own perspective, I think that most people see me as a kind and gentle and generous person. Those who would disagree, though, would be many. Now, this is not unusual for all of us. The shared conflict is that most of those who sincerely say they love me (and I cherish that and them) really do not know me. This is especially true on days like Father's

Day. "I love you Dad" is equal to saying "I need you Dad." If you're doing anything constructive in life then people are gossiping about you. As a result, I enjoy a large arena of gossip. *Gossip is like a blank check—it's no good until it is endorsed!* According to the latest gossip, I am having orgies alone and with others—with man, woman, and beast, dead and alive. *I assure you! If I was to do only half of what I am rumored to be doing, I couldn't walk on my own power!*

When "Father" is producing and providing, I am shy about accepting praise and applause. When "Ken" is weak and emotional and wanting, I feel scorned. Though my friends would say, "If you were only giving 50 percent of what you are presently giving, it would be 100 percent more than what most are getting!" I feel that Calvary is one step closer. When I fail, I do so alone. *Hey, no one ever appreciates a flat tire!* At the same time, I remember being at a priest convocation with some padres I didn't know, and having one come up to me and say, "You're not the arrogant asshole that priests say you are!"

Ouch!

I see a therapist. I am so sure this is obvious to you already! I've got to talk to someone. I've got to make sure that at least one person knows the real me before I croak.

I see a psychiatrist twice a week. *I need the meds.* My weaknesses are my strength!

I am spiritual. I am not pious though. I don't believe that novenas are effective towards curing depression and, while I'm on novenas, they are ineffective when offered for unwanted pregnancies. Just the other day, I had a wonderful family come to me whose daughter was obviously suffering from a hormonal disorder. They were taking her to the neighborhood exorcist when, at the very same time, I have a health clinic and connections to some great doctors here with all the means to help this poor girl. I have a spiritual director (a wonderful man who also happens to be an ex-priest who married a former religious sister).

I deal with the fallout of being so passionate. I pray to be more compassionate. I want to be gentler. I want to be less moody. I am a Cancer. I am romantic. I am a Christian. I am way too sensitive. I would be a great father. I would be an awful father. I am a good priest because I am a good person. I am a man called "Father" but, I assure you, I am more of a mother.

Frankly, though, I had no idea that I was having emotional problems until after I was ordained. Ironically, I have become more psychologically, emotionally and sexually mature after I was ordained a priest—which, at the same time, became for me a lifestyle that was discouraging, frustrating, and suppressing.

If I only knew then what I know now. Right?

Frankly, this writing about MY experiences, life, etc., can understandably appear to sound very narcissistic, hedonistic, etc. Well, I wouldn't be seeing the shrink twice a week if I believed I was so bloody wonderful! Frankly, I am tired of the pedestal that comes with being a padre. It is rather lonely up there. I am sharing this story with you to help build a bridge between "the *you* who you are" and "the *you* you should be." This is what a priest is supposed to do. To help you realize that you are blessed. To help you realize that you are wonderful. To help you realize that all God wants from you is to be who *He* made you to be. Sin is striving to be the contrary.

I am a sinner and believe in the message of Jack Benny: "Never talk down to your audience."

Like all things, this writing about a personal journey is very revealing. It is also embarrassing. It is also not easy. I hope it reveals more about a person who is becoming and who has made some terrible mistakes along the way. I hope it helps you get more in touch with the frequent, inevitable, respectful, and disrespectful journeys that inevitably take us to the cross of change, the cross of courage, the cross of changing course, the cross of not being on the cross.

That damn cross! It's about people making sure we remain on the cross. *The enemy!* It's about how we oftentimes chose to remain on the cross. A true sadness. It's about how we choose to remain on the cross alone. A true addiction to despair! It's about how we refuse to carry the crosses of others because we are overburdened with our own. *Actually, though, helping people with their real crosses IS the perfect way to forget about your own.* It's about how our crosses are usually our own *self-made* crosses. It's about letting others have some attention given to their crosses. Finally, it's about how we are on a cross only because we don't deal with our own.

BUT . . . The intent here is not solely about focusing on the journey, the perseverance and the sacrifice along the journey to the cross. It's about focusing on the perseverance and the sacrifices along the journey to THE RESURRECTION—the Resurrection in *this* life. Though there must be dying essential to be resurrected, the dying is not a physical dying. It is a good dying. *There's such a thing as a good dying?* "Dude, you need to adjust your meds!"

The journey, the quest, we are ordained to follow is not the one we've been taught to undertake by the "Church of old." The journey here is about having joy with the faith. It's about not giving power to those who think that we have to stay in our tombs to be "people of faith," especially people who "sign themselves with the cross" of freedom but present it as an affliction. It's about laughter. It's about the total jazz and total high that come with living a real "Christ-centered" (and/or compassion-centered for you non-Christians) life without being geeky, nerdy, and dorky. It's about getting off that bloody cross! Why? Well . . . why not? Why stay on it any longer than you need to? Or, if it's actually a real cross assigned by the Lord for you to endure and grow with, why stay on it longer than the Lord wants you to?

So though you don't know me yet—TRUST ME! You don't have to stay on the cross forever. If you stay on the cross permanently you'll miss resurrection. Jesus didn't stay there forever.

What makes you think you do? Or, who says you have to? I have to admit the sports cliché NO PAIN, NO GAIN is a line of bull! The cross of Christ is a magnificent cross. But I do resent the sentiment that if you're happy you must be doing something wrong. Though we all need to be challenged to be more loving and true to self and others, my only advice to you who are being tormented by preachers and teachers who proclaim that you must be miserable in order to be loved by God, who died for you, don't listen to them anymore! Though there are a whole lot of people who could use a good cross, there are so many good people who are preventing themselves from enjoying life because they think that's a sin. You don't give until it hurts. You give until it makes you happy!

I was taught, and I believed for forty-eight years that God made us "to know, love and serve Him in this life and the next." Wrong! God made us for one reason and one reason only: to love us. When and if we ever realize, accept, and allow that love, we are called to share it, share him, and share you.

If for any reason we need to get off the cross it's because someone else needs the wood. Usually, the crosses we're on are of our own making anyway. If that ain't getting off the cross, what the heck is? It's also about becoming less of a cross to others along the way, along our journey in life, and being a heck of a lot more life-giving and, actually, a joy to be around!

So—enjoy.

—Ken

I'm not depressed! I've just been in a bad mood for 40 years!
—Ouiser Boudreaux in *Steel Magnolias*

CHAPTER
ONE

BEGINNINGS

1960 (6 years old)

"Oh my God, he's not going to get up and do it again?"

I remember saying this as Dad would stand up at church and read in English from the pews (in the absence of a lector) the assigned English reading from the scriptures at a Roman Catholic Mass in Garden Grove, Orange County, California. I also would remember how tired I was because throughout the night before, my mom had screamed from anger and fear—*I couldn't differentiate between these two emotions of Mom.* But what I most definitely do remember is my mother's screaming in response to a beating from her husband *my father* as I would stand around them and beg them to stop. Usually defeated in this quest, I would return to my room fall on my knees and pray for it to end.

By the way, my dad (the lector) stuttered.

By the way, I wet the bed until I was nine years old. A cross of embarrassment rooted in things that weren't our fault. Yet, deep inside, I couldn't stop it!

1988 (34 years old; 1½ years ordained)

"Oh my God, here they come again!" A baby-boomer, white couple, in their late forties, has made an appointment. They were in the marriage from hell. Yet, they are really good people, just not when they were together. He was probably an alcoholic and she was a frustrated woman of the '80s looking for more in life than being an appreciated wife and never-ending mother. Actually, she was still being a little girl deep inside but didn't know it. By all observable appearances, they violently hated each other. They had two young sons.

Actually, I really liked and still like this couple as individuals. Yet, in a relationship they would be the poster-children couple of constant "garbage dumping." They took out on each other all of their unknown/known and realized/unrealized angers of the present and the past—not to mention the burdens of a nonexistent future. Their Molotov cocktails of depression mixed with their respective shame were constantly hurled at each other. Unfortunately, they unintentionally yet knowingly *(because I told them)* also took it out on some other really innocent bystanders: their kids.

He went to Mass every Sunday. So did she. He would hand out dollars bills to the poor. She would come to church daily and cry alone in the pews. They were both such good people. They should have never been married to each other, though. They didn't possess the ability, capacity—and, definitely had never discovered the ultimate purpose in their marriage or their lives. Finally, when this married couple from hell was in my office one day in the San Fernando Valley, an encounter ensued which reminded me of watching a "midget wrestling" match on TV when I was a kid. Yes, the poop hit the fan! I finally got tired of the constant arguing and abusiveness of their relationship at home and in my office. I went wild! Their constant, never-ending defense and deep-seated, old-Catholic-induced psychosis of "we got married in the Church and we will never get divorced because we made a vow" was like putting a match to my keg of gunpowder. As I tried to determine what their marriage in the Church at the time of their wedding meant, another war would inevitably ensue with their bombing raids of accusations, their launching missiles armed with nuclear warheads of disappointments, and their rattling off of their litanies of profanities based on a history of failures that they had experienced in each other.

Time after time, with their persistent refusal of my encouragement and subsequent support for individual therapy and couple therapy (I really didn't think that novenas to St. Jude "Patron for Hopeless Cases" would even help), I shouted quietly from within, "ENOUGH!!! SHUT THE HELL UP!!!" As their pastor and friend I finally and quite sensitively begged the question, "Come on, guys! I am really wondering if you've considered why a merciful God would want to torture you with a lifetime together. *Helen Keller could call this one!* So finally, now, after meeting with you all these times and each time it getting worse, I have one question to ask you: "Please, I beg of you, tell me one good reason why God wants you to stay married?"

Though I was expecting the usual reply that "a vow is a vow," they responded in unison, "We stay for the kids, Father." Ugh! The secretary in the front office fell off her chair when she heard my cry! My response was one finally filled with the nonverbally expressed *explosion* of my complete disgust, rage, and wanting to beat them over the head with the closest statue of Mary or St. Francis that was available. *You want pain! I'll show you pain!*

"Don't do the kids any favors!" I screamed as I also pounded my fist on the desk. I confess that this was not professional. It had become personal, too personal. "Whaaat?" was their shocked response at my fury when I begged them to get a divorce. I continued the defense attack, screaming with a rage like none other, "Don't do US any favors! At this point, I personally resent more what you're doing to your kids than what you're doing to yourself! You're raising those kids in hell, anger, hatred, and fear! You're killing your kids and screwing them up for years to come!" They left my office. I felt terrible. It kills me to see good people choose to live ugly lives. They finally got what would be, predictably, an ugly divorce—about six years later.

The kids since have struggled with alcohol and drugs. One has had problems with the law and has served time. The younger one is starting to get into drugs and skip school, and both have the self-esteem of a Dixie cup. Dad is looking for another dysfunctional relationship. Mom is at the gym and going to therapy once a week. Dad still goes to church every Sunday. Mom still goes to the church daily during the morning and cries alone. They're happy? No! They're miserable! They are convinced that they're on the cross where Jesus wants them to be—just like I also chose to believe for most of my life. But, I am saved. Finally. I oftentimes will see one of the now grown young adult boys. He'll be okay, I think and pray. The other one has finally had his Twin Towers shot down enough to realize that the road he is taking is one of self-destruction. But, his mommy and daddy will save him like they always have. They have to. They're largely the blame for it. His parents, who I am still in contact with, still won't even let on to me what I already know about their kids. I'm sure they take no blame themselves individually because I know for a fact that they still blame each other. It's so much more fun! They sure don't teach you this stuff in the seminary! Life does.

And the kids . . . they'll be fine. They are white and will have ample opportunities for school, lawyers, counselors, therapy, and recovery.

Ah, the cross. I doubt they'll ever really get off it though I am sure their tendency to remain will lessen in time. Sad. They do have a choice, you know. I can only hope for them, as I hope for all of us, that some day they'll get it. Hopefully they'll quit hating the other as a substitute for dealing with their own crud. Isn't that why people watch *Jerry Springer* anyway? "Man! Thank God I'm not as screwed up as those twin lesbian acrobats from Milwaukee!"

"Hope springs eternal," I once heard. For hope to happen I have a little more work to do with this family just to keep them moving forward and not backward. I will need to sacrifice just a little more and give some extra attention to the boys. I really need to call the mom and dad again and see what's up. I really hope that they realize that the promise of "the best is yet to come" is something to believe in when you finally decide there is a life off the cross.

1961 (7 years old)

"Isn't he the greatest!?" is the sentiment I would express within when Dad would drive to the convent and deliver to the poor Irish "habit-clad" nuns a bunch of fruit, meats, and vegetables. "Man, he looks so happy!" I would think while dreading the upcoming evening at dinner with the drinks and cigars which would anxiously lead to an evening of either a hopeful sleep (even though I would surely wet the bed) or another night of sleep-shattering violence.

Why is Dad so happy with them and not with us?—a cross of confusion.

1981 (27 years old)

"Ken, Dad is sick and dying with liver disease," my sister told me. *Chalk up another victory for the Johnny Walker Black, Red, and Green spirits.* "I will take him in until he gets better," my sister said to me during her surprise appearance at a high school soccer game that I was watching. Instantly, my response was, "No, Terry. You took care of Mom when she died. I was in the seminary when Mom was sick and dying. I'll take care of him."

The arrangement was to have her drive him to my house in Covina the next evening. That evening I finally got home late at night and went to sleep knowing that the man I had not seen for fifteen years and who I hoped to never see again would be in my kitchen the next morning.

Man, oh man! Can you even imagine what it was like coming home and knowing that the father you HATED and have not seen in over fifteen years, who beat his wife and ran out on his kids, was now in your house sleeping in your guest room! I could hear him snoring. I could hear him moving around.

At the age of twenty-seven years old, I wet the bed that night.

The last time I had talked to him was in 1974 (I was a twenty-year-old Capuchin Franciscan brother) when I called him from San Francisco at 11:00 p.m. to let him know that his ex-wife, my mother, was dying of cancer. A young woman answered the phone. "Who's this?" I asked. "I'm Mr. Deasy's daughter," was the guarded response. "That's odd," I replied (as I was imagining myself loading one round of ammunition into my .357 Smith & Wesson). "I'm his son! I guess you're the sister I never had! (Pause.) Now, Sis, do me a favor, will you? Have the schmuck call me!" I hung up. One minute later, "You s-s-s-son of a b-b-b-b-bitch," my dad stuttered. The mother of all father vs. son battles (actually it was son vs. father) had finally begun. The exchange of reactive cursing and verbal threats ensued.

I was calling from the friary. I was a religious brother at the time. Did I actually go to Holy Communion with this mouth? I woke up all the friars in the friary. It wasn't pretty. I wasn't pretty. Man, I'd been ugly for a long time. (I confess again and again and again!) Well, one evening while he stayed with me in Covina we were both watching *All in the Family* when the little girl that Archie and Edith took in, Stephanie, was about to receive her bat mitzvah and the Bunkers were about to throw her a big party. During the episode, Stephanie's father, estranged from her years before, showed up at the Bunker house. My father looked at me. I looked at him. He said, "I'm sorry for the pain I caused you and your mother."

He died a few months later. Before that, I couldn't get back to the father-son relationship again while he stayed with me. For me, he had been dead—out of sight and out of mind—for too long. But, at least, when he died we were friends. I failed to forgive him then but should have told him that I did just the same. I kept him on that cross. In hindsight, I didn't even try to understand him. I confess this constantly. I confess this especially every time I am preaching about forgiveness. I failed miserably with my own father. Why could I understand and be persistent with the couple from hell and not with my own old man? If only I could forgive and forget.

God does.

Whenever I preach on forgiveness I can't help but remember how I failed to be an instrument of forgiveness to Dad. Now, it's too late. He was a heck of a guy. He was alone, confused, emotion-starved. He had survived his own parents' death at an early age. He was sensitive. He didn't know how to say, "What about me?"

He was just like me. I am just like him. The feeling of inadequacy and nonappreciation which, for our emotional/male/Irish Catholic makeup, caused a pain like no other. It just did. It just does. But, unlike for Dad, I have been able to overcome it more and more with the professional and spiritual help that would never have been afforded or acceptable for Dad in his day.

And yet I can still get down on myself and believe, "Thank God I don't have a negligent son like he had!" The cross of keeping people on the cross much longer than necessary is a heavy one. Actually, nailing anyone to the cross is a terrible thing.

1966 (12 years old)

"Oh my God, he's not going to get up and do it again?" I remember saying as Dad would, again, demand that we all have dinner together at the Chef's Inn where, without a doubt, my mother, siblings, and I would end up alone at the table while he would be in the restaurant's bar singing at the piano. He didn't stutter when he sang.

Funny thing, though, is that as I kid I recall saying, "Isn't he the greatest?" when he would be asked to MC the parish's social night. He would come dancing and prancing onto the stage with a big stogie in his mouth. "Your father is just like Jackie Gleason," people would proclaim. "He should be!" I would think. He makes us all sit there in the living room (a Saturday evening obligation) in front of the black-and-white tube and watch *The Jackie Gleason Show* with the June Taylor Dancers, "Crazy Guggenheim," etc. I loved how Jackie Gleason at the opening of the show would take a sip of coffee delivered by a beautiful buxom gal and respond with a from-the-belly exclamation: "Woooooow!" Especially, afterward, while taking a drag from a smoke he would proclaim, "How sweet it is!" Dad would laugh, laugh, and laugh. I am embarrassed with how I really hated him then, especially when as I write this I feel nothing but empathy. I used to say, "If people only knew the hell he would put us through." If only I was sensitive enough to the hell he was going through.

Here is the cross of being the life of the party and the cross of not laughing enough. Here is the cross of being "poor Kenny" while poor Kenny should have been sensitive about "poor Dad."

1973 to the present

"Father Ken," the requester would initiate, "can you emcee our auction of one hundred items on a Saturday night?

"But I have five masses on Sunday!"

"Can you tell us a joke? Can you emcee the cardinal's tenth anniversary celebration as the archbishop of Los Angeles? Can you host a dinner for the pastors and their secretaries?" *I can do wonderful retreats and spiritual talks, you know!* I love doing those things. I love making people laugh and feel connected. How human! How unpriestly? How Dad-like. And Christlike? You betcha! Jesus did his best stuff at parties. No one enjoys a good party as much as I do. No one. No one enjoys throwing a party as much as I do. No one. Especially when everyone is meeting new people, just getting along and enjoying each other's company! Isn't it great to have a meal where everyone is focusing on each other and not on the horrendous floral display in the center of the table that is blocking everyone from really seeing each other?

When I arrived at my parish in Mid-City Los Angeles, I was so unaware of the tensions that have existed between the two cultures of Latinos and African Americans. At the same time, though, I discovered that the Hispanics and the African Americans *really* do not get along because they simply do not know each other. It's easy to understand. They are uncomfortable with each other because of demeanor and language typical to each culture. Why don't they like each other? Why don't they work together? Why don't they want to be together? Why don't they laugh together? How are we going to get everyone to come together? "Good, God," said I, the white boy, "they have more in common with each other than not in common." How can we get them together and discover the wealth that they can lend to each other? Prayer? Novenas? Masses? Rosaries? Workshops?

No. No. No.

Parties?

YES! YES! YES!

It's not so much that the folks in the parish did not like each other. They just were not used to being in each other's presence and feeling comfortable at the same time! You can go to endless workshops on how to culturally integrate diverse communities but the bottom line is if people are uncomfortable—it ain't going to work. What do these good people have in common? Well, one thing is certain. They've got to eat!

I'm a terrible pastor (i.e., CEO) but I am a good cook, cleaner, and servant. The perfect metrosexual! (Metrosexual: a man who exhibits creative, fashionable, and other "feminine"-type charms while retaining his masculinity.) Thank God I can whip up a meal for two hundred when I have the time to shop and cook. Thank God I know how to bartend and make a stiff drink. Thank God I know how to set a table. Thank God I know how to entertain. The cross of making my dad his cocktails has turned out to be a tool of resurrection when I bring people of the parish into my house. The cross of having to work in short-order restaurants before and after high school because I had to pay my tuition has turned out to be a tremendous tool of hospitality and welcome. The cross of having to set the bloody table all the time because of my experience working for a caterer has paid off today. The cross of watching my old man sing, dance, and laugh while intoxicated at the local pub or neighborhood parish dance has paid off today because I have the same charisma.

These are no longer crosses! These are tools of causing resurrection! *Jesus, these five thousand people are hungry. Who's going to feed them? Jesus' response, "Feed them yourselves!"*

At the parish we don't have feedings for the poor. We have "meals." We don't have buffet lines dishing up the slop; people are served and the servers sit down with our guests. We provide meals for people; we aren't feeding the fish. Today, our diverse community of the Spanish speaking and the English speaking, of the legal and the illegal (illegal immigrants), of the gays and the straights, of the elderly (the older) and the young, of the Catholic and the non-Catholic—all come to celebrate together! To confess! To be healed. To heal.

In 1998 the *Los Angeles Times* called it a miracle! I call it "Jesus did some of his best stuff over a meal," and so did my father. Thanks, Dad! I think I am a very sociable and likeable person though I am as screwed up as any other guy. I'm very much like my father. The difference now from then is that I had permissions he didn't have or was allowed to use to assist me in my journey. He didn't have permission to see a shrink, seek help with his drinking, admit failure, admit fear, and admit confusion—the cross of knowing too much too late, knowing what you know now and wishing you knew it then—the cross of being a man with all the stereotypical stuff that comes with it.

1961 (7 years old)

"Oh my God, he's not going to get up and do it again?" I would initially think when we would have to get up at six in the morning and go to church and join up with those old Christian soldiers of the parish. *They must have been at the most forty! God, I take it all back!* These good old boys were there every first Sunday cooking those God-awful Holy Name Society breakfasts (green scrambled eggs and purple ham). Yet, I would observe, Dad was much happier doing this type of work and more appreciated than when he joined us at the house in Garden Grove. When he wasn't cooking for those Holy Name Breakfast Sundays, Dad would be cooking breakfast at home after Mass. It was at this time that he taught me how to cook in the first place. To me, he didn't enjoy it as much. Inevitably, he would suddenly "disappear" after our Sunday breakfasts abounding with French toast and, dare I forget, gin fizzes. He would then disappear for the day. (To this very day, by the way, my drink of choice is gin and tonics—Tangueray or Bombay only, please! Gilbey's? I don't think so!)

Dad felt connected, appreciated and safe at these church functions. He felt celebrated. He was in the furniture business. With his personality he could persuade you to buy anything. *But he could not dissuade the guys that came to evict us from our home in 1967. He was powerless over the guys that confiscated our two cars for repossession.* Church was his family, his home away from house. He was safe there. What he had to offer was appreciated. He was really loved there. They didn't have to live with him and he knew it. In hindsight, church was probably the only place where he was safe and received a break from the hardships of his day, the ghosts of his past. He was safe from guilt (being sorry for what he'd done). He was safe from shame (being sorry for who he was). Boy, it was great seeing him off his cross. Why did I choose to resent him for as long as I did? I didn't know. I couldn't have known, but it sure had been easier and more dramatic blaming all my crosses on him. Life goes on.

From 1967 and on . . .

Bob Bavasi was a great guy from a great family. We would do so many things for others together. Man, we owned our seventh grade nun, Sister Bertrand, and we were partners of business in initiating events for the Boy Scouts, for Mother Mary Kilian, and for our class. We just threw our eighth grade class's thirty-third year reunion. Bob and I worked perfectly together on this.

Rob Johansing. What a great guy. What a great family. We were classmates and he lived up the street from us growing up. He was also at our thirty-third year class reunion. "Ken," he confessed, "I had no idea what was going on at the time at your house. My dad would tell me, 'Be good to Kenny Deasy. He's got it rough.' But I didn't understand what he was talking about until much later. I'm sorry, dude." *Take it easy, Rob. You were only twelve years old, for God's sake. I didn't know what was going on either!*

Rob and I would build forts wherever a hole could be dug. *Deasy is still looking for a home.* He was into rocks. I was into building fortresses of safety and hospitality . . . adorned with pinups of

Playboy Bunnies. I would love to go over to his house on Saturday and watch the ball games with his father, Harry, and his brother, Bruce. We would inevitably go to Finch's Frostee Freeze for burgers and taquitos. Finch's was a great hideout. I ended up working at Finch's as a short-order cook for over four years.

St. Bede's parish—what a great church. I buried my mother from that place in 1974. What a great family. I ended up being ordained a priest there in 1987. The pastor at the time was a monsignor known as "The Monz." He was a character. He always was a character. He died sick and disgraced while under investigation for child abuse at another parish. I don't know anything about what he did in his past and can't believe he ever intentionally harmed anyone. Yet, twenty to thirty years ago a priest had no permissions, empathy, or resources to admit and receive help. Just like my old man!

When I would be home in the rectory when sprung from the seminary he would host these Saturday night dinners and I lived for them. No excuses were accepted for absences. Just like being at home for the family meal. *(Do people still have family meals?)*

St. Francis High School—what a great school and a great family. From here I learned everything about being an organizer, empowerer, and good friend. I ended up being the write-in winner for school athletic commissioner, and I wasn't even a jock. This was revolutionary! The high school was run by the Capuchin Franciscans.

I discerned at an early age a calling to the priesthood and eventually entered the Capuchin order in 1972. What a great group of guys the Caps were. There were some total "not so nice guys" though at the same time. Actually, they were good guys. The formation program was not nice, relevant, and good for me. I take responsibility for staying as long as I did, but, man, I loved that cross.

For five years I was in the Formation program of the Capuchin Franciscan order. This included one year in the novitiate and four years in college in the California Bay Area. I achieved close to a 4.0

grade point average which was a huge achievement from this 2.5 GPA high school graduate. After getting my first college degree at the Graduate Theological Union of the University of California at Berkeley—a BA in philosophy—I was exiled from the seminary along with one other friar to do apostolic work! I was delighted to get the hell out of there for a year. I was sentenced to a year of apostolic work at St. Francis High School, my alma mater. This exile ended up being a heaven-sent gift for me as all former and future initial crosses would be. Hard work and community! It was home and I was never happier; this was the whole reason why I entered religious life. But, I really did not want to endure eight years of academia until I could work. I am a worker. The provincial at the time gave me a second year at the school upon my request—again, a tough and wonderful year of hard work, community, and home. When I was told that I had to return to Berkeley and continue my seminary training for priesthood (i.e., formation) my response was "And why would I return to hell? No freaking way!" So, on that last day of June 1979, after proctoring a final exam before summer, the school bell rang, I collected the test papers and left them on the desk, took off my habit, got into my used but "newly purchased" *Exorcist*-green Volkswagen Rabbit, and drove off to the apartment that I had rented earlier that week.

Ah, my goodness. In spite of the good and bad times, I can honestly say that these "families" were great communities that I try to model mine after, now, positively and enthusiastically. Some say I am pretty good at it. I even think that I am good at it, though I seldom feel that I am part of it.

Please notice that with each of these "family experiences" I sought to connect to them by giving 100 percent of my self. Though some of the above would be total joys, others also had many character-destroying memories of disappointment, abandonment, and betrayal. This is life, I suppose. But some of these people of my past literally took my soul and stepped on it. Yet, the funny thing is that I don't resent them for it. They just didn't know any better. With all these "experiences of pseudo-family," I entered, stayed, moved on, etc. There were so many times that I felt stuck and had to remain to prove something. That I was right? That I was good? Eventually, time would tell, I was not stuck. I will not be stuck only because I cannot be stuck!

For Dad, though, he was stuck. Finally, he decided to uproot himself. He made a good decision to move on. He left his family. He didn't leave us high and dry because he had nothing to leave us. The way he chose to leave us, though—as the old protector of the Grail said to the poor guy who picked up the fancy, diamond-adorned chalice in *Raiders of the Lost Ark*—"he chose poorly."

The man who demanded that his kids have style and class could not have enough class to just tell us the truth that he couldn't do it anymore. He didn't know how. We wouldn't have listened to it anyway; poor guy. We were delighted when he finally divorced Mom. He didn't even show up at the divorce proceedings. He couldn't I suppose. I can't blame him. He couldn't admit his failures. *Unlike the rest of us, right?* The cross of Christ is inevitable. Yet, Jesus does not want us to hang on it any longer than we have to. But, also, make sure you don't get off it any earlier than it was designed for.

1958–1960 (4 to 6 years old)

"Oh my God, he's not going to do it again?" I would cry to my mother when Dad would fall asleep drunk in front of the fireplace. "Santa Claus is not going to like this! He's not going to be able to deliver our presents when he sees Dad like this." (Dad drank and ate the traditional glass of scotch and two Abba-zabas that he would leave on a plate for Santa.) It wasn't until I was sixteen, by the way, that I realized that the traditional Santa's meal was supposed to be milk and cookies. The next morning, I would be so excited for all that Santa left me while never realizing that Dad was Santa. Poor dude never got any credit. The cross of not winning even when you're the champion is a hard cross to accept.

I never said thank you to my parents. Not once do I ever remember saying thanks, at least, for trying, and you actually succeeded! "You did your best. You really tried your damnedest during some tough times and after some tough calls." I wasn't a spoiled kid. I worked hard to help with the bills, the rent, and tuition. Mom and I would go out to dinner on a regular basis and I would flip the bill at the age of fourteen. Working has always been for me and will always be a good escape/release from my own self-afflicted and other-afflicted torments. For me, achievement was the key to being a man.

DOING = SUCCESS

SUCCESS = APPROVAL

APPROVAL = LOVE

If hell was ever made for anyone it was made for the schmuck who said, "The more perfect you are the more lovable you are. The less perfect you are the less lovable you are."

This shows itself in men living by other empty creeds: (a) The one with the most toys win, and (b) never ask for directions; just keep on driving until you get there. So what if you have to go to China before you find the house three blocks away. Think about it. We really rule our lives by this motto. To confess is to admit fault. To admit fault is to admit imperfection. To admit imperfection is to admit that you are not as lovable as the other guy who is seemingly more perfect and/or successful. Man, that really is isolating and causes a painful sense of real aloneness. It's unreal! So my question is why do we do this?

Thank God men are getting their faces done up these days while walking around with purses, having manicures, and eating quiche for lunch. It is a sign of freedom and being self-assured. Doing this stuff is no longer a "chick" thing. So what do we guys do to compensate for this conflict, confusion, and/or tension? We overcompensate for everything. We think that bigger is better, more powerful. (Look at the church that men have built. Big! Expensive! Ornate! Cold! Uncomfortable!) The most expensive is the most revealing. It's the object of a gift, which is more important than the sentiment behind the bauble. Men love Hallmark cards because they can't say it themselves. This is probably also why the men of the church need to have every prayer written out beforehand, and any sense of self-disclosure would be un-Catholic and unmanly.

I can remember during my ordination rehearsal when the cathedral master of ceremonies said to us, "When the Cardinal says, 'Let us pray,' at the invitation before the Opening Prayer; you are to bow your head *as if to pray!*"

Today, even I am constantly overdoing it by overstating my need for glory and appreciation. I CONFESS! A good example is when someone does something good for me and/or the parish. I just feel that I cannot say thank you enough in overreaction to the way the institutional church doesn't convey thank-yous or positive affirmations.

Or I just don't believe that my appreciation is worth anything! *If they only knew me.*

I believe that not affirming people enough is one of the main problems today. We either (a) look at a gift horse in the mouth (Nice presents under the tree, Dad. It's your job, by the way!); (b) demand a gift (which, subsequently, demeans the gift into payment/reward; a gift is never earned); (c) focus on the object that is the "gift" rather than the gesture behind the gift. *(No jewel or ruby could ever equal the love I have for you)*; (d) we are so into our own needs that we wouldn't know what object/gesture of giving would really be meaningful to the recipient *(like the guy who buys his girlfriend roses when, actually, the seven other times he did, she told him she was allergic to them)*; or (e) don't know how to receive a gift. The best part about giving a gift is how it is received. I can remember times when I would be so excited about giving the gift that, after it was received by the lucky person, you would have thought by his/her expression, or lack thereof, that I just pulled the plug on the life support system of his/her favorite aunt.

So, since when did giving a gift, a real gift, become risky, threatening? When it became a real and more revealing expression of your self and your feelings while also accepting the vulnerability that comes with being accepted, rejected, or disappointed.

How many times in our history of so-called gift-giving have we actually convinced ourselves that we were giving the gift out of love and care when, actually, what we were doing was baiting the recipient to respond to our own needs for affirmation/reassurance in some profound and probably intimate way? In other words, we were expecting repayment for the gift by being reassured that we were okay, or this would lead to me getting something in return rather than just giving for the sake of giving. I mean, come on! How many times do we say, "I love you," only to hear "I love you, too!"

This is the cross of knowing, whether Dad hears me or not, that I now love him and am left with the conflict that this expression is way too late in coming. This is a hard one. I know how he felt now.

1960 (6 years old)

"Oh my God, he's not going to do it again?" When I was about six years old Dad bought a bicycle tire pump. Cool! I'll help out Dad and pump up the tires on the car (which didn't need it). As I screwed the pump's attachment onto the tire's nozzle, I was shocked with all the air that was coming out of the tire. "Air's suppose to go in! Why is it coming out?" I ran for my life and quickly forgot about it while playing with the other kids. "Well, at least I tried to help," I remembered assuring myself!

"STOP IT, DAD!!! OUCH! THAT BELT HURTS! THAT FIST HURTS! THAT ROD HURTS! THAT WALL THAT YOU LITER-ALLY THREW ME ACROSS THE ROOM INTO—IT HURTS! OKAY! HELLLLLLLP MEEEEEE, SOMEONE!" I screamed. "HE'S COMING BACK FOR THE SECOND ROUND, THE THIRD ROUND! WHERE'S MOM?" I recall thinking as I was being thrown in the air across the room, crashing into the wall for the second time.

"Thank God tomorrow is school," I would say to myself in my childhood. It was safe there at school—St. Columbans in Garden Grove, California. I could go take a nap in the church. It was quiet and safe. God was there. I quickly figured out how to light the votive candles in front of the statue of the Blessed Mother. I remember how cool I felt when I had the art of lighting matches down to an art. I would get some pennies in my pocket in order to make the appropriate CLANG into the coin slot before lighting the thirty to forty votive candles. The Irish Sisters of Charity at St. Columbans were really cool to me. Father Garrity could really kick that ball so high. I couldn't wait to serve Mass. Why were they treating me so special? Why did they keep referring to me as "poor Kenny Deasy"?

Sister would ask me one day after a rough night at home, "Where did those black and blue marks come from, Kenny?" The Irish sister (with that nun smell that I thought was the smell of religious sanctity. *It was body odor*) with the parish nurse now said, "Lift up your shirt will you? How did you get so bruised, Kenny?"

"Dad was mad at me last night" was my response (loving the attention and care given to poor Kenny).

"Your Dad? Mr. Deasy?" Yes. "You better go to class now; you don't want to be late."

"Can I go and sit in the church?" It's safe. Jesus is there. Mom loves going there also to cry all day long. Maybe, even better, Father Garrity will be there! Maybe he'll ask me to be an altar boy though I'm only in the second grade! In second grade I would absolutely marvel at the young God, Father Garrity, who could kick a kickball higher than anyone I had ever seen. I also vividly remember he went home to Ireland. I also remember quite vividly when Father Garrity, while in Ireland, died from cancer. He was twenty-eight and ordained two years.

SLAP!

"Kenny Deasy, why did you light all those candles? Why are you in here? You should be outside playing with the kids. It's recess! Go outside before I box your ears!" the nun screamed at me while giving me a good whack on the back of the head.

"Okay, I'll go outside." They were picking teams. As usual I wasn't picked.

Weeping!

"Dad, no one likes me," I would convey looking for comfort. His response, "Kenny, that's impossible. Not everyone has met you yet!"

Hardee-har-har! At the ripe age of seven I thought that Dad was funny as hell. I have his sense of humor! Thank God tomorrow would be school, again. Safety, away from home—the cross of being sad, and still faking that everything is okay.

1999 (45 years old)

RING, RING—"Kenny Deasy," the Irish, female voice proclaimed then identified herself. "I was one of the nuns at St. Columbans who learned your whereabouts after a newspaper article appeared on good ole Father Ken. I'm calling after all these years to say I'm sorry to you for something that happened almost forty years ago that came to me while reading about you in the paper." Confused, I replied, "I don't understand."

"I remember those bruises on your body that day in school. I'm sorry. I didn't know what to do."

"You've done more than you can imagine, darlin', by just admitting it and calling me to say 'hey.'" This is a good example of the cross of remembering and, once meeting that cross, having the courage to be freed of it.

1967 (13 years old)

"Oh my God, he's not coming home again?" We would be sitting at the table never knowing if Dad was going to come home. As we were finishing up—CRASH! Mom would look up and say, "Your Father is home," as she would react to Dad driving into the light post again at the entrance to the driveway. We would react as if we were performing a well-rehearsed play. This had become a regular occurrence. He'd show up late with a few drinks already under his belt while we were finishing dinner. We would have to hurriedly reset the table and eat again. It was better than having another sleepless night. One lovely evening at the table came the announcement about my brother. Dad was mad again and, while intoxicated, made the proclamation, "You adopted bastard!" My brother is adopted? That explains everything! No wonder we don't get along. No wonder he's different. Boy, did he get screwed getting adopted into this family! This is the cross of being mean/nasty in reaction to life being mean/nasty—those who hurt—hurt.

2001 (47 years old)

Abuse. It is such a strong word. It covers such a broad amount of vulnerabilities, dimensions of life, world history, local history, socially acceptable abuse, illegal abuse, sexual abuse, character abuse, financial abuse, and trespassing. Forgive us our trespasses . . .

Though I get "shrinked" often to get relief from the abuses inflicted on me by the past, with each day of my own healing also comes a new discovery of someone being abused, somehow, somewhere, by someone of our time. I just don't understand it. Wounded wounders.

One of my greatest gifts and one of the greatest curses placed on me is feeling the pain of others. Oftentimes, I hit the sack at night feeling that I have been totally inadequate. I don't know how to fight, though I'm a fighter. I don't know whom to fight, because I am not patient enough. At the same time, I don't want to fight whom I should be fighting, because I am a coward and they are not supposed to hurt others. I oftentimes just don't have the energy to fight, because I am already tired from fighting all day; especially fighting myself and fighting off the baggage from the past—*the waxy, yellow buildup of the old Catholicism.* I am limited. I am imperfect. I don't know how not to be. I shouldn't even have to worry about this! But, no one likes a water heater when it doesn't work.

The cross of having been assigned the role of being a pseudo Messiah because of my profession and my life story—I am really good at it when I can focus on one fight at a time, though. I guess it's enough that I just try. As Woody Allen supposedly said, "90 percent of success is just showing up!" "Lord, take care of your church, I'm going to bed!" is a good prayer. It's a great prayer.

Humility is being content with who you are and who you're not. But I just wish people weren't so complacent. "How can people sleep at night?" I often wonder. If only people knew the power that they have to help the helpless! If only the helpless knew how powerful they are to teach us. You think faith in God is a tough one? Faith in one's self is much harder. Why? It's because we don't have faith in ourselves that we fail to have faith in the goodness of others and, consequently, are threatened by the stranger or the oddball.

I can remember reading a story about what happened in San Francisco in 1989 when the earthquake hit hard in the Marina

District. People were homeless. People who routinely had fought to rid their streets of "these bums" (homeless people) had no place to take shelter from the elements of this shaker of an evening in the Bay Area. It was those very homeless, the stranger who was at one time the threat, the enemy, who helped those with houses (not necessarily homes) through it all.

Take and drink. ALL of you. Do this in memory of me.

1967 (13 years old)

Thank God school is tomorrow! Thank God tomorrow is Boy Scouts! Thank God I am helping the nuns tomorrow decorate their Christmas tree! Thank God I am rehearsing for Christmas Midnight Mass! Thank God that I'm always picked to do the job when there's a job to be done! Damn I'm good! As long as I can do—I am good. They really love me. They really NEED me! I can do anything. Yeah, that's it. DO and be loved! Thank God! I have found the secret—do for others and you will be loved! WRONG.

The cross, which eventually led to another resurrection, is a result of feeling the permission to actually accept that I have needs also. The need? To be one's real self and to quit being whoever others want me to be. A hard one for a guy trying to adapt to everyone! This had become a very unhealthy pattern of my life and, thus, quite exhausting. I couldn't say NO. I couldn't say YES to myself.

2001 (47 years old)

The theme for our parish is "We will make this house a home."

It's life that teaches you about being a good Christian and, subsequently, about being an affective parish priest. *(Wait! I'm an American man! Aren't I supposed to be effective?)* The seminary really teaches you nothing practical about being a parish priest. It doesn't encourage work. It doesn't focus on relationships. It is exclusive and removed from most normal reality. It teaches theory and theology. It teaches a wide range of stuff that a parish priest seldom uses in a parish experience. It seemed to be interested in forming theologians (i.e., making faith understandable) and not servants ordained to minister to the people who, seemingly, need continual reassurance that the Lord loves and that they are lovable. I used to often think that they underestimated Catholics as simple people burdened with the ultimate Catholic Question: "Does this Saturday wedding count for Sunday?"

During Leonard Bernstein's Mass *I remember the adage, "I believe in one God. I believe in three. I'd believe in twenty gods if they'd believe in me!"*

Why seminary courses such as soteriology, eschatology, ecclesiology, systematic theology, fundamental theology, etc., were mandated in order to be ordained a priest today continues to baffle me. Actually, the content of these areas of theology was fine if you wanted "knowledge for knowledge's sake." But, we were not taught to apply the theology to ministry. Theology was taught in the same manner that history was taught when I was a kid. Know it! Give it back on a test! There was no attempt to make it applicable and relevant in ministry.

Frankly, if I was the servant-king, the two necessary requirements for candidates to even be accepted into the formation process for a diocesan priesthood would be: (1) You're a nice person (i.e., you possess a basic pleasantness about yourself when among people); (2) you like people. (*You would be surprised.*) (3) you're a hard worker; and (4) you've dated and are capable of relationships (and, preferably, not a virgin). *Sinners need apply! Holier-than-thous—don't call us—we'll call you!*

It was after being sent to St. Agatha's in Los Angeles, an inner city parish in the "hood"—following a five-and-a-half-year assignment in Santa Monica where the parishioners were extremely nice but where the rectory life was hard for us all—that the most major epiphany of God, self, and world was to occur. At the very get-go—

from day one, when I showed up to say my first Mass in this parish of strangers—the people who were the "in crowd" were so welcoming and loving to me. They didn't even know me! Though I wasn't black, though I didn't speak Spanish, though I had no idea what being an African American or an immigrant from Mexico or Central America was, I knew what it was like to be the black sheep of a family. Historically, there was always in me a sense of shame, inadequacy, and guilt when in the presence of an institutional and conventional church. I always looked forward to enjoying priests' meetings, workshops, conventions, and retreats as a seminarian, yet I just didn't feel a part. I don't blame anyone for it. Who knows why? Obviously, the need for affirmation, which in church chat is synonymous with "promotion," had been great, and the sense of blame for all the rough stuff in family and church had caused in me a tremendous sense of inadequacy. Call it being an adult child of an alcoholic. Call it having an inner child that felt so immature when compared to where I thought I should be relationally, socially, and financially. Call it being constantly reinforced as being a loser by those figures in my life who I expected (begged) to affirm me of being anything but. But, I must confess, before arriving in inner-city Los Angeles, I had felt from my own life experiences that I was just as black as the blacks. I felt I was just as Mexican as the Mexicans. I felt that I had snuck through as many borders as our legal and illegal immigrants had done. Yet, I also had felt underestimated. I also felt misunderstood. I had also felt misjudged and labeled. It was so good now to be gone from a life where I couldn't live up to those I wanted to trust (and worked so hard to try to gain their trust) and to be among those who would understand, give me a chance, and who sought the same out of life, love, and God.

Being here at St. Agatha's has been a wonderful beginning for me. I now believe in a loving God. I now believe that the Jesus of Nazareth is alive and well beyond me and within me. I have learned about and experienced the Holy Spirit. I have learned about how my life direction needed a radical change. I had been dead. I had been on the cross. Finally, after forty-eight years of life—I am accepting and allowing myself to feel resurrected. And I am not even dead yet!

After my first night here at the parish, where I slept in what I saw as a filthy rectory left by my predecessor (Was I a snob or what?) I was in total fear of the unknown: of the inner-city neighborhood, of being surprised upon hearing roosters, resting up for the next day's cockfight, crowing in the night *(I thought they only cock-a-doodle-dooed when the sun rose)*; and of a nightlong sequence of police helicopters circling over a newly committed crime somewhere close by.

I awoke on my first Sunday in the parish to go down to the church to say hello to my parishioners. It was the seven o'clock Spanish Mass. *"¡Buenos dias!"* I said in a Spanish that sounded like how John Wayne must have sounded after a two-day drunk, *"¿Como estas?"*

The people looked at me, the gringo, with obvious looks of disappointment, threat, and despair. *Oh my God they hate me!* They hate me before I even had a chance! Excuse me for not being a Latino! Forgive me because my Spanish sucks. Don't worry, I'm just passing through. A little senora came up to me and said, *"Mira, padre. Lo siento."* [Look, Father. I'm sorry.] She pointed to the door of the sacristy's PA closet that was vandalized my first night there. God! We're robbed already! And in her broken English she begged, "Please, don't hate us!" Ugh! Oh my God. My God! "Don't hate US?!" I will never forget those words. They did nothing wrong but would take the brunt for some stranger who violated *them*—not me. That was when I decided, I'm sticking around. My initial plan was to stay for my six-month stint and just leave it all . . . even if I had to settle for a job at the local supermarket.

Well, I've been here for eight years. The first year we were robbed at least eight times. I had to spend thousands of dollars on gates, fences, and security systems. The cops said to me as if proposing a dare. "They're testing you, Father. You're the new guy and they want to show you who's the boss and scare you away. Good luck." Every time they broke into the place, though, I got stronger. The break-ins were definite crosses at the time but they became opportunities of resurrection, empowerment. "If you think I am going to do this alone, you're in for a surprise. It's your parish. I'm just passing through."

No one could have had any idea how a burning passion for these good people arose in my entire being. I was on fire—nothing could exhaust it at that time. Thank God the fire lasted for a couple of years. About three months into my temporary six-month stint, the search formally began for a new pastor. One Sunday, and I can remember the exact time and place, some people from the parish came forward and said, "Father Ken, we know you're only supposed to be here for a couple more months, but would you think of applying for the pastorship here?" It's been a great trip these eight years since. It has been a very successful apostolate in so many ways. This what was thought dead parish has become a vibrant example of what can be done when you allow people to be church, when you allow people opportunities to get off the cross and enjoy some resurrection. This once upon a time "dead Church" is now alive and vibrant. So am I. They did to me what they did to themselves. Give me God!

I preach my experience of the Good News here. Oftentimes, it seems, what is preached in churches is nothing but bad news! Life is hard enough. If you want church to be a place where the people get beat up, this place is not going to be the place. There are more than enough churches around town that will gladly fill that need for you. Not here. We're a place where all are welcome—even if you aggravate the hell out of me.

Yet, as with Jesus, when you try to build bridges; when you're different; when you try to give a new view of church, God, self, and the world—you're going to meet Calvary. No one likes Calvary. With every compliment a voice continuously rings in the back of my head: "One step closer to Calvary, Deasy!" Calvary came about five years into my assignment here. During Holy Week 2001 some of the people who originally welcomed me here and invited me here were now passing around a petition to have me removed as pastor. I was accused of everything from discrimination against blacks to encouraging lifestyles/views contrary to Church doctrine. I had hurt them. I had sold them short. They truly were committed people. Yes, I was not correct. Yes, I was tolerating peoples, groups, lifestyles that are not exactly up to par with the doctrines of the Catholic Church. These good people felt that I had totally sold the Catholic Church down the river. If they only knew who really sold them down the river!

A few years back I can vividly remember an older person of color coming up to me quite upset because there were noticeable numbers of homosexuals coming to church. "What are you going to do about those queers that are coming here?" I just can't believe how easily people forget how harsh life has been on them and now want it on someone else: victims of racism being racists; nationalized migrants ignoring the needs of their sisters and brothers who have no legal status in this country; the hungry rich ignoring the hungry poor.

For the life of me, I can't understand how former illegal immigrants—now legal immigrants—refuse to lift a hand to help other illegal immigrants. I can't understand how people harshly nicknamed "nigger," "beaner," or "honky" can call someone else a "fag." I can't understand how people who teach Bible stories about the struggle that ensued with the early apostles over integrating the Jews with the Gentiles can, at the very same time, totally be insensitive to the racial tensions among their own brother and sister Christians called to coexist.

Anyway, because these people were upset with my unorthodox method of ministry (being creative, inclusive, and not putting up with bigotry or any of that other nonsense), they wanted to turn me over to the same church authority that they thought wanted to close them down. Man, I really was devastated! The plotting to remove me broke my heart. Granted, I had made mistakes. Granted, I was a totally different character than the normal stereotypical priest, but I just couldn't believe the manner in which this was done. It was a sad time for me. As a result, I had become cynical, angry, depressed, and—though I turned to my God for solace—I felt it was unfair and something that I just didn't need. It took me years to get over it. Yet, during the darkest year of my tenure here, the fact that this was being done during Holy Week, when Christ was being betrayed, was absolutely ironic and, at the same time, gave me courage to deal with all the issues this brought out in me.

Though I had support from the majority of the parishioners, I focused only on threats and rejection. Though I received a lovely and personal note from Cardinal Mahony, I still chose to feel mis-understood, unappreciated, and rejected. In other words, I CHOSE TO HANG ON THE CROSS AND STAY THERE! These issues were lack of trust in myself, lack of trust in God, lack of trust in church authority, and lack of faith in resurrection and the possibility of having a joyous intimate life as a celibate Catholic priest. I was revisiting old wounds of abandonment, rejection, and a history of misunderstandings. Again, these people who I had called "family" were now trying to rid me of my job, but they were also running me out of home, again, instead of seeing the growth of new life, hope, church membership, and ministry.

Finally, two of the accusers arose from the darkness and the shadows and confronted me. They told me that they were not going to send the petition in. Frankly, I didn't care. On reading, it revealed to me a history of built-up sadness and fear that I could relate to. What the hell! Since these "accusations" had already been spread among the parish and the damage of divisiveness had been done I felt compelled to send it to the archdiocese myself, and if they thought I should be removed—go ahead. Actually, I was hoping that they would! Like, I need this crud? I might as well hang my own dirty laundry on the line.

In it all, though, I didn't feel the need to be right as much as I wanted to be true! I knew I wasn't correct . . . and I was unwilling to be false. But I could not downplay my experience of God, community, inclusiveness, love over law, etc., that I experience in my drive to live the Word. On the other hand, the age-old personal doubt arose: "Maybe it's me." It probably is me. When am I going to learn not to trust anyone? When am I going to get healthy again? Why do I believe in this stuff when there seems to be more resistance than resilience? I haven't had a complacent moment in my life! And, man, I am getting tired of this cross!

I tried to handle this with class and with Christ. My anger, though, was evident in my preaching and my appearance at the same time I was drowning in my fears. And, through it all I'm still here and I haven't been the same since. Actually, I have become better—really. The cynicism is gone. My wanting retaliation is gone. The fears are gone. Now, instead of giving God my fears and begging him to take care of it all, I pray, "Hey, Bud, if it be for your glory . . . bring on the worse that can happen!" I really don't want to keep on this cross or any cross too long. Historically, the Lord has never allowed that for me.

1968 (13 years old)
La Canada, California

"Mrs. Deasy, we have a warrant for your son's arrest! Is Kenneth Deasy at home? He's being arrested for breaking and entering into a number of homes in the area." I remember hearing those words while watching *Frankenstein Meets the Wolf Man.* I immediately shot out the back door and ran like hell. I didn't even get out of the backyard until the realization came, "So where am I, a thirteen-year-old punk, going to run to?" I returned to meet my fate. Sergeant Jim read me my rights. *I'm only thirteen years old, you schmuck!* The other two kids, my best friends, who were also in on this breaking and entering, totally bailed on me, set me up, and denied being involved. I took the entire rap. Sergeant Jim was cool, though. He got the "victims" together. These victims were the owners of the houses that I entered and played around in after finding an open unlocked door somewhere. (We stole nothing. There was no damage.) There were seven houses; I mean homes, by the way. The Sergeant encouraged the owners not to press charges. Thank God for Sergeant Jim! Instead of being the "official cop," he saw through his own experience a good kid who had some potential that had yet to be discovered, and never would have been in the penal system. Sergeant Jim intuitively saw in "poor Kenny Deasy" some hope that he had the power to participate in by bending the rules. He said, "You better come down to the station," which scared me to death. I went. Alone. Mom had to work.

Whenever I preach on the Gospels pertaining to raising Lazarus from the dead and the command of Jesus to "roll back the stone," I think of Sergeant Jim. He rolled back the stone and let me free though I had to pay a price of meeting the people whose house I had trespassed into. He would have been right in the eyes of the law to have sent me to trial. See? He didn't feel that the need to be right was as important as allowing an experience of care—a perfect example of the power of love over the enforcement of law; mercy being as important as justice. In hindsight, I just wanted to see other homes. Therapeutically, this has been an issue for quite some time: the search for home. I was fascinated with what "families" were all about. I was intrigued with how families lived in other "homes." To this very day, I still am in that search.

To this very day, I wish I had family and a home. Throughout my priesthood, this is a major motivating factor in the formation of community, family, and protection. I project that we are all in one way or the other looking for that "family," for that "home."

This is why I truly believe that to have a legitimate faith experience in a parish setting there must be that sense of welcome, care, and openness to sacrifice for one another. Funny. This has not been my experience of church, generally speaking. This definitely is the parish "charisma" here at St. Agatha's. My imprisonment was hardly anything, a few hours in the station being drilled over as the Number One most wanted on the FBI list. I was so scared. *Oh man. I got to go see Father Lesser. He'll help me! No! I better not.* He might not let me be an altar boy anymore! Father Lesser was huge, and the young associate pastor of my parish, St. Bede's. He was the LYP—the lovely young priest. He was huge physically and in demeanor. From my perspective then of being a little overweight eighth grader, he was huge, scary, and my priest. He was so extraordinary to me and such a miracle—my savior. He was one of the many godsends (though I often only focus on those that disappointed me. Love that pity pot!) who would be sent to catch me and pick me up when I fell off the cross. To this day I don't think he knows that simply "my priest being there" was enough for me.

What did Father Lesser do? He did the same thing that Sergeant Jim did, which by the way, they don't teach in the sheriff's academy or the seminary. He took the time and listened. He spent time with me. A whole thirty-five minutes of hope. I dug him for that and I dug how much he enjoyed helping my poor, screwed-up family and me. I dug how the Church (the people of church—priests, nuns, friends of my poor folks—those who were present and not all talk) really enjoyed helping me out and helping everyone out. They were such happy people, caring people. Happier than any of the other adults who I had seen up to then. As the adage goes, "There's no place like home." Back at my house, though, upon my return from two hours at the sheriff's office, there was good news. Finally Mom is getting a divorce! They finally are getting divorced! Scandal. I'm going to have to watch *Divorce Court* every day hoping the Deasys would be on it. I bet Mom five dollars that Dad wouldn't even show up at the court. *She never did pay me*—mixed crosses. Mixed blessings! It's called life.

1987 (33 years old)
Woodland Hills, California
First year of priesthood—a baby priest!

The best and most powerful experience for me as a baby priest was getting involved in juvenile detention ministry. I would go weekly on Saturdays (when the three-wedding-a-Saturday circuit allowed) to the juvenile detention facilities of Camp Miller and Camp Kilpatrick to celebrate Mass and visit with the "homies." The most beautiful, ugly-ass kids you've ever seen. These poor, ugly, beautiful kids—most born from unwed teenage mothers and having no father (or a father that didn't give a rat's ass) while taking charge of their younger siblings when not incarcerated. There was this one kid, my favorite, whom I gave the name "Rose Man." After I would celebrate Mass on any given Saturday, Rose Man would insist that I go for a walk with him. In the course of this lap around the baseball diamond we would come up to this rose bush that by all appearances had the potential for only one rose. "This is my rosebush, Fadda Ken," he would proudly say (as if boasting of his newborn child). "And a lovely rosebush it is," I would affirm. This rosebush was his sole charge.

He would run across the baseball diamond when he would see me on Saturday and help me with setting up and packing up my Mass stuff. Then the ritual walk would occur, a walk to the rosebush. This ritual, for me, had more reality than the Mass I just celebrated. "This is my rosebush, Fadda Ken."

"And a lovely rosebush it is," I would affirm. Every week it got better, especially the one Saturday when there was a rosebud, then the next Saturday when there was more than a bush and a bud. There was the flower. The rose, his firstborn. This young man started acting strange, though. He was sad and unusually quiet; sneaky and secretive; almost embarrassed. Scared.

"Wassup, Rose Man?" Silence.

That morning, as he and a few of his homeboys were allowed to venture outside the wall and put my stuff in the car—*a big privilege!* Rose Man was really quiet. He kept sneaking around and acting suspicious. As I walked the boys back to the office I had noticed that Rose Man had disappeared. AWOL! My heart was broken. I was devastated. I had concluded that he made a break for "the outs." I told the other two young people to go back to the office and say nothing. If there is any news to break, I will break it. *I'm screwed. Rose Man's screwed.* As I walked back to my car I caught him sneaking out of the backseat. He was hiding something.

"Rose Man, what the hell are you doing?" Nothing. "Were you trying to sneak away with me?" Nothing. "Talk to me, *mijo*." Nada. *I confess I had thought he was trying to rip me off or hide in the backseat and escape.* I returned him to the office, though, just thankful to God that he was back and safe. He wouldn't say good-bye to me or even look into my eye. I walked back to the car. There was the rose on the dashboard. What a gift! Yet, he feared that it would not be celebrated, accepted, or appreciated. The kid taught me what giving a gift is all about and the vulnerability and sacrifice that make a gift "a gift."

As time went on, I saw my earlier life now being lived in the Rose Man: He was rearrested in 1990. His mom was murdered in 1993. He had a baby that died at birth in 1994, and he had no place to live in 1996. As he approached eighteen, I found him staying with not the most desirable of people. Consequently, I cosigned with Rose

Man on an apartment that he would share with an older retired man who needed someone to split the ren. Eventually and not surprisingly, he started taking drugs again and was sharing his room with a gal who also was taking drugs. His senior roommate did not like this. Neither did I. The "Rose" was becoming a thorn.

I was able to find him a great job with benefits, with a very good friend of mine. I was able to get him a brand new bicycle so he could get to work (actually it was the guy of the marriage from hell who helped me get the bike for him). I was able to get the bucks needed to open a checking account. I was able to show Rose Man how to use makeup to cover the "FUCK YOU" that he had tattooed behind his ear. Lovely. Why don't you just hold a sign up that says, "I'm a loser"? (His boss, my friend, was really happy about that tattoo. NOT!) I was not able to help the Rose Man keep his job. I was not able to help him wake up for work every morning. I had learned that his boss was tolerating his behavior because of our friendship. I was not able to help him get his GED diploma. I was not able to help him pay his rent. I was not able to be the dad, big brother, or full-time savior that he needed. So, what was I expecting?

The Spirit is willing. The flesh is weak, incapable. The time investment was impossible for both of us. The software really wanted to work. The hardware couldn't hold it. I tried. I felt like I failed. I hope the kid is okay. I hope he is happy. I hope he is alive and, more importantly, happy to be alive.

1968 (14 years old)
St. Francis High School
The first test-grade I got in high school, Catholic high school, of course, was an F. I got a 21 percent on my summer reading test. *Hiroshima, Tale of Two Cities,* and *Lost Horizon.* Father Bill was really disappointed in me. I had known Father Bill before high school

because he helped out on Sundays at my parish church. He knew me personally because I had served Mass for him a hundred times. He also was cool. That summer was the summer of my arrest, the summer of my parent's divorce, and by then I was washing dishes at a steak house. I was a million pounds overweight, I was still building forts (homes) with my buddy down the street, and we were evicted from the house. Poor Kenny Deasy, again. *Man, this is getting old!*

Father Bill let me take the reading test over again because he was sensitive to the realities that were distracting me. This time I got a 24 percent. He never included this failing mark in my grade average. After that one test of my reading skills and Father Bill's compassion, I received B's. Father Bill left at the end of that sophomore year. He got married. I was disappointed in him for that then. Not because he got married. He didn't say good-bye. I really thought he liked me. I thought we were friends. He probably felt like a failure. I'm sure that in 1969 the superiors of the order and the Church didn't say, "Good luck, buddy! Have a happy life." I would have. The search would continue.

The search would never end, though, with my taking the crosses of my past and being thankful that they have been raised to the level of dignity in how they have bettered my person and how they have made me a more sensitive man—*way too sensitive!* Yes, Virginia, there are such creatures as empathetic and sensitive men in priestly ministry, in the world. Even in America.

2000–2001 (13 years ordained a priest)

"Oh, my God! Make them stop!"

One day it all began, again. My car radio announced, "KFWB news-time, it's three thirty." The Vatican reiterated today that Catholics who have been divorced and remarried without receiving an annulment are not allowed to receive Holy Communion."

Boy, we sure needed that dose of Christ and the Church's wel-come, didn't we? Just when you thought it was safe to go back to church, the institution has spoken again giving indication that it has no clue of what type of pastoral ministry it has come to be or it would not have made a statement attaching such exclusivity to the inclusive mission of Jesus Christ.

Another day: "KFWB news-time, it's one thirty." In Rome, today, Cardinal Ratzinger of the Vatican reiterated, "Catholicism is the only way to salvation." What I read in the Gospels is to avoid religious zealots. Perhaps the method of communication, listen-ing, openness, etc., is really not conveying the Good News here, is it? I don't recall Jesus asking the blind, the lame, the dead, and the leper, "Are you Catholic?"

Another day: "KFWB news-time, it's ten fifteen. Today the Vatican's press spokesman, Joaquin Navarro, declared that homo-sexuals do not belong in the priesthood." Did you discuss this with the homosexual clergy who are already tirelessly working with the poor and repairing the burned bridges caused by institu-tional rhetoric? Attaboy, Joaquin! We're opening doors out here and your statements are continuing to shut them. Frankly, in my experience, the most personable and caring of the clergy are those who are gay and comfortable with it. And then there's the oppo-site. And guess what?

Another day and another day and another: "KFWB news-time, it's one nineteen. The pope, during his weekly papal audience, reiterated that only Catholics are to receive Holy Communion." The poor pope! What a huge hero. I mean really! But, I just don't know who feeds him this information that on Holy Thursday when we celebrate the institution of Eucharist and priesthood that we need to be selective as to who is invited to the table!

Someone needs a cruise!

"KFWB news-time, it's six thirty. The canon lawyer for the Vat-ican has announced that bishops shouldn't turn over to the legal authorities any information about allegations of the clergy sexually abusing minors." This canon lawyer needs to go on the same cruise. "Heya, Monsignor! Howzabout another Bahama Momma cocktail?!"

"KFWB news-time, it's twelve eleven. The Holy See announced today that there would be no discussion pertaining to celibacy and the ordination of women priests." Holy See? Do you see what I see? Obviously, not!

And the most recent, August 3, 2003:

"KFWB news-time, it's six twenty-three. The Vatican announced today that it would deliberately be addressing legislation in Western Europe concerning same-sex marriages. At the same time, it also discourages legislation allowing homosexual adoptions because the Vatican views homosexual behavior as deviant. Archbishop Mahony of Los Angeles issued a comment on John Paul II's July 31 statement: "I welcome and offer my full support." From where I sat, the cardinal's need to begin his comment with this opening sentence was not his usual style. "Someone" in corporate Rome was putting a gun to this progressive cardinal's head to show unquestioning allegiance "to the Man." You would think that with all the pressing issues of the world dying for attention and resolve (AIDS in Africa, world hunger, terrorism, priests and bishops sexually abusing children) that same-sex marriage (and now same-sex Anglican bishops hooking up) would deserve their immediate attention? Obviously, someone must have plenty of time on their hands.

The hilarious thing about all of these Vatican statements and figureheads is how much people pay attention to them. The pope says this! The pope says that! The bishops say this! The bishops did (or didn't do) that! We've got some great personable padres, deacons, nuns, laity, etc., in the field (i.e., the real church; the real people of God) who are doing a heck of a job at their parishes bringing a fresh and joyful face of God, church, and self at the cost of a lot of sacrifice, loneliness, and aloneness. These guys and gals are bleeding themselves in loyalty to their people. When "church history" is discussed it's ONLY about "the history of the papacy" and not the real/majority church. Yet, some overeducated and tired bishop, cardinal, or pope stomps into town and everyone loses their water in excitement! To me this parallels the earlier misconceptions of what a new messiah was to do in the times of Jesus. "He'll fix it for us!" Like John Paul II is going to return your call in the middle of the night when you need a priest? Like the local bishop is going to visit you in the hospital? That's the job of us parish priests who work among the flock. Hey, who wouldn't want to be ministered to by one "closer to God"?! I assure you I have met people in prison who have greater powers of holiness than me!

You joyously and enthusiastically work your tush off trying to extend a personal Christlike welcome to people, especially those damaged by religion. Yet when an official Church figure says something as off-the-wall and out of context as just expressed, these repaired people will leave the Church, again. How convenient! They leave over a statement by someone whom they'll never meet because he wears a hat and red (or white) buttons. Amazing. Where are the prophets?

All of us are in need of growth and direction in our spiritual lives. This means the hierarchy *whether they act it or not* are people of God: priests, nonpriests, children, prisoners, queens, kings, princes, terrorists, liturgists *(like the rest of us . . . children of God)*, men, women, gays, straights, legals, illegals, wealthy, butt-poor, and so on. The Jesus Christ of Nazareth as well as the Jesus Christ of the present speaks just as strongly to the local community; i.e., in our parishes, as to the select chosen (ordained) male Gnostics. I am just saying let's have some balance here! I know that there is a need for order, structures, etc., but there is also room for affection, understanding, listening and mending. It's time to teach the people where God is and not just where sin is; it's time to teach the people about heaven and not hell; it's time to say I am sorry and make amends "not to sin again." It's time to be the poorest of the poor and not the high and mighty. It's time to not just teach about the seven sacraments but time to empower the 1 billion potential "sacraments" who call themselves Christian. It's time for the children of God to become adults of God. It's time for the adults of God to become children of God.

Frankly, if one really discerns that the Lord doesn't speak, affirm, and walk with you in your parish community, and that your community's unique charisma is restrained, you need to get the heck out of that parish, or you need to really ask how to be involved in your parish. If one really and truly brings their personal gift of self to the altar and you truly discern that it is not being recognized, welcomed, affirmed, and celebrated as such, then one is right in continuing the search for a more relational community. This is totally healthy. You go where you're fed, baby! Just make sure you are also challenged. Growth is always a challenge. How can Christians be comfortable in today's world?

So this may sound a little unorthodox. Christians are called to be different because we are trying to speak to the local parish community's experience and not an experience that is foreign to them; i.e., doctrine and "church-chat" that only speaks to the reality of the overeducated and to people who have nothing else to do with their time but to fuss over doctrine. May the peace of the Lord disturb you always. In all fairness, though, the Church never speaks in "one-liners" as presented in the media. To the best of my experience, she never comes out and speaks with a "this is the bottom line" approach. Usually, there is quite a lengthy, biblical-footnoted treatise that very sensitively approaches a matter of faith and/or morals that it is presently concerned with. And, again, the Church has not issued a "decree" as legalistically and bottom-lined as is thought.

This is what the media does. I believe this is called the teaser that is used to attract attention to its "show" by its viewers. This is also what the clergy has done. A lot of the clergy have and continue to present the Church as the Judge Judy of divine guidance, divine protection and divine justice. Any relevant teacher of the faith knows that this method is antiquated and unhealthy. Yet, it has been from the pulpits and the media that "bottom line" theology has been presented without going into the wealth of scripture and sacred tradition from which the document has drawn its authority and consistent revelation. When done through the pulpit, a minister only has a couple of minutes (if he's lucky) to do his magic. So as a result, there is no way in which the document could be presented clearly, affectively, and with discussion. Secondly, if the padre and/or catechist (a person who helps us teach and integrate the Jesus of Catholicism) wanted to go into it more fully, it would have to be outside of the Mass, which also means it probably would not fall on Sunday. Most "religious zealots" only believe in the hour-on-Sunday Catholicism; the "does this count for Sunday?" way to salvation. Thirdly, many Catholics haven't learned anything about their faith since receiving their First Communion in second grade.

Have you ever asked a Catholic to explain their faith? Most can only explain the religion.

This is why I NEVER wear my collar on the plane. This is why I never ride with the funeral director in the hearse on the way to the graveside! This is why I never admit to being a priest while boiling away in a hot tub where other strangers have also gathered to be poached. I don't want to be stuck answering questions about the religion in the manner of a lawyer discussing law. Who cares about Limbo? Who cares about Purgatory? Who cares if Jesus had brothers or sisters? Who cares about what are the seven cardinal sins? (You want their addresses?) Now, while still enjoying the bubbles and while sipping on a mai tai, you want to talk about sexuality, intimacy, and their relation to living a truly compassionate life? Let's go! You want to talk about forgiveness in a condemning world? Let's go! You want to talk about how the heck someone who makes a minimum wage can afford a seven-hundred-dollar-a-month one-bedroom apartment for a family of five, and still be happy with life? Let's go! You want to talk about where I have experienced the ultimate love of God beyond apparitions and bleeding statues all without having sex? Let's go! And to do this without using the "G" word while admitting that I am a "P"? You ALSO want to talk about a good restaurant, disco, bar, vacation spot, etc.? Yes! It's called talking out of experience and not doctrine. As the historically told salvation stories of the scriptures help us to look for love in our day, so are the doctrines meant to do.

The resource and references inside the doctrines are usually more valuable than the doctrine. Yet, its method of presentation and delivery (always in writing; always written with the globe in mind and not individual cultures) is the problem. The documents, believed to be inspired by the same Holy Spirit behind the revelations of scripture, is written out of the Latin Church in Rome and distributed to the non-Roman world. As a result, we have the bottom line method of presentation of Catholic doctrine. The Church does not write documents concerning topics such as "Going to church is a mortal sin" without going into huge detail about the value of the love of God, the goodness of the world; the wealth of its Judaic-Christian tradition; and the intimate view of God, self, and each other presented through Jesus. She will go into the love behind what God, in Jesus, did for us then and now. She will talk about the historical doctrines of how the Eucharist at Mass is the continued reliving and reexperiencing of that salvific moment when God allowed himself to be betrayed, abandoned, and executed by religion and politics. To miss out on this great gift would be a slap in the face because therein God is offering us the gift of himself to us, again, in the Jesus of the Eucharist.

Now, taking all that in becomes my job, as a priest and preacher, to add my own witness to how the experience of the Eucharist is intimate and something that I choose to receive and strive to become. It is my job to make the Eucharist conducive to the charisma and particular personality of the parish. It is my job to discuss, sell, and entice with how, for example, when we choose to go to Mass we avail ourselves to receiving the love of God in the word, Eucharist, and community, and we allow ourselves to be the word, Eucharist, and communal revelation of God to someone else. We stand at the cross of Christ and the crosses of others and say "We're not alone" anymore. We are resurrected! Will we allow resurrection? Will we accept resurrection?

Yet, I have to admit when I originally wrote the above paragraph I took the negative approach and had to catch myself. The preceding paragraph initially read: "When one chooses NOT to go to Mass, not only do you fail to receive the love of God in the word, Eucharist, and community BUT you also fail TO BE the word, Eucharist, and communal revelation of God to someone else."

Becoming the Eucharist is so huge to my own personal walk. When I celebrate the Mass it is a reliving and a wanting of an intimacy like no other. And when I see the faces of the people who want the same, I'm on fire. When I see the faces of the spirit-suckers chewing gum (which only is an external sign that they are not getting it yet) I know that I have work to do, though it aggravates the hell out of me. *When I hear someone say, "Mass is boring," I say, "No! You're boring!"*

Again, the official teachings of the Church do not simply pronounce stuff like: "Sex outside of marriage is a sin." "Gays are going to hell." "Remarried Catholics without annulments are going to hell." "Marry outside of the church and you go to hell," etc. Even though, in such matters, the magisterium of the Church presents beautiful teachings that go into the great dignity of the ministry married life, the intimate experience of the love of God therein, the role and beauty of sex in regards to enhancing the sensual and affectionate dimensions of love, etc., it is the manner in which it is presented that conveys the exact opposite.

Bottom-line Catholicism:

YOU MUST COME TO THE BANQUET
BUT NOT ALL ARE ALLOWED TO EAT.

Miss Manners would call this rude and impolite. This is why people no longer come to the banquet. People are being yelled at in the confessional. People are being denied the sacraments. People are being told to go away. Why? Because as long as you live under my roof, you will do as you're told! And, if you start crying, I'll give you something to cry about.

Again, the Church does not believe in this approach. But we present it still as such and, as a result, we lose some great people because they have had the Spirit sucked right out of them. They feel abandoned by their religion. Therefore, they feel abandoned by their faith (which is impossible for faith to do!) and in this religion that enhances a Christ who was given to us for the forgiveness of sins, due to the shock of rejection people leave. The bread goes and the crumbs stay? And yet, having said all this, one of the truest pains of ministry is coming across Catholics who still believe in a condemning God and a condemning religion—that for which God gave us Jesus to rectify.

People still want the bottom line. People still want that cross. At Gold's Gym in Venice, California, people approach me for three reasons: (1) Father Ken, is it a sin if I do this or that? (2) will you write a letter to this priest in Boston who won't let me be the godparent of my brother's baby unless he knows that I go to Mass everyday, and (3) Father Ken, look at her! Do you think they're real?

Especially in reference to issue (1) Father Ken, is it a sin to do this or that? I would prefer to enter an answer of "Let's talk about it." What's your name? Who's your Daddy? What is your story? What did you do that you think MAY be a sin? What is sin to you? What were your thoughts and intentions at the time of committing this "possible" sin—deliberate severance from God due to ignoring him or failing to act in the manner of his son?

I confess for what I have done and what I have failed to do. "Bless me *father for I have sinned.* It has been three years since my last confession and I have not committed any sins. I go to Mass every Sunday. I fulfill my Easter duty. I haven't killed anyone."

OH REALLY!

And what have you failed to do? Have you helped the poor? Have you taken in the homeless? Have you learned about this God whom you supposedly have a relationship with? Have you prayed? Have you really tried to be a disciple of Christ? You haven't sinned? Let me ask your spouse!

Again, outside of going to Mass on Sunday is there any other evidence that you are a follower of Christ? But, people don't want to share in this discernment. They want a quick fix—a drive-through McDonald's Value Meal of Grace. They want the car wash approach. Just put me through the process and let me know whether I am a good boy or a bad girl. If we treat sin as simply law, that which governs only our external actions, we have not grown since the times of Jesus who came not to abolish the law, but to take it a step further. "If I have not love, I am nothing."

Spirituality? That's just for priests and monks.

No!

You've got the power!

This is why I love to enhance and invite people to a new church—the same way Jesus invited others to see God, self, and the world in a new way. Especially in Los Angeles, where we have a Religious Education Congress where over fifty thousand catechists come to learn about their God, their people, and making the "good news" relevant and "real" to the present. YES! There is such a healthy and Spirit-filled momentum of true religious and spiritual integration going on which, by the way, is encouraged by the local bishops; as long as it's orthodox in content (being orthodox in acting with that Roman persona is not demanded). Yet, if there are 5 million Catholics in Los Angeles, what's fifty thousand?—a start. They're the center of the broadcast of good seed on quite fertile ground.

During such religious education and ministry conventions there is such a unique connection and revitalization of Spirit because there is a feeling among Catholics that they seldom feel at home, a feeling of *us*. It is an often expressed regret by the attendees of such conventions, though, that the next day they, and the other fifty thousand, must return to THEM—the parish; the bottom-line, Sunday-going parishioners who see the love of God as something completely unattainable and unexperiential. All of this other stuff is just touchy-feely.

Thank God I am here in the hood and at St. Agatha's. I am so blessed to have been given their spirit. It has been through them that I have come to finally realize in life that I am blessed. I have learned that the Lord above and within and among does not want success; all that is demanded is faith accompanied with the confession of St. Paul, "It is in my weakness that I am strong." I, who used to gaze upon the pomp and circumstance of Rome as one would upon a member of the Royal Family, have come to recognize and appreciate that.

May 13, 2001 (46 years old)

Someone dropped off this bulletin cover that was from some parish in the Bay Area, and I immediately had to print it on ours. I treated this adopted missive as a God-sent affirmation that I was not alone.

ST. AGATHA PARISH FAMILY

2646 South Mansfield Ave.
Los Angeles, CA 90016
frkendc@stagathas.org

"We will be a place where all are welcome!"

STAY AND EAT . . .
People of all faiths and all races.
Divorced and separated persons.
Families with children and children without families.
Straight people and gay/lesbian people.
Homeless persons and people with houses but no home.
Loving relationships and struggling relationships.
Single people and married people and people who live together.
Those in recovery again and again and again.
Travelers from far and near.
Widows and widowers.
Visitors who are invited to visit or be members.
STAY AND SEEK . . .
To live the Gospel of Jesus Christ.
To gather as a community and tell your story.
To break the bread, share the cup, to be the bread and the cup.
STAY AND CELEBRATE . . .
Our diversity and commonality.
Our spirit of hospitality.
The unity that God wills for us all.
The enlightenment of those who seek the Lord
That we reach out to alienated Catholics,
Protestants and non-Christians.

That we revere the dignity of each person.
That we care for the less fortunate.
That we empower Christians to realize their calling and talents.
That we provide an oasis in a desert world
That we honor and show understanding among all faiths.
That we nurture our gifts and share them.
That we pursue new ways to serve Christ and others.
Becoming a good neighbor.

**STAY, EAT, SEEK, AND CELEBRATE
COMING OFF THE CROSS BECAUSE SOMEONE ELSE
NEEDS THE WOOD!**

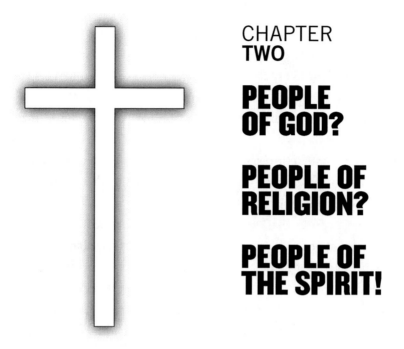

PEOPLE OF GOD?

PEOPLE OF RELIGION?

PEOPLE OF THE SPIRIT!

I don't want to get off the cross! I don't want to get out of the tomb! *Yeah! It's so nice to be insane because no one asks you to explain!* It's easier to be dead, then no one expects you to be alive. You've got to admit to stay in the tomb, to remain ignorant, to be in denial, to be complacently unaware, is safer, more reliable, and, if you choose, more permanent! *And for a lot of people, a whole lot of fun!*

GET OFF THE CROSS, DEASY!
SOMEONE ELSE NEEDS THE WOOD!

Oftentimes, I confess, whether alone or with others in my life, I could easily enthrone myself on the pity pot—another version of hanging myself on a cross I made myself. Oftentimes, the download of the litany of those negative voices that reassured me that I was no good, of no worth, and totally screwed up, could instantly play itself in a snap when triggered! There are times when the smallest minute little thing would trigger this. This harsh litany can get us all drunk on the angers and depressions that come. Feeding this drag would also result in complacency and permission to cop out from doing anything good for yourself, let alone anyone else.

Hey, I personally confess this myself and I am embarrassed to reflect on how my behavior has often revealed this. I have personally drunk from this martini of 100-proof self-pity and a splash of the vermouth of "woe is me." Jeez-o-man! I am sure you can relate! Once anyone is accused of being the perfect black sheep there seemingly comes a response that is quite ugly though, sadly, oftentimes too socially acceptable. As long as we are convinced of being the perpetual ugly duckling we don't have to even worry about sharing, discovering, and being affirmed; about realizing all that personal talent, potential, and life to be had which is attainable within and beyond. The staying on the cross, in the tomb, gives us cause not to have the courage to live a life of compassion and passion. Sadly, we are stuck (nailed) and this cuts us off from being resurrected by those real attainable opportunities of affirmation by peers and strangers of being a "helluva nice guy/gal." You are my beloved!

It pains me to see people in such pain. It pains me to see people feel that this pain is necessary to be a child of God. Not only will we not allow ourselves even to consider the possibility of a resurrection experience in this life, we will most surely believe that we will be lonely as hell as a result of feeling blessed. We can believe that no one will want to be near us, and we will not allow anyone to be near us. To be blessed does not mean we will be holier-than-thou. We cut ourselves off from this experience and the experience of God. *That's why it is called hell, numb-nuts!* "But that's okay!" we say defensively and with conviction. Believe me; I know what I'm talking about! I have spent most of my life selling myself short and blaming everyone else. I am the poster boy of allowing others to convince me that I am worthless while not allowing my own self-knowledge to be affirmed by others, especially when I couldn't do it myself.

Helping everyone with their own crosses and hopeful resurrections, while ignoring my own, has surely, and with all humility and surprise, won me some recognition, popularity, and success as an "affective" priest—a guy who is just beginning to explore his humanness and actually see it as a plus. This is a big deal on both counts. Humanness as good! *How non-Irish!*

I realize that it is NOT normal and NOT divinely commissioned that I am ordained to "aloneness." Though the vacation plans of diocesan priesthood are glorious (at least seven weeks a year; four-month sabbatical every seven years), the nights suck. But, that's the cross. The least adorned room in my house is my bedroom. I mean, who's going to see it anyway? People will love me or need me because "Father gives up so much for his people!" Maybe they will also love me just because of who I am. There is the fascination of the cross, the curse of being Irish, and that of clinging to the cross because it is so easy to do. And, what drama! Why look for penance during Lent? It finds me quite well on its own!

Clinging to the resurrection though has finally been my salvation. This healing, freedom, release, renewal, and reconciliation is so empowering and a huge slice of heaven, which is pretty cool seeing that I'm not dead yet! We do have a choice, you know—it is not a matter of being right or wrong. It's a matter of how much life or death do you choose to take advantage of in the short time we are allowed on this planet. True, we can always find something to agonize over. That's easy. But to actually find something/someone to celebrate, and trust in that, would be sustaining more than a quickie turn-on? Hot damn!

To find and stick to the cross is a safe bet—always accessible and available. It is seemingly much easier to identify with the crosses of life than with resurrections in this life. Just open the newspaper. Just read the tabloids. People pay for bad news! Just drive through any major metropolitan city and see the contrast between the crosses that afflict the inner city and the self-inflicted crosses of the affluent! *Lady Bentley, I regret to inform you that your Waterford razor for your legs has broken!* Just go into a naughty chat room on the Internet. Just look at how your kid can't spell! *It must be the teacher's fault. Now, who is his teacher, anyway?* Just look at how new parents are already volunteering at private schools four years before their kids will apply so they can get them enrolled? Just look at how a lot of "orthodox Catholics" behave! *The only thing more embarrassing than Americans in Europe are Roman Catholics participating in spontaneous prayer! Honey, if it ain't in the "missalette" it just ain't gonna happen!*

I am a person who seeks to define and live his own truth, in touch with what is spiritually and humanly ultimate. I am constantly meditating on the next step, the constant calling forth for and the new adventures the Lord puts before me. In the process of this quest, I am consciously and unconsciously in search for my capital-*T* truths. Capital-*T* truths concern such things as ultimate purpose, ultimate convictions, ultimate choices, ultimate goals, and personal stories. This is the ultimate spirit software that motivates our hardware. I have also become frightfully aware of my small-*t* truths: those things which are so insignificant, trivial, and petty but which we deify. Small-*t* truths are such things as being like everyone else, worrying about tomorrow, accusing others, or accusing oneself. Most bet the farm, focusing and sending most of their energy on their small-*t* truths because of being overwhelmed by the quantity and shallow quality of them. They are endless. They are insignificant in the long run.

But I also fight like everyone else to find the balance between these two levels of truth. This is why I hope that I am known not for having the answers but for knowing and having dealt with the questions. I ask them constantly. After studying world religions for many years I am totally aware of the conservatives/liberals, the right-wingers/left-wingers, and the progressives/suppressives, especially in religion. One of the saddest things that I have learned in sixteen years of priesthood is how Catholics often know more about their religion (when to go to Mass, when to fast, when the holy days are, who was pope before Pius XII) than they know about God, faith, spirituality, salvation, and affection. Some of these dear souls become "Catholic soldiers of religion" (we priests call them the Liturgy Police, Doctrine Nazis, etc.) and are, for example, so quick to defend the church's "bottom-line doctrinal stance" on pro-life as being an issue that solely protects the unborn babies. With the best of intentions some will furiously tell you this and that happens to the fetus in mommy's womb at two months, three months, five months, six months, two weeks, and six weeks. They'll parade with bloody pictures of fetuses while yelling names such as "baby butchers" and "murderers." Name-calling has always been so mature, huh?

They may even feel empowered with the authority to claim one as excommunicated and condemned to hell. At the very same time, though, these messengers of God's law will also be pro-racial discrimination, pro-sexual discrimination, pro-nuclear bombing, and pro-capital punishment. They will pay their housekeepers a nondignified wage (without benefits, by the way), etc. Some will even, when arguing with a pregnant girl outside of a clinic, simply walk away feeling successful and victorious if they have convinced her to keep the child. I applaud those who not only argue the case but make the sacrifice of helping the girl mother the child, then provide the loving care and support needed in raising it. But to gloat because they saved another baby born into a fatherless home, who statistically will probably grow up in a neglectful family, is mad. Some of these folks infuriate me! It is imperative and mandated that, if you're going to debate and rant and rave, you can't refuse to lift a finger or spend a dime to help the mother bring the baby to term and, also, help raise the child. Woe to the zealots who open their mouths quoting the laws of religion but don't open their homes and share their faith. It's not either/or. It's BOTH/AND.

The religious zealots—God loves them. But these poor people will and can literally destroy a Thanksgiving dinner for the cause of arguing religion. I have personally witnessed these people disown their own daughter if she decides to marry someone outside the church or someone who's been married before or, even worse, who doesn't want a thrilling, action-packed church wedding. (I know many think Catholic weddings can be a total drag.) I've seen these "people of religion" not attend to their own son's deathbed because he had caught the AIDS virus because of sexual improprieties and/or careless drug use. "My presence at your wedding (or at your deathbed) would send a message that I condone this type of behavior!" they'll say when challenged to be present to their dying son/daughter. *Get off your self-righteous cross! Your son is going to die and needs his mom and dad.* These "good" (scared, hurting, confused) but complacently ignorant people need to be right all the time. That's what they were taught. It's not their fault! They are so afraid. They are already so ashamed. They hate in themselves what they see in their kids. Who did this to them?

It really blows my mind that there are "good old Catholic people" who still furiously need and want Latin Masses (while not understanding a single word of Latin) but who are violently opposed to attending a Spanish Mass (while not understanding a single word of Spanish—a Latin language). I am amazed at how married people with a thousand kids will argue vehemently for mandatory celibacy for priests in the diocesan priesthood. They, personally, have no intention of living celibate lives themselves—not knowing where the whole idea of celibacy came from (it only was instituted in the eleventh century because of nepotism)—and they could care less about the implications it has on one's person and ministry in the twenty-first century. After all, *why should Father be happier with his sex life than we are with ours?* Of course, they are stating this while these good "in the know" Catholics are still making love frequently, *hopefully with their spouses,* and making more babies; but not as many babies equal to how many times they have sex, make love—whatever you call it these days.

What really blew my mind was when we in California had Proposition 187 in which illegal immigrants would have been denied any type of federal help—medical, educational, legal, or social. The U.S. Catholic bishops even voted against supporting this proposition. NO on Proposition 187. *Attaboys!* First time I can remember them speaking forcefully about something other than abortion and birth control. I can remember a young African American bishop, who is since deceased, who said to me after I asked him how his first national bishops' conference went, "Those damn white bishops! All they know how to do is talk about abortion and birth control." Disgustingly, in my opinion, this discriminatory Proposition 187 won the popular vote, and the majority of the Catholic population must have supported it also. How can we recite the scripture of "Love thy neighbor as thyself," if it only is applicable to those who are white, legal, Catholic, and "in a state of grace." Right?

A most vivid thing that comes to mind is at my own parish, St. Agatha's Parish Family (I don't emphasize the "Catholic" title so much because it is synonymous with "GO AWAY" for many people) in Mid-City Los Angeles. We are a lower income neighborhood community which is approximately 75 percent Hispanic and 25 percent African American. The worshipping community on Sunday, though, comes from all over. On Sunday, our worshipping community is 60 percent Hispanic, 20 percent African American, and 20 percent white. Getting souls to heaven is important, but also just as important is getting them to Tuesday while assuring that the parish family has the same dignity, benefits, and rights that are afforded any human being. In other words, I definitely would really like them to get to heaven but I don't want them to get there any earlier than possible. In the meantime, I want to minister to them my experience of the healing and survival of Christ Jesus in the church community while providing the solace needed when life is hell.

One of the many ministries that we have in the parish (and they don't teach this in the seminary) is a twice-a-week tutoring program where adults of the parish "just show up" to be with the kids from the neighborhood who "just show up." They are taught the ABC's and the three R's and also experience the comfort that comes with being in a safe, friendly, and caring environment of faithful, wonderful people. This amazing program came from a dear woman who has struggled with her own stuff, Ashley Merryman, who wanted to provide a little caring and sharing to the kiddies. Kudos, Ashley! We also have a weekly "reach out to the poor of the neighborhood" called SHARE in which meals (not feedings) are provided to the disadvantaged of the neighborhood. These are a sample of the true ministry of Jesus, hands touching hands. And this was begun by Marjorie Nickleberry who came forward originally to provide a meal on Christmas Day, which developed into the weekly Saturday SHARE reach-out to the neighborhood. We have ESL (English as a Second Language) classes for the Spanish speaking. We also have SFL, Spanish as First Language, for the Spanish speaking who cannot read or write in their own language, let alone try to learn a new and more difficult language as English. During the summer, when kids are out of school and more vulnerable to getting into trouble the most, we have a summer camp, an "asphalt" camp, which is huge for the neighborhood: CAMP GOOD IN THE HOOD. Then, one of my most favorite ministries is, simply, going with some of the senoras to the local market (bad enough the markets in the hood have lower quality vegetables, fruits, and meats than the markets in the suburbs. What is unnerving is that the poorer quality stuff is also more expensive). This is so annoying and unfair. As a result, we take the time showing the people of the neighborhood how to selectively shop and not tolerate poor quality fruits and vegetables. "It's okay to complain and speak your mind. They need you more than you need them," I encourage them.

"Now, Father, why are you getting involved in this stuff? You should spend more time saying Mass and hosting novenas!" Mass! Mass! Mass! Why do we have to have Mass at everything? "Say the magic words and win salvation!" Don't get me wrong, folks. I love celebrating the Eucharist but we are supposed to live what we receive. We are called to be the Eucharist and not just watch it from afar in the bleachers! As my mother said, "Beware of people who go to daily Mass!" *By the way, she went to Mass, daily.*

Now, the ministries that I mentioned above would not even be of importance for the traditional Catholic. While well-read religious writers write about the injustices of the world, did you know that many of my senoras don't have anyone to teach them how to count their change? So, at the grocery stores in the hood there are these coin-counting machines. Ain't that great? Such a wonderful help to our people. Yes? NO! The coins are surely counted electronically but 7.5 percent is deducted as a service charge. Again, where is the justice in that? I tell the folks, "Come in to my office! I'll count your change or even better, I'll teach you how to count your own change!" And what blows me away with these dear, sweet, saintly people from Mexico and Central America is that when I make this offer they look at me with horror! "Padre, you should be raising the dead and curing the sick, like Jesus!" Ugh. It really annoys the local "hospitals for profit" in the area when I horn into their territory and raise their dead and cure their sick. LOL! Plus, Father should be golfing, counting his stipends, and drinking Scotch like the padres back home.

And now, for your further ministerial enjoyment, one of our signature ministries at St. Agatha's ("Signature ministries"? See how white I can still sound?) is a service that is a total gift that fell from the sky: our health clinic, Queen's Care. Our nurse, Angelica, and her cabinet—the Queen's Care Foundation, a fund which was created from the sale of Queen of Angeles Catholic Hospital in Los Angeles—approached me one day after I had lunch with an old friend, Big John Brodhead, who introduced me to this guy, Rick, who worked in the Development Department of Queen's Care. *It's all about who you know and telling the story.* Imagine, what a blessing! Queen's Care called me to say, "We would love to put a health clinic in your parish! Interested?" Are you kidding? "YES!" Surprisingly, my initial reaction was rather shocking to them! *I was surprised by their surprise to my response!* Apparently, Queen's Care had made this offer to other parishes and faith-based communities but, alas, they were met with apathy. "Well, what did you expect?" I cracked sarcastically. "What does having health care and a health-care clinic have to do with saving their souls?" I was amazed at how some of the leadership of these faith-based communities could miss an opportunity to serve the sick and empower their membership to be involved in a healing ministry.

The health clinic's task is to provide health screenings and provide health education to the people of the neighborhood no matter what their religion, nationality, creed, legal status, etc. There is a "health cabinet," who are representatives from the neighborhood/community, which informs the RN (again, our parish nurse, Angelica) about the needs of the folks on the streets and in the homes of our parish. In addition, the membership of the neighboring six parishes and their geographical areas are invited to come to us for assistance. The families and individuals are served, referred, and provided funding for necessary prescriptions, dental, vision, in-home care, etc. It is a total gift for the parish in its mission to serve and minister, empower ministers, and to invite those who were "blessed" by this ministry to bless and minister to others in response. Oh my Good and Gracious

God! The many miracles that have come out of this ministry are huge.

So, now we have to associate ministries (such as those mentioned above) which will help us determine the difference between those who see themselves as primarily "people of religion" (people of conditional love, people of the law, left-brainers, right-wingers, people who put in the collection) and those who see themselves as primarily "people of faith" (people of unconditional love, people of compassion, people of love, right-brainers, left-wingers, people who do not put so much in the collection as they put forth in ministry). One day a man of good intentions approached me. He was from an upper-class neighborhood, a very traditional suburban Catholic parish, *i.e., smells and bells,* who attended daily Mass and had more money than God. He's a good man, really. This man said, "Father Ken, I want to make a donation to your clinic. I think it's great what's going on down there and I want to donate thirty-five thousand dollars." "Great," was my reply. *I'm always up for progress!* As we proceeded to nail down this great gift (i.e., as we were trying to cut the deal), we came to a hole in the road. "But I got to tell you, Father," he said as he finalized the offer, "it has to be for U.S. citizens only." Huh? Render to Caesar what is Caesar's? Render to your political views? Render to God what is God's? Render to the IRS what is the IRS's? Render to Immigration was is Immigration's? UGH!

"Uh . . . thanks for your offer but I guess I can't accept it. I really don't know, and couldn't discern who around here is a legal citizen or who is an illegal, a noncitizen, or a no-green-card alien," I replied. "Well you surely must inquire, don't you?" he inquired, shocked that I was turning down thirty-five thousand dollars! *He was shocked? I was shocked! "You're killing me Larry," goes the Sit 'n Sleep commercial.* My response to his method of inquiry was simple: "Sir, I do not ask those questions. I don't even ask if they're Catholic." When Jesus served the poor he did not ask them if they were registered in the synagogue, were legal or illegal, were insiders or outsiders, or whether they had a criminal record. Therefore, anyone who comes to our door is Christ looking for care. Period. I even tell my secretaries and volunteers who are seeking service that we don't immediately do what many parishes do. Normally, when you call a parish for a wedding appointment or even more serious, a sick call (and someone actually answers the phone) you are immediately put under the modern-day "Inquisition":

> *Are you Catholic?*
> *Are you a member of the parish?*
> *Do you tithe?*
> *Do you attend Mass weekly?*
> *Do you register?*
> *Who's the present pope?*
> *Or:*
> *"I'm sorry we cannot serve you. Call St. Agatha's. They serve everyone!"*

I refuse to ask who's legal or illegal. Who's Catholic or non-Catholic? Who's in "a state of grace" or "not in a state of grace"? *Like I would know? Like anyone would know?* It wasn't an issue for Jesus when he was with the sick. I really was tempted by the man with the thirty-five thousand dollars! Who would know, anyway? We really could use the money to help our fellow sisters and brothers (Catholic and non-Catholic, legal and illegal) fill their prescriptions, get in-home nursing, etc. Even Pope John XXIII said when he announced the creation of the Second Vatican Council in 1959, *"I am here to help the Holy Spirit,"* and *"Beware of the prophets of doom."* Anyway, the donor was obviously devoted to some other agenda. His final response: "This changes some things, Father. I'll give you a call." Obviously, *it changes everything!* He never called back. No donation. Not a penny. Not even a call back when I followed up. I never give up on the first pitch.

Unfortunately, I have found this to be quite typical. I hope that his "rendering to Caesar" and his "agenda" will be there for him when he is on the cross and there's no one to relieve him of it. Believe it or not, though, I will be there. Why? He doesn't know any better. He is just stuck. Please don't think I am condemning anyone here (though they, the people of religion, would, and have, condemned me in a New York minute) because there is room for all kinds of people in this world to coexist in peace and harmony. It just makes me wonder what people think is more important in life and in the eyes of the God? Religion gone amok! People still think today it's all about the rules, the rules, and the rules. "What are the rules about fasting, Father? What are the rules about getting married, Father? What are the rules about sex before marriage, Father? Is this a sin? Is that a sin?"

Following the rules and laws of the Catholic Church (as also with Judaism, Islam, or even Frank's Free-Rocking-and-Rolling Baptist Church) can oftentimes be the priority. It's only in exploring spirituality (that driving force that makes us want to move ahead, to unite, to connect) that we would want to ponder on how much joy would come if we simply tried to love as Jesus, Moses, or Muhammad did? I can't help but feel very saddened and passionately frustrated by the infinite amount of spiritual wealth and self-value that people are depriving themselves by being people whose "religious ideas" are more important or more prevalent than "spiritual quests." For these sad and complacent and typically not-so-happy people, the possibility of a spiritual quest is so "otherworldly" and reserved for people who stereotypically have been assigned an "otherworldly" calling: monks, clergy, and religious women. We must remember as the little ones who are of this world, that the Father gave us Jesus his Son to remove the distancing between him and us that was constructed by unhealthy aspects of religion. God is of this world. Where? Look inside!

Alas, the problem. If we can't even see God in ourselves, how are we supposed to see this divine source and urging in one another? My heart breaks for those good people of my Catholic parish family (heck, for many Catholics in general) who just cannot and will not come to believe and trust that God loves them, that salvation is a gift that is just for them to participate in. These poor people can't shed themselves of all that Catholic guilt that has accumulated throughout the years of their "religious" formation. *I am not sure they even know that we've grown!* It pains me sitting in the Reconciliation Room at church every week (i.e., the confessional or the box) and hearing these saints who are convinced that they are going to hell because of, for example, a minor sexual struggle. Or, even worse, a bad thought. They honestly believe that no matter what good they do (which is more than most) that God will not look beyond this minor problem with masturbation, dirty thoughts, and awaking in the morning with a woody. Everything is still a mortal sin. They are convinced that pleasure and joy are inconsistent with the message of Jesus Christ.

"Bless me Father, for I have sinned. I have a gambling problem."

"Yikes! Gasp! Panic!" my actions conveyed.

"You okay, Father?"

"I just remembered that I didn't buy my Lotto ticket today. $190 million, baby."

This despair really saddens me and when I try to offer some type of hope, some Christ-centered assurance that God loves them, they walk away so disappointed in me. I failed in my duty to make them feel bad.

"Where are my twenty Our Fathers and fifteen rosaries, Father?" On file? A floppy diskette somewhere? You want fifteen rosaries? I'll make you read the whole Bible if you press me!

"I would suggest sitting in the church for three whole minutes and listening to the Lord." This is sheer torture for suburbanites— a whole three minutes in silence. Listening! This means shutting up and not torturing God with petty requests and pleas for mercy. Just listen to him love the living hell out of you! There is something that they've been conditioned to believe that makes them not accept salvation when it is handed to them on a silver platter (which it is during the Eucharist, by the way). This also happens just as often at Mass when we share our platters of food with the poor, the neighbor, the stranger, and, *here it comes,* when we even share a meal with our spouse and children! When was the last time that happened? (This means no TV, no Walkmans, and no cellular phones, by the way.) Yes, it is not a capital crime to actually not answer the phone when it rings. At my parish I announce before each Mass, "Please turn off your cellular phones. If it rings during Mass, we'll just have to start all over!" This works, by the way. The other thing that works is that when the cell phone rings I say, "No problem. We'll all wait until you've finished the call!"

Let's face it, for those of us Catholics who are either (1) baby boomers or are (2) that older generation that did the booming that made the babies, we know our religion perfectly but we don't know God. We know exactly how to go to hell and not have a clue as to how to get to heaven. For us, the only way to get to heaven is keep out of hell! It's as easy as that! Just don't murder, don't rape, don't swear, and don't touch yourself! Why go to Mass, for example? To avoid committing mortal sin and thus keeping out of hell just in case I was killed in an accident and there was no priest to be found, which there seldom is. We're off blessing jungle gyms and houses like they did in the old days. Frankly, the guilt with obligating Catholics to attend Mass (i.e., celebrating the Eucharist) under pain of mortal sin is brilliant! This "rule," alone, has saved many a parish from going down the tubes because their liturgies end up being a Spirit-sucking experience, an experience of ritual devoid of any spiritual relevance or human solace. The mortal sin deal doesn't really work at my parish where, I am told, our liturgies are a rave party in comparison to theirs back home! And parents of the baby boomers still wonder why their adult children no longer go to Mass any-more. It wasn't real! The people looked like they were in pain. Too many rules—you break the rules, you go to hell because of mortal sin! Why not eat meat but only fish on Fridays? To avoid commit-ting mortal sin and going to hell. Yippee! It's Lobster Friday!

Why not have sex before marriage? So to avoid committing mortal sin and thus keeping out of hell. This is "give me the bot-tom line" Catholicism. I really don't think God is as concerned about our sex life as much as the boys with red hats are. Whatever. The whole sexual deal is covered in Catholicism within a scholas-tic field known as Moral Theology. Catholic Moral Theology is a huge compilation of directives, which have accumulated over a two-thousand-year period, pertaining to how to live a moral life as Christ would want us to. Though morality covers a lot more than sex—it covers economics, life, capital punishment, social justice, family life, and world hunger—for most it still seems to be about just sex. Therefore, moral theology has become a collection of thousands of different sex-centered directives concocted by celi-bate churchmen who tell us, the faithful, "If you don't knock that crap off you're going to go blind."

I love the comic piece by Father Guido Sarducci in his album *Life at St. Dominic's* wherein he is giving a lecture to a bunch of nuns on what criteria determine whether someone gets into heaven or hell. It goes something like this:

You see, it's-a like-a this. When we are born we are-a given a cer-tain amount of money, and it's-a placed in a big-a bank account in heaven. Every time you sin, money is deducted from the account. Depending on the amount of money left in da account by the end of your life-a determines whether you get into a-heaven or into a-hell. For example, let's say you begin your life-a with a thou-sand dollars. When you murder someone, that's-a gonna cost ya one hundred dollars. That's a biggie. When you steal, that's-a twenty-five dollars. When you cheat, that's-a ten dollars. When you-a masturbate, that's-a twenty-five cents. For the masturbation, that doesn't seem to sound like a lot, but it adds up-a pretty quick! You wanna know what my nightmare is? That when I die, I go to the pearly gates and I'm a short-a twenty-five cents!

Let's take time for a sidebar!

Now, what did I tell you was the number one truth sought out by Catholics after a wonderful, Spirit-filled celebration of, for example, the sacrament of marriage on a Saturday afternoon which began at 2:30 p.m. (Over by 3:30 p.m.) Answer: Does this count for Sunday, Father?" Do you really want me to answer that question? You won't like the answer.

(The number one thing I learned in the seminary and still live by to this very day: NEVER ask for permission. If you get busted you can always say, "I'm sorry.")

I generally never wear my collar when on a plane. By the way, nowadays if you see a nun in the airport who is recognizable by her wearing a veil, she's only wearing it in hopes of getting bumped up to business class or first class! If I do happen to wear the collar on the plane for a short flight while on business, I'm trapped. There was a time I especially recall when I did get trapped on a plane and some dear old lady was asking me endless questions about "the faith" (for her that meant about "the religion"). She was sweet and I thought I was really doing a great job explaining to her the passion of God's love for us, of how we are empowered to be dynamic "Christs" in the world today. Her response: "That was lovely, Father. Now, what I really wanted to know, Father, is whatever happened to LIMBO?! Where do those unbaptized babies go? Also, do people who went to hell because they ate meat on Fridays get a reprieve since it is no longer a mortal sin? And, whatever happened to all those pagan babies whom we brought from Africa in the 1950s and 1960s?" HELLLLLPPP!

While on this matter of getting trapped and tortured with trivia, I have another little experience to contribute. When going to the cemetery after a funeral I never travel in the hearse. Whenever I do a funeral, and I've been doing them for sixteen years, these guys from the mortuary always ask me if I want to ride to the cemetery with them! Are you kidding? No way! Not only do I not need to sit in a car with a dead person housed in a lovely piece of furniture (aren't coffins a waste?) but I need to avoid being ambushed and, inevitably, tortured with the same ridiculous questions concerning religion and, ultimately, nothing of any significant salvific importance.

The litany of questions goes like this in order of frequency, and it hardly ever varies.

Who's going to be the next pope?
Answer: John Paul III?

When are priests going to be allowed to get married?
Answer: When we first teach them how to be vulnerable in relationships!

When are women going to be ordained?
Answer: When you can find one who isn't a threat to the male church.

Why did you want to be a priest?
Answer: Because I can work until I am seventy-five years old, enjoy an hour-and-a-half retirement, and drop dead—broke, untouched, and not found in my room until three days after my clock quit ticking! This would make Jesus very happy, I am told. I really can't wait to hear the bishop stand before my coffin and say what a wonderful priest I was. I am a man, NOT AN ANIMAL! I am just the Elephant Priest! By the way, if you ever really want to see someone rise from the dead, I dare any one of you to open my coffin! I'll reach up, grab you by the throat, and drag you in with me!

Are you a virgin? (Why do you need to know that?)
Answer: In every dimension of my life, I can say emphatically, "I wasn't born in Bethlehem."

What do you really believe in?
My response after having endured round after round of such questions: Right now, trading places with the dude in the box in the back of this coach.

Because of the sentiment above, I almost never go to wedding receptions if I don't know anyone at the table that I would be sitting at. The rule: I got to know at least ten people who are fun. Funny thing is, though, I love to party and meet people. But not at the weddings that I just presided over. Again, I love to socialize but it's the same torturous questions over and over at wedding receptions. Can't someone have a conversation with me as you would with any other person? Can't I sneak in a dance without everyone taking photographs of the priest kicking up the rug with some babe? No. So, you walk around and get interviewed over and over again. *Where did the days go when people bought the padre a drink or three?*

Just because I'm a priest it doesn't mean that I can't talk about sports, sex, romance, the world, tell jokes, laugh—be engaged! But, I'm a priest. No one thinks we can have conversations. Therefore, it is a three- to five-hour interview. I don't need this. Sorry. I can survive on my own, thank you. But you folks really should think about the unrealistic demands you put on the padres! I guess we have asked for it. But not all of us. Did you ever notice how you never see anyone place flowers on a priest's grave in a Catholic cemetery? The priest section is as barren as Death Valley. Frankly, as far as I'm concerned, they can put me in a Hefty and put me in the trash bin for the morning pickup.

I can remember a time when I was still not wise enough to socially find polite ways of "ditching" wedding receptions. Once in the Valley, I remember a woman from the generation who "did the booming that made the babies" who came up to me and started to engage me in a discussion over celibacy. *Now dear, go buy Father a drink. Do you expect me talk about this sober?* I began with a huge exhortation of what intimacy is, how compassion (carrying the crosses of others) is truly that which is fulfilling and intimate, (i.e., that one can have intimacy without having touch). *Calm down, we'll get to this later!* And, I said after that, "I can honestly say that I have intimacy in my life on a regular basis"! *I meant it at that time!* Then, I gave it to her. *What the hell.* "Yet, I think that celibacy should not be mandatory for a diocesan priest and that a priest would be more effective and affective if he had a wife and kids, a loving responsibility to human relationships."

Could you imagine how the other Catholic women in the parish would treat the wife of a Catholic pastor? Could you imagine how the wife of the pastor would treat the wife of the associated pastor? Let's face it—the only reason that there is celibacy today is that if there weren't, you'd have to pay us. You think my wife is going to put up with this?

She got really upset with me because I had challenged one of the sacred cows that she felt was necessary to inflict on us priests without having a clue as to the practical, emotional, and relational implications of celibacy, positive and negative. An hour returned and she came back to me (three glasses of wine later for her) and said, "You know, Father, I gave it some thought. *(A MIRACLE!)* I agree with you. *(Another miracle!)* I think priests should have the option to get married. Who could it hurt?!

"Who needs a wife?! I need a mistress!" *Just kidding.* I am surprised I didn't share this thought with her. I usually don't have an unexpressed feeling! Anyway, the very next day, my pastor came up to me and said, "Ken, some lady said that at the wedding yesterday you were talking about having sex (she obviously didn't hear a word about my definition of "intimacy") and looking for a wife? *Swell. Off to Priest Prison!*

Sadly, I really can't blame people for not knowing how to talk to priests and, more importantly, how to talk about or go about the development of their spirituality. If you really think you are going to hell anyway, does it make a difference? If Father is on the pedestal, why embrace him? He's too high! He's out of reach! Besides, why worry about spirituality? All I have to do is get to the confessional after killing someone or committing adultery and it's washed away in a jiffy! Have you ever noticed that everyone knows the Ten Commandments (the "thou shall nots") of Moses's time, but don't know the eight Beatitudes of Christ that we take the Christian spirituality from? Beatitudes: attitudes to be and live. Why should people who think they are going to hell even be remotely interested in spirituality if it isn't going to do any good? Spirituality means that you believe in hope. It means that for you being a Christian is not a title achieved but, rather, a personal goal to attain. "Heaven can wait," literally, according to people of religion. Why? No one can fly direct to heaven. There is a layover. Where? PURGATORY!

If we were ever to get to heaven, it would only be after spending hundreds and thousands of years in purgatory. For one like myself, who still often relapses back into his yellow Catholic waxy build-up, I still thank God that there is a place, a state of being, called purgatory. There is hope for me! As a child I would pray at night, Lord, get me to purgatory! I can especially remember thinking as a kid, "If I died and woke up and saw a sign that said, "Welcome Ken Deasy to 5 billion years in purgatory," I would be exuberant! I made it! But, I didn't deserve it. I still deserve hell, and Jesus is only sparing me.

"Kenny Deasy," my second grade religious-sister told me once while pronouncing sentence on me for the crime of shooting a spit wad at the girl across the room, "You must write one thousand times, 'I am personally responsible for the wounds of Christ,' and get it signed by your parents." I did it. I believed it. But no way were my parents going to join in on this momentum of public executions! Jesus would understand. He disobeyed his parents once when he did his own deal conversing with the wise men. My parents never signed it. I forged their names. I forged their names on everything: lines, conduct slips, progress reports. You see, in Catholic school I became and remained a master of forgery. My mom used to make me bring home to her the Sunday bulletin as proof that I attended Mass. I would bring her home the bulletin, but I would simply go to Church, pick up a bulletin and then go off with my buddies.

As she was getting suspicious, she would begin to drill me. "What was the Gospel about?"

"Jesus."

"What was the homily about?"

"Love."

This is also, I guess, where my preparation for giving homilies/sermons began. I would now have to take home the missalette and prepare my own homiletic discourse. I had her going for a while. But because my own homilies were too personal, she became suspicious. Mom thought she was really smart.

"Kenny, I not only want you to bring me home a bulletin, not only do I want to hear what Father preached on, BUT I ALSO WANT MONSIGNOR TO SIGN IT!" Not a problem. Again, I thank Mom for this experience. Being a master forger got me through a lot of tough times. Also it contributed to my becoming a good preacher. If I am a good preacher it's because I have been resurrected by all these wild and twisted, good and bad experiences of life, in the family and of the Catholic Church. Though I have had my most painful difficulties with people of "church" (my only enemies to my face have been priests), I also experienced the goodness of their charity and kindness to me during some really lonely and devastating times. They, like Jesus, literally walked into my hell and took me by the hand and brought me out.

CHAPTER THREE

IT'S YOUR RESURRECTION

"Lazarus come out!"
"But I don't want to!"
Could you imagine?!

Most unfortunately, and most erroneously, Catholics can be known by many to be those whose actions convey that they are still entombed in those medieval traditions and, thus, assigned such titles as: "idol worshippers," "papists," "people who worship Mary," "rich Ca-zillionaires," "Vatican folk," "Romans," and "descendants of the thirteenth-century Crusades." For me though, and based on my own experience, Catholics predominantly are people of prayer and sacrifice for others. Yet, we still get thrown into the bathwater of being total robots of Roman papacy. Unless someone has been blessed with the types of experiences of faith that I have, this is very understandable. This is why

I am trying to paint a different face on it all. Yet, there is little consistency and, thus, mixed messages:

We pray for peace.

We pray for justice.

We pray for the end to bigotry.

We pray for healing in struggling marriages.

We pray that Michelle Pfeiffer will marry me someday.

We pray that the St. Louis Rams will win the Super Bowl. *They lost this year's.*

We pray that I will win Lotto.

We pray that the Lord will rid the world of people living in sin. *Though they are lots of fun.*

We pray that the homosexuals will change their ways so that the Lord will not punish us with their AIDS. *I have actually heard this one.*

We pray for this.

We pray for that.

We pray for sunshine, rainbows, happy faces, and balloons. Ugh!

God says:

Quit whining! And fix it yourself! As I have done so you can do. Don't get me wrong, kids. I don't want you to shut up. I would love to fix this stuff for you if only you would allow me to. I can fix it, again. But YOU have to shut up and listen. You have to hear me want you and empower you to be my hands. You have to hear me want you and empower you to be my tears. You have heard me want you and empower you to be my tools. Get off your high horse! Get off your tush. Get off your high crosses that you have carved for yourselves but continue to blame me for!

NEW FOOTPRINTS IN THE SAND
ONE NIGHT I HAD A WONDROUS DREAM
ONE SET OF FOOTPRINTS THERE WAS SEEN

THE FOOTPRINTS OF MY PRECIOUS LORD
BUT MINE WERE NOT ALONG THE SHORE.

I THOUGHT OF THE FIRST FOOTPRINT HOPE
IT'S MEANING FOR MY LIFE TO COPE
I REMEMBER WELL THE FOOTPRINT PSALM
THAT THE LORD WILL CARRY ME FAR AND LONG.

BUT, THEN SOME STRANGER PRINTS APPEARED,
AND I ASKED THE LORD, "WHAT HAVE WE HERE?"
THOSE PRINTS ARE LARGE AND ROUND AND NEAT,
BUT LORD, THEY ARE TOO BIG FOR FEET?

"MY CHILD," HE SAID IN SOMBER TONES,
"FOR MILES I CARRIED YOU ALONE.
I CHALLENGED YOU TO WALK IN FAITH,
BUT YOU REFUSED SO I'D CARRY YOUR DEAD WEIGHT.

A FREE RIDE YOU EXPECTED! YOU WOULD NOT GROW!
YOUR WALK OF FAITH YOU WOULD NOT KNOW.
SO AS NOT TO ENABLE YOUR PASSIVE "RUT"
THERE, I DROPPED YOU ON YOUR BUTT!

BECAUSE IN LIFE, THERE COMES A TIME
WHEN YOU MUST FIGHT AND YOU MUST CLIMB
WHEN YOU MUST RISE AND YOU MUST STAND
OR LEAVE YOUR BUTT PRINTS IN THE SAND.

—Author Unknown

This is so true.

Oh sure, we all want resurrection, but we got to get off our asses (crosses) to attain it. We pray for freedom, paradise, celebration, and companionship during our journey here in our own lifetimes, but we also want to tiptoe around (avoid even) the cross at all costs. Yet, funny to say, because we allow our resurrection experiences to be short-lived because of new complications in life that inevitably come with being vulnerable, our return to the cross and staying there in favor of another short-lived resurrection is inevitable.

No matter how many warranties, insurance policies, guarantees, defense systems, and backups we create to ease the crush of an unknown future that we fear, there are going to be crosses in life. Something or someone else is sure to come our way and throw us back on the tree. So, it's better to stay on the cross to ease the disappointments than to rob us of our resurrections. I mean we might as well stay there and not let anyone get the upper hand. *It is better to expose our own dirty laundry before having someone else do it for us!* To choose to remain on the cross means that you have no motivation for trusting and accepting the joy that can come when off it. Again, you surely can't have resurrection until you go to the cross. But, I have also learned that you have to allow it. Allow the cross. And . . . allow yourself to live the resurrection and allow resurrection to hold on to you. Resurrection? I have to rise from the dead? I have to rise from physical death?

No.

Remember Monty Python? *"Bring out your dead! Bring out your dead!"*

"But I'm not dead yet. I was just going for a walk!" Well, at least I wouldn't wait for that though it is totally possible.

Resurrection means being able to rise from despair and to allow hope! It means to heal from wounds inflicted or self-inflicted and live unscarred. It means to believe in our real goodness even when we are challenged to be bad! It means to believe and celebrate simply because with living a Christ-centered, "in this world" life the possibilities for life and zest are endless. The resurrection still remains even when we allow ourselves to feel like failures and are made to feel like trash.

God doesn't make trash. We do!

Let's not judge God's will and life's purpose the way we read the stock report in the *New York Times*. We pray to believe in "the possibility of return," especially when we are told "to go away"! *What's better to say—"Here's where I am going by this time, on this route, according to this agenda," OR, to say, "I don't know where I'm going but I'm on my way!"*

Resurrection is about believing in getting up when you've fallen. It's about resignation. It's about surrender. YIKES! Remember when words such as "resignation" and "surrender" had positive and romantic connotations? Now, they connote disgrace, defeat or what you must do when you are doomed to failure. Remember the stations of the cross? The devotion has Jesus falling three times. This devotion also has him getting up three times, by the way! Resurrection is also being able to pat yourself on the back and allowing yourself to be patted on the back! Real resurrection happens especially when you have tried and bled and sweated but did not attain the results you wished for. I really believe that the bottom line of life is when we die and meet the Lord at the security screening station to heaven and he says, "Did you try to love me?" We will ourselves give testimony to this effort or lack of effort, contrary to believing that in the "Judgment Center of Heaven" there will be a record printed out displaying what we have done and what we have failed to do. It's all about results? I don't think so.

SIDEBAR

Three couples are drinking and driving on the way to Las Vegas. They drive off the road at three in the morning and are rushed up to the Judgment Center in Heaven where an awakened, grumpy

Saint Peter meets them. Impatiently thumbing through the three case folders before him he declares, "Let's do the men first! Mr. Johnson, stand up! Heaven or hell?"

"Heaven, Saint Peter!" He replies.

"HEAVEN?" Saint Peter shouts in disbelief. While continuing the sentencing he adds, "There is no way that heaven is in the plan for you, Johnson! Look at your life! You loved and sought only money and wealth every day of your life. You loved money so much you nicknamed your wife Penny! TO HELL WITH YOU!"

Wham! In a flash, Johnson goes down.

Saint Peter continues. "Mr. Howard! Heaven or hell? The obviously ruffled "Howard soul" responds with a tone of doubt, "H-H-Heaven?"

"HEAVEN?" Saint Peter belly-laughs in disbelief while continuing, "There is no way that heaven is in your plan. Look at your life! You loved and sought only food, feeding your face every moment of your life. You're three hundred pounds overweight because of intentional gluttony. You loved food so much you nicknamed your wife Candy! TO HELL WITH YOU!"

Wham! In a flash, Howard goes down.

The third soul, the palefaced Mr. Jones, looks at his wife and says, "Oh, oh, Fanny! I think I'm screwed!"

So, where is the resurrection in today's moment, in our life on this planet? Bottom line: Allow yourself to be connected, to feel connected in today's moment by seeking and believing in ultimate meanings, purposes, and "hints of an explanation" behind the crosses of life—meaning, behind the utter disappointments, behind the abandonments, behind the rash judgments, behind the addictions, behind the unjust condemnations—the list of crud that goes on and on.

Resurrections are various and numerous. They occur and begin to occur when, even though we fall short of living a fully human life as shown to us through the story and dynamic mission of Jesus, there is forgiveness. There is always the opportunity to begin again without shame. Reconciliation. There is resurrection when you ever so slightly begin to hear and believe that there is dignity and more to be had in "getting up" rather than the safety of "staying down." There is resurrection when there is reconciliation. It is very important to know that not only is there resurrection in forgiveness but when a reconciliation is attained (i.e., when the relationship harmed is graciously "wanted" to return right back where the relationship was before the offense).

RECONCILIATION = FORGIVENESS WITHOUT GRUDGES THAT PREVENT RETURN

This is what surely was the challenge presented by Jesus to the people of religion of his time. Jesus came to bring a more intimate and touchable and sensual face of God to a people who were experiencing loss, defeat, despairs, and judgment without mercy.

As many of my Jewish friends have said to me, "We really blew it with Jesus. Not only did he shake up the boys of the synagogue, but also he was a happy guy who was a carpenter in a town that had no wood. Things would have been different for him if only he was a doctor!"

So, resurrection is just psychobabble, right? No. It is having a God experienced in the deep-felt urgings, desires, lustings, and wantings for more in life. It is believing and trusting in a God who, in Jesus, can say to us when we're in our crud, "I have been there!" We have a God that can relate to our life situation of "doings" and "beings" even when it doesn't work as dramatically, as easily, as speedily, and as permanently as we would like. And resurrection is having the people who call themselves "people of faith" (again, this does not necessarily apply to those who present themselves as "people of religion") be the actual godsends in response to the prayers of others. So, where is the resurrection? Or, why is the resurrection not so evident to us today? I have two responses—not answers, mind you.

1. We need to shift a little. Budge a little. Take the initiative to develop and grow into a new look at faith, life, God, and self. Try it you'll like it! Let go and let God! Get lost a little. Resurrection is happening all over the place! I see it thirty times a day and sometimes thirty times an hour. I also miss it thirty times a day and sometimes thirty times an hour. I mean it. I see resurrected people who conquer their tombs, inflicted or self-inflicted, whether it be accompanied with a lot of FLASH (a cure) or a taken-for-granted good day, feeling, and happening. I see miracles happen everyday with as much dramatic flare as a whisper in the night. (I would love to hear a whisper in the night!)

Take a moment and ponder the smallest and most minute joys and good things in life: The ability to go to the store in a car. The ability to afford a car AND insurance. The ability to have hot water. The blessing of a good friend. The blessing of opportunity. Done? Good. Now dwell on how this joy has an infinite amount of potential and power in it. This joy has the power to lift you up high. This joy is a total mystery.

A mystery? Remember when the dear sisters taught us that everything was a mystery? "How can the bread change into the Body of Christ?" "It's a mystery!" was the typical response. How could God always be? It's a mystery. How could Jesus rise from the dead? It's a mystery. How could God be three persons, but one and the same? It's a mystery. Shut up and look at the three-leaf clover, will you? If, in fact, we turn into a pillar of salt if we smile in church, why didn't Father Martin become "salt-a-fied" when he smiled at the sign of peace? It's a mystery.

"A mystery" was the answer given to the unexplainable. "Mystery" is the term given to those treasures of our faith that have an infinite amount of meaning and empowerment for us about God, ourselves, others, and the world. By the way, I have this Trinity thing all figured out. It can't make sense? Well, if faith is such a cognitive thing then three can't be one and, congratulations, it's a mystery. But if we think in terms of relationality—a relationship is that which God wants for us and from us the most—it makes all the sense in the world. The Trinity is God continually revealing himself to us in different personas. The character on which the movie *Jerry McGuire* is based has a mentor, his uncle, who says to him as a valuable piece of advice, "It's all about relationships." Therefore, I will take the same approach much to the chagrin of theologians who think faith is a mystery when it clashes with reason.

In the beginning was the Father—all is destined toward the Father.

In the beginning was Budweiser.

God the Father's original expression of himself to a people thousands of years ago was as a providing father. He fought their fights, he made them a home, he fought off other gods, etc. But after doing all this, after being the providing father, he came to realize that at the fall of the Judaic empires of Israel and Judah, a fall interpreted to be a result of the people not keeping and adhering to the covenant, that the love needed in response to his doing things wasn't happening. As I see it, God the Father was thinking, "Why don't these folks get it? I do everything for them and yet they don't get how much I love them. Hmmmmm. It's not their fault. Maybe I need to rethink their needs. Maybe I need not to do so much but to be with them mutually and lovingly and vulnerably."

The original Budweiser is great but far more people need to be attracted to it and stick with it to keep it successful. So, even

Budweiser had to rethink people's needs. Avoiding calories! The people of two thousand years ago needed a touchable God; a mutual God; a relatable God. They needed a brotherly God. "I will give them myself in Jesus." The people of Budweiser needed a good tasting beer but with less calories. So, Bud gave them Bud Light. Likewise, the next step of growth in this relationship . . . the touchable, lovable, adorable, and vulnerable Jesus of Nazareth.

We spend a lot of time learning about that Jesus "then." In so doing, we learn not just about God experienced in the person of Jesus, but we learn about ourselves, our capacities, our power, our need for love, and our need to share love. We learn about what is most important: Love. That God is loving. That we should be loving. That we are forgiven for the times that we are not loving. That love hurts. God hurt. We use the story of Jesus like a pair of spectacles by which we can see the Lord working in our lives then and now. In addition, we can also see where the Lord is summoning us to say yes to his invitation to "come and see."

The Christian people of today, who absolutely adore the Jesus of Nazareth, now need to feel that this Jesus, who has not only been resurrected but has ascended, is still around and is not a museum piece, an old love letter, reminding us of value and love. The Budweiser people of today realize that tasting great is good. Fewer calories is good. But a little extra kick wouldn't hurt also. Did God quit talking when the Bible was compiled and published? After Jesus, did God quit transmitting like a malfunctioned, worn out satellite on Mars? No. As a matter of fact, God was just beginning to serve the choice wine.

God gave us the Holy Spirit. Budweiser gave us Bud Extra Dry. Father, Son, Holy Spirit. Budweiser, Bud Light, Bud Extra Dry. Whichever one you can relate to, you're going to go for it. In other words, whichever one you pick, it's still a Bud. Whichever one you identify with, it is still God. How about that one, Sista? Your "mystery" has become a surprise! A gift! A joy! A beer! So drink up!

Let me tell you about one of the resurrections that I think of often. It is a total mystery. It is total resurrection. It is about Eric and Eileen, Eric the resurrected, and how Eric was resurrected by the Christ in Eileen—the Eileen who was and is one of the many Christs who exist today. How the Eric on the cross resurrected Eileen. I pray that Eric knows that he is the power, also! They both were another avenue of resurrection for me.

There is Eric, a homeboy from the hood whom I had the honor to meet when he was imprisoned in a juvenile detention facility about fifteen years ago. He was in a gang and had absolutely no intention of ever leaving this lifestyle "family." He was a powerful young man. He was one of those guys who surely would exit the detention facility and immediately return to his gang family, risking parole violation.

Don't throw stones at the gangsters, folks! Though I've never seen so much despair and waste of life and potential with these guys in the gangs, there is sure more spirit of family, twisted as it is, than I have seen in many of the so-called perfect American families. His reasons for being in the gang are textbook. On the streets there are no jobs that he could qualify for and, at the same time, that could pay enough to meet the practical demands of family. On the streets there are no presumed expectations and encouragements for the guys/gals to believe in, in order to achieve a little of the best that life has to offer.

We all presume that humans are born with an inbred agenda that you go to high school, college, have morals and good manners, and become law-abiding and love-abiding civilized people.

WRONG! Nothing could be from the truth.

But resurrection has happened for Eric, though, like us all, he can surely ignore, deny, and discard it. It began when he was in jail. A seed of hope and faith was planted by Christ, through the Holy Spirit, by Eileen and countless others throughout his life. Though Eric seemingly ignored it for a long time (whether he was

IN or OUT of jail, gangs, and work), the seed implanted was not apparent but, as time would tell, neither was it deliberately discounted. Though Eric did return to prison on gang-related crimes a few times after the time I met him way back in 1988, now he is married with two kids. He works graveyard shifts in a warehouse. He is a family man. He is a father. He is a husband. He is alive. Man, I am so glad that he is alive. I thank God that he is alive. So does he. He doesn't have a fancy car. He doesn't have a fancy job, apartment, neighborhood, or wardrobe. But, he doesn't need that stuff either. You see, he conquered the odds. Most kids in prison stay there and return and return most of their life. Well, at least until they are shot because of gang retaliations or selling someone bad dope. Hey! Why work at McDonald's for $7.15 when you can make $715 a day selling drugs?!

You see, Eric has allowed resurrection to happen for him, and thank God he had stayed alive until the time (i.e., survived without being killed) occurred when he was ready to allow it. It didn't happen because of novenas, candles, and "spiritual devotional aerobics." It was a gift from God. It was a gift from God named Eileen. Eric was also a gift of God to Eileen. Eileen McDermott, whom I had invited to minister at two juvenile detention facilities in Malibu, was the godsend to Eric. This will play out more as I continue to set it up. But I will say right here and now, Eileen is awesome! Just plain hot-damn AWESOME!

This brings me to my second response to the wonderment, where is the resurrection today? Or why is the resurrection not so evident to us today?

2. Resurrection is not as evident today because we don't share the resurrection that we've been given. We hide it in a bushel basket and/or don't even know that it has already happened. If being a Christian were a crime today like it used to be would there be enough evidence to convict us?

We talk about it. Decorate Easter Eggs on the morning we celebrate it, but we really don't believe it. We believe in the defeat of the cross and not the triumph of the cross: the power of hope. And, we don't believe that our actions will reveal that there is a resurrection or, sadly, that there is nothing to reveal. We speak of resurrection, but our actions reveal our nonbelief.

Remember the story of the "doubting Thomas"! Poor guy. Thomas is known for all time as being a doubter, unfaithful to Jesus. Well, let's look at this gospel and see really why Thomas doubted. It really wasn't his fault. (*It's not your fault! It's not your fault!*—Robin Williams to Matt Damon in the film *Good Will Hunting*.)

John 20:19–31

On the evening of that first day of the week, when the doors were locked, where the disciples were, for fear of the Jews [people of religion], Jesus came and stood in their midst and said to them, "Peace be with you." When he had said this he showed them his hands and his side. The disciples rejoiced when they saw the Lord. Jesus said to them again, "Peace be with you. As the Father has sent me so I send you." And when he had said this, he breathed on them and said to them, "Receive the Holy Spirit. Whose sins you forgive are forgiven them, and whose sins you retain are retained."

Thomas, called Didymus, one of the Twelve, was not with them when Jesus came. So the other disciples said to him, "We have seen the Lord." But he said to them, "Unless I see the mark of the nails in his hands and put my finger into the nail marks and put my hand into his side, I will not believe."

Now a week later his disciples were again inside and Thomas was with them. Jesus came, although the doors remained locked, and stood in their midst and said, "Peace be with you." Then he said to Thomas, "Put your finger here and see my hands, and bring your hand and put it into my side and do not be unbelieving, but believe." Thomas answered and said to him, "My Lord and my God!" Jesus said to him, "Have you come to believe because you have seen me? Blessed are those who have not seen and believed."

Just some questions? Thomas has always been presented to me as a flake, an unbeliever. Please note that he was not in the room behind locked doors with the other apostles. Unlike the others, he was not hiding out of fear of being associated with the one arrested, accused, condemned, and crucified. He obviously left the cross once Jesus of Nazareth was removed from it also. He had stuff to do. He was still alive and free to go about his business.

The reason Thomas couldn't have believed that Jesus was raised was because the behavior of the apostles didn't give evidence to it. They were still behind locked doors. They were still in fear. Though Jesus was resurrected they, themselves, were not resurrected! In other words, we talk resurrection but WE DON'T SHOW IT by how we act, how we make choices and treat others. This same lack of evidence to the resurrection (called "personal witness") is furthered when "children of God" believe more in the betrayals, misunderstandings, accusations, rash judgments, etc., that lead to the cross and pay little attention to these things that the cross of Christ was supposed to conquer: death and the gossip, defeatism, smut, false ambitions, jealousy, and fatalism associated with it.

Thomas was being told by people behind locked doors that Jesus was resurrected. But the apostles remained behind these locked doors showing that they didn't get it. They were still locked into fear. They didn't fathom that what they saw happen to Jesus, as a loving response from God, could actually happen to them. As the locked doors were more evident than resurrection apparently was, the apostles didn't believe the full impact of Christ's resurrection from the tomb as having a dramatic effect on their own tombs. Two thousand years later I am not sure we do either.

Now, I can understand and totally empathize with the disciples hiding out of fear. I can also totally admire Thomas for not being locked in with them. Yeah Lord, you were right—Blessed are those who can still believe and hope in the resurrection especially when we Christians who claim the resurrection still keep our faith locked up in our heads and memories. This is surely not the case of Eileen McDermott who was the source of resurrection to Eric the converted homeboy. She was the conduit of God's resurrection for Eric, the onetime homeboy, now father, husband, employee, friend, and taxpayer.

Eileen has been involved in Detention Ministry for over fifteen years now. She heard an invitation from some nutcase, wild-man padre (me) to prayerfully consider if she would be interested in visiting the youth who are jailed in two local juvenile detention facilities in Malibu, California. It was love at first sight for Eileen—love of the jail, the jail's love for her. She has been hard at it now there in Malibu (as a volunteer minister) ever since. It is there that she has met hundreds and hundreds of troubled youth; mostly gang members. She has met hundreds of young guys way more expressively hopeful, "wanting," and reparable than Eric who was not one of the guys who would look for and admit to much-needed attention. He wasn't a kiss-ass! He wasn't looking for special favors. Nor was he wanting to make any type of contact with people in the outs—especially bleeding-heart white folks! He was quiet. He was different. Eileen was persistent, motivated by the potential of Eric's goodness and the sadness of "lack" in Eric's life. Her being able to see his potential that must be realized made her realize her own potential also—her "calling" to be a mentor for Eric.

When Eric was eventually rejailed, she walked with him. When Eric had trouble she walked with him. When Eric dared to live a life away from the gangs, she walked with him. She didn't have the answers or the power to tell him to do this and/or do that. She was persistent and continually present. She was present when Eric fell. She was present when Eric lost his job. She was present as Eric started to learn to be more present to himself and his future. She gave him faith in himself. She was present at his wedding. She's the godmother of his two children. She took the time.

"Watch and wait. My hour is almost here."

Could you not stay awake? Watch and wait will you? Sure. Will you watch and wait even when I screw up? Of course, my sweet man; of course, my sweet girl.

Eric would call her and also share good news. Eric was so concerned for Eileen and her life. It was wonderful watching Eric and Eileen be resurrections for each other. You should have seen Eileen at the baptism when Eric affirmed her as the godmother for both of his kids. Eric invites her out to breakfast. Eric is her son. I know he is. Because Eileen never gave up on him, Eric did not give up on Eric.

Eric must have seen Eileen's determination to believe in the hope, salvation, and the potential of an "Eric" he had yet to meet. She believed in him. She believed in him when Eric did not believe in himself or Eileen. Eric had to be curious as to what the hell she saw in him! Once he took a look for himself, he discovered a whole lot of life that can only blossom. Eileen's belief in Eric and in the resurrection caused Eric to believe in himself and experience resurrection. Now, he must allow it and fight to hold on to it as the crosses of his living situation can still be a total hindrance, obstacle, and distraction. Eileen's job is not over. Eric's job is not over. Eric's resurrection is not over. Eileen's resurrection continues and she continues to share it with other troubled youths.

And the job of those who claim and truly believe that they are resurrected is not over. We must constantly and continually allow it and accept it. We must feed it, fondle it, caress, and honor it. We must defend, empower, and know that "it" continues. We must continually allow it. Accept it. When we lose it . . . we can always get it back! The Holy Spirit does not hold back. We do. We humans do a total transference thing on God.

At the same time, I have seen hundreds of young men break Eileen's heart and the hearts of many of good-hearted, faith-filled ministers like Eileen. We have seen them rearrested time and time again. We have seen them dead in the coffin time and time again. We get so discouraged and disappointed. Yet we don't quit. Save one life and you save a world. The harvest is great. The laborers are few.

What are the main obstacles which prevent people from believing in and living their own resurrections? First of all, we official "people of the cloth" don't help the people recognize that they are resurrected (instead, many still love to remind them that they're sinners!), and don't empower them to cause Christ's resurrection in others. Secondly, the good people want permission. They need permission. They are afraid of failure. They are afraid of the unknown. They are afraid of rejection. They are afraid of sacrifice. Ministry without sacrifice is not ministry. Ministry without perseverance when defeat comes our way is not ministry. And ministry is ministry even when you don't know if your efforts have been worth it. Man, oh man. In this "time productive" society based on quantity production, I can tell you right now, I would make a terrible farmer. I don't have the patience. This is my biggest problem. I demand immediate results . . . or, at least, a sign that it's working!

I pray to accept God's will. But I also pray that his will may be similar to mine.

I have been too "result orientated," protective, and sensitive. I am growing to be more surrendering and projective and less self-centered. I don't have the confidence and usually overcompensate as a result. I become overextended as a result, and my efforts are laced with useless worry and fear.

Could you imagine me as a farmer? If I was, I would plant corn. It's quick. The results are fast. I would plant the seeds, spend hours fertilizing and tilling the soil beforehand. Then to just sit there and wait would be hell on earth for me UNTIL I saw the first sign of life, the first tiny green stem of the vegetable fighting its way out of the topsoil, to let me know it's working. A farmer depends on this sign of life for his livelihood. That was not my problem. Mine was: if they're okay I am okay; if they're not okay, I am not okay. This conflict no longer keeps me on an old cross either.

But as I grow in faith (i.e., that God believes in me), then I believe in me and believe in others, finding myself more willing and less willful. More and more, it is no longer a matter of if people like me or not; I am becoming less stuck. I am finding myself more free from the institutions and conventions of church and politics (let them stand on their own merits or lack thereof), and less blameful of them (less preoccupied with them).

My prayer is often for resurrection from the self-doubts and aloneness that only I entomb myself within. Yes, I oftentimes need to know that it's working. When it does it is a slice of heaven for me: God saying, Attaboy Deasy! A usual reaction of mine when becoming aware of this graced moment is a more deliberate wanting to affirm others. I presume that they are wondering if it's working, too. I am projecting that they too are wondering in the process the same thing we wonder but just don't confess: "Am I okay?" They're more than okay. They are beloved!

Now, we don't need any more pseudomartyrs who present themselves as pain-filled exhibitionists. In other words, we don't need these modern-day bleeders who day in and day out list all the sacrifices they are making while complaining, "Where is everyone else?" or "Look what I had to go through for you." I call these people "Spiritual Lamaze Monsters." Well, these ministers may do the task well, but they are not effective ministers. They are effective volunteers. We don't need volunteers. We need disciples. We need ministers.

Actually, these dear poor people, the martyrs alluded to above, are pains in the butt and prevent resurrection more than cause it. To give life you also have to have a life! Oftentimes, I will have to ask a volunteer who is well-intentioned to choose a less people-oriented task because they are just not nice enough in order to be an affective minister and , thus, an effective minister. They have the tools but they're so negative! These miserable Christians can suck the life out of the leg of the Lamb of God! They can scare the "happy" out of Easter! They can make you want to intoxicate the HO HO HO of Christmas with the BLO BLO BLO of Jamaican weed! But there's got to be sacrifice. But there also has to be a reason. Joy? Resurrection? Fulfillment? Peace? Spirit power?

So I need to focus on resurrection in this life which will also afford me to perhaps be offered salvation in the next life! Notice I connected the resurrection in this actual moment of life—with heaven. I mean we are not only doing this stuff so we can get to heaven after we're buried (or sprinkled), right? *You're scaring me!*

Oh please, this afterlife thing we have to deal with later. This fascination with the afterlife and end of the world stuff is really boring, stupid, and packed with unnecessary fear and permission for powerlessness. Do you think that I am going to wait until after I die, or that God wants us to wait until we're dead, until the award or the gift of the "experience of heaven" can be realized? True, the fullness of heaven can't be attained until after we're dead, I suppose. But why do we have to wait for the whole pie when there are little slices of heaven given to us along the way. But, again, we have to allow it. We have to want it. We have to believe in its attainability. And again and again: *WE HAVE TO GET OFF THE CROSS* (once we get to the cross) in order to travel on, in order to get to the top step: resurrection.

Though we seem to be "Christmas people" by our using this commercial season to buy gifts, sing songs, donate more, splurge, plan, and party—we are supposed to be "Easter people"—"Resurrection people." People who begin opening the gift of God at Christmas (which is Jesus, by the way, in case you've missed it because you didn't get enough bobble-heads and glow-in-the-dark statues) should realize that this gift is our God walking his walk and living his talk, that "there is no greater gift in life than to give one's life for one's friends."

I urge everyone to allow resurrection to happen. To recall the resurrections that have happened, that have occurred in your life, by remembering the crosses (the needs, the hopes, the hungers, the darknesses) that first were there to sensitize you to how much we are in need for purpose, real love, hope, happiness, joy, peace, security: God.

I find myself today more than ever inviting people to allow resurrection to happen. I find myself sounding like a salesman trying to convince others of a greater joy and purpose that they might want to invest in. I'm a regular Father Tom Sawyer. Habitually, naturally, imperfectly, soulfully, and compassionately, I find myself trying to sell people the conviction (based on the experience of trying to live a life of "yes" to God which oftentimes also means saying no) that we must really begin to allow resurrection to happen for ourselves and also to allow resurrection to happen for someone else. Now that we have experienced this resurrection personally and intimately ourselves, which is foremost, we have got to do something with it.

Believe it or not, this experience now arms us with the same authority that Jesus had: "I know how you feel. I will walk with you to your cross on Calvary. I also know the way but I will also invite you not to stop there. I will walk with you to your own resurrection. I will help you. Feed you. Direct you. But, you've got to take the step." Yes, we can go to church. Yes, we can read prayer books and pray all day telling God how much we love him when actually a lot of us have been taught to be scared lifeless when putting ourselves "through Him, with Him, and in Him."

"You better not pout, you better not cry, you better not shout, I'm telling you why: God is coming and boy is he pissed!" Again, I have got to ask, did you ever think of just shutting up when you pray? And add some balance to that whining when you pray!

I am now forty-nine years old. My inner child has got to be around, say, seventeen. My physical, emotional, and sexual drives and energy have got to place me around twenty-five years old. Given all that, I could be easily labeled as immature, a wild man (the cardinal's secretary, Eileen, calls me "wild man.") As a child, I was raised being known by the adults in town as "poor Kenny Deasy who is all over the place working at this and that!" It kind of became my main modus operandi in receiving affection, recognition, and affirmation: doing adult things that a boy normally doesn't do at his age. Actually, I acquainted pity with affection, recognition, and affirmation. I'm really working on that. Poor Kenny Deasy—God, I am so embarrassed that I spent so much time in this awful "place."

DEASY, GET OFF THE CROSS. SOMEONE ELSE NEEDS THE WOOD!

Again, it was a childhood buddy of mine who shared with me this awesome pearl of wisdom handed down to him by his mother. So, as I focus on the harsh realities and disappointments of the past (all of which I not only survived but became a heck of a good person as a result of) I focus on those "little slices of heaven" that the Lord gives us to get us off living on the cross, especially crosses that only we design and assign ourselves.

As a youth, I had many godsends that were the vehicles of resurrection from the crosses of my life. The Father Garritys (rest in peace) who could kick the ball into the heavens and who allowed me to be an altar boy; the Father Lessers (the once associate pastor whom, when I was a kid, I sought help from during my run-ins with the law); the Father Bills (married) who gave me a break on my summer-reading test because during that summer my parents were getting a divorce; the Father Endas (dead) who, when I was a kid and a young Capuchin, bailed me out of trouble constantly. He was the one who entrusted me enormous tasks and levels of responsibility at the ripe age of fourteen. There were the Mother Kilians who would sentence me to hours in the convent cleaning and scraping when busted for this and that in grammar school. (She's still alive and well. She's a million years old which blows my mind because when I was twelve I thought she was already a million years old). There were the Sister Bertrands (still active in her religious Order), the Sister Fechens (changed her name, thank God), the Father Chris's (in recovery and accused of sexual improprieties when he taught the high school I attended), the Father Martins (the first priest that I ever saw smile during the invitation at Mass to "offer each other the sign of peace"), the Monsignor Boyers (a former business competitor who eventually reintroduced the idea of my being a priest. Actually, it was in 1982 when I crawled into the Good Friday service following a three-martini lunch.) Ah, and there was the good Father Chris. Let me tell you what Father Chris did for me.

It was in January 1974. My mother had just died at the age of fifty-one. I was eighteen. Dad was long gone and there was just myself and my three sisters. I, striving to take the responsibility of being "the man of the house" but who didn't even live in the house, just thought that I would spare my sisters the tensions of arranging the funeral and took on the responsibility myself. I thought this was a great gift to them and I enjoyed playing the hero, again. Well, during this process of arranging the funeral for my mother, my middle sister, Veronica, comes to me and wants to discuss the flower arrangements. I told her not to worry about it and that I would take care of it all. She continued to inquire and

I continued to insist that she didn't have to be concerned. It was all done. Finally, she screamed and cried, "Damn it, Kenny! She's my mother too!" I was devastated, crushed. I had hurt my sis. I had also felt rejected and unappreciated. I ran to see Father Chris. He was just present. He was just Chris. He let me cry. He let me mourn my mom for the first time. Thanks Chris.

Sadly, Father Chris and Monsignor Boyer, the latter being deceased, have been accused in the whole priest molestation tragedy. I don't know where you are, Chris. But I hope you know that I still love you and appreciate you for what you did for me.

They were all so cool. They gave me such a good experience. They were so happy helping out a dirtbag like me; frankly, and quite simply, they were just happy. They smiled. They cared. They laughed. They were present. They were not supermen. They were just women and men who really cared. They gave me an experience of connection, safety, and care. This is exactly and ironically what Dad loved about the church. In hindsight, I can now see why he would escape from the house in order to be in the safety of God's home.

Man, you can't imagine how I have moved from hating Dad, ferociously, to now empathizing with him and the disappointments he must have encountered. Yet today, he and all of the good people I just mentioned, were the role models of religious life whom I now hold as an anchor in my memories. I hope to share in the same experience of joy and hope, to share it with others like me—people on the search. In the process, I have to and have had to constantly fight stereotypical expectations that come with being a padre in order to keep these salvific resurrection experiences in the forefront of my thoughts and prayers when the disappointments would inevitably return. Oftentimes, in spiritual direction, I share with my director the exhaustion that comes with the seemingly never-ending battle to keep centered in this parish priest assignment—and to be fulfilled, be honest, and to be real in it. I have always struggled with how I act in contrast with the stereotypical behavior of what a priest is. When people say, "You don't act like a priest," it is usually meant as a positive remark. Though I have the faults of an Irish temper (which is indicating my inability to say, "What about me?" and actually think that someone gives a rat's ass), I am not disconnected, not high and mighty; I hurt, I laugh, and I fall. At the very same time, though, I used to really want to be part of the Church family, the boys' club, and it pained me that I am not. I would tirelessly and endlessly say yes to this opportunity and that opportunity, in taking on extra committee work, fund-raising, retreat giving, etc., just to be included. No more.

I have returned to being comfortable with distancing myself from that which is stereotypically "Roman" conventional behavior and remember the heroes of my youth, including Dad. These dear superstars whom I have referred to were the instruments of resurrection for me in my early youth. They were my bread. They were my saviors. Though the many crosses would be inevitable, it was during those formative years of my life that these prophets of God's love for me (a wonder to this day) would become the foundation of allowing future resurrections to occur for me and from me. They were and are my motivations, among many recent others, of getting off that damn cross and participating in resurrection. The battle is maintaining the balance between "God loves Ken" and "Ken has been disappointed." I could have a thousand people say, "Great homily, Ken," but only remember the one that criticized it. I could move mountains, but when some mere mortal would throw me off the track of my own goodness by a negative remark or a rash criticism, I would be awaiting the ax to fall, again. Prayer would lead me back, though. I am taught that God loves Ken, but . . . So why don't I always believe it?

Fear. Fear of being disappointed. Fear of getting my hopes up. Fear of being discovered. Fear of Calvary. With every positive affirmation comes the little voice, *Don't get a big head, pal. You're just one step closer to Calvary.*

The Gospel about the temptation of Jesus on the Mountain: Luke 4:1–13

Jesus, full of the Holy Spirit, returned from the Jordan and was led by the Spirit into the desert for forty days, where he was tempted by the devil. During that time he ate nothing, and at the end of it he was hungry. The devil said to him, "If you are the Son of God, come and change this stone into bread." Jesus answered him, "Scripture has it, 'Not on bread alone shall man live.'" Then the devil took him up higher and showed him all the kingdoms of the world in a single instant. He said to him, "I will give you all this power and the glory of these kingdoms; the power has been given to me and I give it to whomever I wish. Prostrate yourself in homage before me, and it shall all be yours."

In reply, Jesus said to him, "Scripture has it, 'You shall do homage to the Lord your God; him alone shall you adore.'" Then, the devil led him to Jerusalem, sat him on the parapet of the temple, and said to him, "If you are the Son of God, throw yourself down from here, for Scripture has it, 'He will bid his angels watch over you'; and again, 'With their hands they will support you, that you may never stumble on a stone.'" Jesus said to him in reply, "It also says, 'You shall not put the Lord your God to the test.'" When the devil had finished all this tempting he left him, to await another opportunity.

What were these temptations for Jesus? For all men, being confronted with the manly urgings of wealth, fame, and power is huge. Heck, just being given a piece of bread when you're starving is tempting enough. Why didn't Jesus go for it—wouldn't you have? Wouldn't I? He was given an opportunity to win the Most Super of Lottos! Jesus wasn't following a script. Jesus wasn't concerned with what was stereotypical behavior assigned by a religion and religious/cultural tradition. Instead, he had a personal vision of God, self, and the world that he believed in more than any other mortal power. He had a "why" for life that he had chosen to commit to every day. He had to reaffirm and rededicate that commitment every day. Jesus did not come loaded with doctrine. As he grew he attained an experience that kept him grounded. We see Jesus walking, talking, and speaking from that experience only. We see Paul the apostle, later on, speak from the experience of "I didn't get it, but now I do!"

What was that experience that Jesus held on to? What hope did he hold on to that allowed him not to degrade himself, his purpose, and his potential before that which was sinful and/or not of the Law (i.e., not of God)? This experience must have been HUGE! I mean really huge! It was the experience of being "beloved" by the Father at the Jordan River that immediately preceded this pericope (section of the gospel) above. Jesus, Son of Mary *(an accusation of being illegitimate by the way, or he would be "Jesus, Son of Joseph")*, went to the Jordan in John 4. Notice the wording: "Jesus *allowed* John the Baptist to baptize him." Jesus, being affirmed by the Father that he was beloved at the Jordan, wasn't going to participate in this alone. His life was not about just his authority and identity.

The attempts by "the devil" to distract Jesus from holding on to that experience of being beloved are the temptations: "BUT you're hungry—here's some bread"; "BUT you're feeing powerless—you can always use some power and I'm the one to give it to you"; "BUT you're lonely—you can always use some fame and I'm the one to give it to you." These are traits that typically hinder rather than enhance belovedness for all of us—even in a God embodied in the human Jesus, in our own humanness.

So, I'm left feeling only partially and conditionally beloved. "Yeah, I'm beloved but . . ."

> Yeah, I'm loved by God . . . but . . .
> Yeah, I'm a good guy . . . but . . .
> Yeah, people love me . . . but . . .
> Yeah, I'm supposed to love myself . . . but . . .
> You mean I can only love myself IF it is to get me to love my neighbor? So even when I am a screwup . . . Can I stay?

Remember what occurred after this Jordan event when Jesus is affirmed, empowered, recognized, bonded, connected, and dignified by "This is my beloved Son" expressed by the Father? Remember what occurred after the man, John the Baptist, heralded the mission of Jesus by saying, "Look! There's the Lamb of God"? Jesus splits (commonly called today a "retreat") to take a little time alone with the Father and his experience.

On his journey to solitude there are two dudes who are following him at a distance. (Surprised? Here is someone being called the Messiah. They were curious. We would be skeptical.) Jesus turned to them. *Oh man. Busted by God.* Jesus asked, "What do you want?" They responded, "Hey, can we stay with you?" They simply wanted to be allowed to stay in the presence of him who could have been for them the hopeful fulfillment of an ancient promise. The joining of the hopes of the past religious traditions are now about to be discovered in the present experience. This is the long awaited Messiah. This is God. Wow! Did you ever think of why a lot of others didn't decide to follow Jesus up the mountain? Only two did.

How many would follow such a figure today? I have to admit, this very same question was put to me by my spiritual director,

Wilkie Au, who also happens to have authored great books called *Urgings of the Heart* and *The Enduring Heart*. "Ken, imagine that you were one of the guys trailing behind Jesus. Now, when Jesus turns and surprises you with the question, 'Hey, Ken, what do you want?' What would you say to him? Remember," he would continue, "this is God giving you directly an invitation to ask any question you want of him. This is the magic wand–type of 'make a wish' chance of a lifetime. What you are asking for is a simple answer to one of the most fundamental questions of human existence: 'What are you seeking at this moment in life?' Remember, you are the one who decided to check this guy out by following him."

What am I looking for?

Initially, I responded with this "on the spot threat to my ignorance and complacency" by asking the very same questions a candidate for the Rose Bowl Parade royal court would put forward: "Can there be peace on earth? How can we get rid of poverty? How can we stop despair in the world?" Sounds like I was running for the Miss Universe beauty pageant, doesn't it? I was stumped. So, as I hemmed and hawed, an answer really hit me. Remember, whatever the answer, if it's real it's going to hit hard because the question posed is one that causes me to seek the Lord in myself and, as a result, empowers my main motivation in life. At the same time, how I experience this question has to have something to do with my wanting and failing to help people discover the Lord in their own lives. This is the question that those who have the answers must return to and ponder. I started crying. "Wilkie, I know what I would ask God if I was one of those clowns on the road. Hey God . . . Hey . . . God! Am I OKAY?!"

I have finally come to perceive through the experience of being loved by God that I was especially beloved during the most hideous times in my life that I have tortured you with in this writing. All of this is the pivotal experience that motivated me to begin and continue the long search to living priesthood, thus far a sixteen-year stay in "ordained" priesthood (forty-nine years in baptismal priesthood), and the hope that the joy will continue to allow me to choose staying in priesthood.

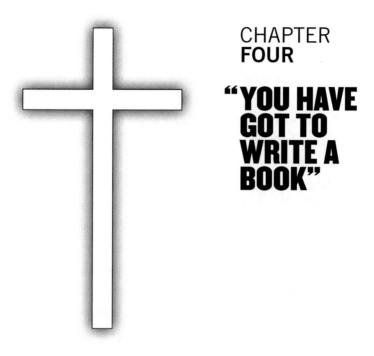

CHAPTER FOUR

"YOU HAVE GOT TO WRITE A BOOK"

I have heard this so many times. I am already up to my "tuchus" in things that I "got" to do. Really. But, write a book—why? Like I have nothing else to do between raising the dead and curing the lame? In my earlier years I thought the life of a priest was sipping a little scotch and playing some golf. I am busy professionally and socially. But, I have finally decided to take a stab at it obviously. *Thanks for buying it!* But what do I really want to achieve? I can remember reading Scott Peck's book *The Road Less Traveled* and I can remember Peck's first sentence: "Life is difficult!"

Someone said it. Alleluia! Praise the Lord! Hot diggety dog! Hot damn! Someone finally said it. Life is hard and someone with a PhD after his name said it. He connected with me. He understands! Ah, the connection. Frankly, after that first sentence I put the book down for at least ten years. I was completely content. I was completely satisfied in just reading that one line of empathy when I had been drowning in the apathy of my surroundings (when I, in order to be an affective Christian, needed to be excited about the present, about tomorrow, and not chained to the crosses of the past).

Man, this is the whole reason why I am still alive and living like I am alive. The graced (cursed?) ability to identify, bleed, and feel for those who feel anonymous in life, who bleed alone, and who are unnecessarily burdened with no hope for a rescue/companionship/celebration. So, if anything, I am a man who really has been touched by the lovely Jesus then and the lovely Christ now—a man who is driven, who is drawn, and who prays that his ministry is to be someone of credibility and not assigned authority, who shows the world that someone in this institution cares.

It's so important to use the crosses/resurrection experiences of the past and share them with others as "someone who has been there" in their continuing Christ mission of making someone else feel more empowered, understood, celebrated, and worthwhile. That is, having been someone who has had a job and been unemployed; had relationships and knows what it is like to be loved and dumped; experienced death, divorce, jail, depression, and condemnation, as well as bereavement, marriage, freedom and medication—someone who has been there and knows the joys and pains of life.

I believe this "I know how you feel" empathy is what drove our Father God to give us himself in Jesus. Following, Jesus continued himself then, and Christ continues in us now through the Holy Spirit. This is my drive in life. This is my goal in life. This is the experience that I present for others to believe in. This is what I am looking for in my own life:

To help people know their power by acquainting them with the Jesus of the past and helping them resonate with the Christ of the present. In other words, we read the sacred scriptures of Judaism and Christianity as indicators of "this is where God was then and this is where God is now." At the same time, sacred scriptures teach us of God's mercy along the way. Clearly, the human person is portrayed as a "one step forward, two steps back" entity.

Now, whether you are buying this or not is not my concern. All I know is that this has worked for me. Insofar as I allow it for myself, I allow "it" as an invitation for others to come into this experience of response and joyous meaningful continuation of our respective salvific life stories. Personally, it has changed me from being a wounded wounder to striving with God's grace to be a wounded healer—a servant, non-holier-than-thou leader—as Christ was and is for me. So many good people feel stuck in a pot and not rooted and grounded in a vibrant energetic life no matter what their financial, sociological, emotional, cultural, and historical story. This is so obvious to me. I say this without hoping to sound judgmental. I share an observation as one who has been there.

I am very grateful for my faith. It is the most important thing to me which, by the way, doesn't mean I no longer sin, doubt, worry, fear, and lose my cool. But, I can actually and finally attest that I love soulfully, and resonate with Lord Jesus' message. As a result, I can experience his presence, urgings, and healings in my life, daily. I love, adore, and am totally in awe of how God has made himself very affective (and, thus, effective) in my life by having someone take the time to break bread with a schmuck like me.

I certainly am a man with urgings. I love that word. I am drawn and driven by my urgings. In other words, my urgings for life and love draw me forward and drive me to enhance the lives, and urgings, of others. God is love. God is the entity behind all of our urgings. Regrettably, we have either been taught by the dear Irish that our urgings are sinful or, more unfortunately, we have underestimated these urgings by medicating them with booze, drugs, alcohol, food, anger, pity, and violence. Too bad—these urgings are God's urgings for us.

Every human person experiences extreme and powerful urgings: to be loved and excited, fed, satisfied, wanted, accepted, discovered, enhanced, worthy, lovely, totally healed, freed, and held. Everyone needs a time to mourn, to be missed; to be looked forward to; to be stimulated and comforted; to be clothed when naked; to feel liberated when imprisoned; to be alive when told dead; to be young when told old; to be on fire when told "extinguished"; to feel wanted when dumped; to be dignified when betrayed; to be secure when you lost it all; to be worthwhile even when you have . . . nothing.

So, I am writing this because my urgings are for connection and participating through, with, and in the God in others and the God in myself. The God in others just turns me on when I experience people allowing it. The God in others validates and draws forth the God in myself and the true power of the world. This is so much better than looking for the crap in others.

It's a battle though. Most good people, in my experience, are stuck in the old religion and refuse to believe they (not just the THEM of religion, politics, and industry) have the power! I was conveying to the shrink the other day my frustration that I was directing at someone who was acting so helpless and powerless. When I offered this person a possible solution it was thrown back in my lap. Every time. I threw a lifesaver and he would discount it. "Why does this guy drive you so crazy?" the shrink asked. My immediate response: "There's something about this guy that I hate in myself!" Get off the cross. Get off my high horse. Allow a slice of light and purity into the darkness and filth!

Recently, my shrink said to me after eight years together, "I think we should take some extra time, three sessions a week, and spend some real, concentrated time on your family, your parents, and your childhood." My response? "Screw you, Doc!" And

I continued to rant and rave, "I love it how I come in here feeling great and leave here feeling worse! Why do you want to torture me some more? I come in here week after week, working my butt off, staring at my two size-12½ feet alone on the coffee table every night. I readily and generously spill my guts out. You should pay me to come in here! You know that I'm your favorite and most dramatic client! And now you want to take me back to the crap of the past so I, again, have to go home alone to sort it all out? I don't think so! Maybe you just don't get it yet—I know I am off-centered and self-extended!"

We preach, "The doors are open!" Someone has to be there to let them in. I know that I am alone. It's not like I can bring home a honey. I know that I'm great at being a "human doing," and I suck at the human being thing. I was taught that for forty-nine years. "You think I am just going to give that up now?" I continued, and was burning mad. "You're the doctor! You are being paid to do the work, not me. I am bringing myself in to you as I would bring in my car to a mechanic. I can't fix the damn car. I can't fix me either. So don't give me any more work to do!" YOU FIX IT! Ugh, I'm thinking, what a putz.

It's been three weeks now—though I only gave in to two sessions a week, my concession and victory over total surrender to the dude and his desire for me to play "let's beat up mommy and daddy" three sessions a week. It's been a great experience (and I didn't even take a swipe at the parents). Thank you, God. It has made me even more tender and free and accepting of myself and my behavior. Consequently, it's made me more sensitive to others who are stuck or who are just beginning to give in to the need to be rooted. Funny, isn't it? At exactly the same time I become healed, tender, and liberated, I develop a greater acceptance of others.

I am not a Freudian (i.e., I am not going to beat up on my childhood for the rest of my life). I am more Jungian; I search to see and appreciate the multidimensional aspects of my own being: my own maleness and femaleness, and my own past and its influence on my present and my motivations towards the future. I am actually enjoying bringing the demons out of the darkness and dragging their sorry tails into the light. I must confess here, as time goes by and I grow, I find myself being more softened, less mad, less blaming, less revengeful and more positive, spiritual, human, and peaceful. And if you think this final draft is rough, you should have read the former three. Now I know why I have so few priest friends.

When I began this thing a year and a half ago the priest abuse scandal was high and out there. Everyone was talking about the bishops, the abusers, the money, the lawsuits, the cover-ups, etc. I was getting sick of hearing "the Church" said this, "the Church" denies that. When I think of "church" I think of us! When I hear of "church" I resent being included in the "them" of the hierarchy. They are not the whole church. It's the Church that has abused itself, the Church. I had felt a need to simply offer another perspective of who we are, of who the Church is. We're the little people. No better. No worse.

So, if I air the good and the bad, the yin and the yang, my love and anger with self, people, church, and God maybe it will help someone to resurrect—themselves and me. Apparently, it is what I do best: trying to make the different, the unusual, the characters of our world and not the "status quo-ers" of the world (who get all the attention and the bucks) feel connected and welcomed without condition. Unconditional acceptance from another is "I love you for who you are *and* for who you're not." Unconditional acceptance of self, as just expressed, is called humility. The opposite of unconditional acceptance, obviously, is conditional acceptance. We talked about it a little earlier. It is the "I love you, BUT . . ."

Finally and honestly, another reason for writing this book? Well, let me put it this way: If bin Laden walked into my church I would welcome him out of charity. But I would also call the FBI pronto. Why? Because of justice? Yes. But I also need the cash. I can and will say that a lot of the real things I want to do in ministry require a lot of prayer and a whole lot of bucks. I am totally into funding more halfway houses for guys/gals who've been incarcerated for such a long time (there is little rehabilitation in the correctional system, by the way) and who need some instrument of reentrance into society, probably because they are worse off than when they began their sentence. They usually return to the same, if not worse, crap-of-a-life situation at the time of their arrest and incarceration. If I could open a halfway house for recovering Catholics the waiting list would be endless!

Maybe this writing will help me get people to listen more sensitively to, especially, those illegal immigrants who were smuggled into this great America of prosperity when they were three years old. Now that they are sixteen-year-olds seeking college, they don't have the funds to pay a tuition that "citizens" don't have to worry about because the taxpayers foot the bill. I am totally into providing classes for Spanish-speaking people who can't yet read or write in their own language before they can even begin to read and write in English. I am totally into summer camps, prevention programs designed to help kids know that there is a choice from the oftentimes hellish situations their parents (who should have never been parents just because they made a baby) raise them in. I am totally into building nondenominational communities and missions of support and faith. Yeah, having some extra cash and extra attention would and will surely benefit those "lepers within our midst" who are the sweetest and most kind people I have ever had the honor to have called "friends, family, and significant others."

BUT this is just one of the things that I want; there are two others. I am presently forty-nine years old at this writing. I am not going to be always physically fit and able to pull off a full day's work. When I retire, I want to retire. I sure don't want to live in a rectory and continue to carry the load in someone else's house. I need my own home. Not just to buy a house, but also to have something that is a home for me and for others. Privacy. Dignity. (Now I am looking to get away from the attention that I already have.)

Privacy: Already, I have people watching me every minute of the day. Believe it or not, I have had stalkers. If I did only 10 percent of the things I have been accused of doing, I couldn't even walk! I've been rumored of having drunken, wild parties in the parish house; it's been said I have had wild orgies with men, women, and beasts. If I am tired and not with it (after working a third thirteen-hour day), it's because I am rumored to be hung over or just in from a wild night. "You know Father Ken—in bed by ten, home by three!" I hear it all the time outside my window: "He's got white people over. He's got black people over. He's got girls over. He's got gays over. He only likes this person and that person."

SHUT UP! Though I want to say, "Shut the hell up!" I smile or, actually, go in my room and mourn

Am I not allowed a place of my own? I am not looking for a mansion. Just a place to call home and where I can invite over whomever I want, whenever I want, however often I want, and be myself—Ken. Okay, I confess, Ken with a pool would be nice. But, I also know me, I would share it with the world. How am I going to pay for this? Well, here's the kicker: the profession would have to adjust its salary scale—one does not go into priesthood for the bucks. Speaking about profession, career, and "what would you like to do when you grow up," if I had to work for money my true, lifelong dream has been to own a corner bar. I'd be doing the same thing I'm doing now!

For real—when I was a kid I wanted to be one of two things: a TV game show host, or a barkeep. I can see it now: K. Herbert's, a typical neighborhood corner bar for all to come in to enjoy, just like *Cheers*. Just like the pub Archie Bunker would go to. And, what type of bar would this be? I don't care if it's a biker bar, a gay bar, a straight bar, a froufrou bar, or a hard bar. It's a place where everyone knows your name, people come to be known, and people are nice. If you can't be nice, go somewhere else. (See? I told you I'd run it like I run my parish.) This is exactly my mentality and spirituality and how I operate my parish—creating a place of welcome and refreshment, for being known and for being served, that encourages laughter, the telling of stories, and the sharing of lives. Man, if that ain't what church should be, what is? Besides, it's all over good spirits. Who said I had to suffer? Who said I couldn't dream?

Not on $800 a month! (That's approximately $550 in salary and $250 in tips and stipends.) I'm not complaining. Believe me, I am not starving, and I don't know of any clergy member who is. Actually, I probably have it better off than most. My friends call me "America's Favorite Guest." People are nice to me and very supportive of me. Though I never ask for anything for myself, and it is so much easier to ask for things from others for others, people support the parish because I have been honored to have supported them at some point in their life.

I don't live with any priests. Not having to live with people you work with has become a good thing for me. I have fashioned for myself a nice house to live in with my dog, Spirit. We are provided a company car and room and board. Though the nights are lonely, I am blessed! *I was just informed that I get another two dollars annual monthly raise: YIPPEE.* Holy Mother Escrow, I'm looking for you! I would not mind living on top of my fantasy bar. I've been living on top of where I work for a long time. It's called a rectory. By now, I would suppose, some are very disappointed in how I talk and write. I am embarrassed myself because I know this is not going to help me fit into the status quo. But, I could have lied and been dishonest and appealed to those who wish clergy to be the holier than thou. This would have appeased the right wingers who seem to believe more in "corporate Rome" than in walking the road through, with, and in Christ. I could easily have claimed that I have received some "divine calling" to tell my truth. That in being ordained to a higher calling there comes more "special ins" to God, and because I have been blessed with the opportunities to attain a BA in philosophy and an MA in theology that makes me a special Gnostic. To this day, I am amazed at clergy who ascribe the initials of the academic successes to their names.

Anyone who knows me, and whom I am not paying to know me (like my spiritual director and shrink) would die laughing in disbelief in hearing me talk in pious church platitudes. "The Lord has called me to do this!" "My dear sistas and brothas in Christ!" Ha! Or: "The devil made me do it!" I don't talk that way.

I don't even come close to having the faith, trust, and confidence to make such a statement of certainty in regards to being divinely commissioned because I assume I am supposed to have it all figured out by now. Well, I don't. I guess I feel inadequate and a failure because I am supposed to be strong, all-knowing, and all-powerful. I'll leave that for the boys with the red buttons and red beanies, while praying for the day when there'll be some women wearing the same.

It seems apparent to me that most of those who have felt the need to make such a self-declaration of their own "righteousness," and to whom I have given allegiance, have been the hugest disappointments for me. As time would tell, their real motivations were their own need for control, fear, lack of freedom, and not personal betterment. In other words, I got screwed. I am a very trustful person and I used to get screwed often as a result. I am just amazed at how untrustworthy, unhealthy, and/or downright evil some people can be and justify it along the way with goodness and godliness.

Politics hangs itself on this constantly and I am totally amazed at all the fuss and dollars that come with voting for the right person. It's as if we are betting on a horse! The business end of church, I am sorry to say, can be that way also. Even as a pastor, I have to oversee all the business affairs of the parish. I don't enjoy it, but I am good at it. But, to be a businessman and a leader is truly a conflict for me—a totally weird balancing act. The more personal, available, and accessible I become, the more people want to take advantage. The doorbell rings all night. I finally cut the wire. The phone rings all night. I disconnect it before I go to bed. The need for funds at the door for rents, bills, utilities, medicine is endless—I am a man, I am not an ATM with legs. I have friends who actually think they are doing me a favor by directing couples seeking marriage from all over the nation to give me a call. Then, the more professional I try to be, establishing working procedures and personal boundaries, the more I am accused of being a bigot and a "coldhearted SOB like the rest of them."

And, as I said, I am really good at administrating, fund-raising, collaborating, organizing, motivating, creating, and taking care of all the business of a parish. But, because I have ten other plates spinning on ten sticks at the same time commanding me to be the person of Jesus Christ, it's a conflict. The inability to balance the personal call with professional demands will be my downfall. If I had wanted to run a business I would have gotten a business degree and worked in that field. But, as a result of my business demands, I lose the certainty of my calling, confidence, priorities, and self. I become less sure of the mission.

There were certainly times, though, when I thought I was more focused and certain. There have been endless times that I not only thought that the Lord was going to give me a "divine command" (and/or a swift kick in the ass) but also felt that the Lord was walking with me for a specific purpose/mission.

My own typical in-the-box confession, I must divulge, continues to be how I reluctantly surrender to and prioritize these special commissions and blessings that have certainly been powerful experiences for me. I don't want the responsibility of living up to being "blessed." If everyone thinks you're blessed, then I can't act cursed. I don't want to be responsible for being and acting blessed when I would rather feel condemned, inadequate, and misguided. Walking around with a cross certainly gets more attention and pity.

"Give me a sign," I constantly begged my Maker. Most times I would ask for a sign to leave this all rather than to stay. It must happen a hundred times a day. Or, to be really honest, it hasn't been until the last five years that I have allowed myself to listen, see and trust in the calling. Now I believe in it. This is the problem. I've been given way too many signs of being called to stay. I have been transformed. Even with the memories (crosses) of the worst betrayals and abandonments of life that have come with this vocation, transforming miracles for me and for others have occurred.

And besides, I have become less sarcastic and cynical. Drinking alone, and having to drink socially, is gone. The "hornies" have lessened, thank God! I have made huge advances in curbing my Quick Draw McGraw tongue. I am way too quick for my own good and have learned to control it a little bit more. I had been very sarcastic and cynical concerning the many apparitions and moving statues of our Catholic faith. Now, I am just a little more gentle and understanding with them, even though I remain a bit suspicious of claims that the Lord conveys his "I am with you" by sending bleeding statues of Saint Anthony of Padua, and faces of Our Lady appearing in tortillas and garage doors and cloud formations as special "FedExes" of his presence.

Just talk to me, will you Lord? Why do you whisper? Why do you communicate today so passive-aggressively? Any shrink will tell you that You need to talk to me the way I need to be communicated to. Why can't you be certain and direct? What's the big deal? You have got to get over the Adam and Eve thing! You've got to get over the Ten Commandments bomb. It's not my fault that the Holy Land isn't holy at all. It's only holy if you teach a "God of history." As for revealing the God of the present—it needs some work. It was and is certainly holy insofar as being the root of our salvific beginnings. Even today we know that it's not how you begin, its how you end. There's a new Holy Land in town! It is in Los Angeles among a million other places. Its name is Agatha, First Church of Christ, Nate 'n Al's, jail, and Wal-Mart. Most importantly, at least for me, it's the hood. It's "Good in the Hood." Why?

Because the Holy Spirit entrusted to this place in L.A. teaches you to see the divine in yourself and in your own house, work, spouse, child, and enemy. I don't teach it. I just help people see, recognize and participate in the experience. Let's face it, the present Holy Land in Jerusalem is an experience of religion and how the need to be right has screwed up everything. Jerusalem, to me, and the Jewish, Christian, and Islamic traditions it has given birth to are simply indicators of the need to start all over—renewal.

Come on, Lord! Of course, you surely have revealed yourself several times since Jesus and we just missed it. Even worse, we killed you again. I don't even want to think of that. Catholics usually don't refer to themselves as "born-agains." I do because I am. Actually, I was "born again" about thirteen times this morning. Yet, of course, I don't always feel this way and the Lord and I have a love/hate relationship. We aggravate each other! Actually, I look forward to him lovingly aggravating me. Tangled extension chords are one of his favorite tricks to send my way!

If God and I were in marriage counseling, I am sure that the counselor would say to God, "Now, Lord, you really need to talk to Ken and let him know that you are sensitive to his needs." But, the Lord talks to me all the damn time. I just often choose not to listen. Though skeptical about apparitions, etc., I have prayed constantly for one to come my way. It sure would make things easier. Again, though, the apparitions I pray for are ones that say, "Get the hell out." But, like everyone else, I need a little flash to get it.

I know one was being sent my way about thirty years ago. I can remember a special place for me that I discovered in 1973 when I was a Capuchin Franciscan novice at a place called San Lorenzo Friary. I was sitting in a small valley in the Santa Ynez Mountains, located on the grounds of this novitiate and friary. I discovered and named this valley my "meditation spot." I was sitting down with the two German short-haired pooches of the novitiate (Carlotta and Max) puffing on a Marlboro Light (supplied graciously by the Order) and at total peace. I also was celebrating quietly to myself. I had survived another attempt at being thrown out of the Order during the quarterly "votation" (voting) evaluation. In the novitiate, one checks out the Order and the Order checks you out!

I wasn't doing too well on the "being checked out" end. Each votation, in which the padres vote on whether you should continue or not, were close calls for me. It all depended on what padre was or was not there at the time. I remember making sure that the elderly Fathers Columban and Cyprian were in good health and caffeined up at votation time.

Before we go further with this, for years during and after this experience, and surely not before, I changed from feeling pretty lucky to have survived to, well, damaged goods. In regards to my behavior then and to this day, I wasn't and could never be the poster boy of sanctity and pious religiosity. Additionally, during early adult years (around age eighteen), I became so emotionally and psychologically unstable. I was crazy, but I was lovable crazy. I laughed. I cried. I liked to throw parties. I liked to live on the edge. I was horny and didn't feel good about it. How does ASHAMED about it ring? I was only eighteen years old!

So, after seven years in seminary formation (phase one) I continued to ask myself why I was constantly in trouble and being threatened with being thrown out by the superiors. I mean, what was the big crime about being me? My intentions were always good. But, I just couldn't be controlled!

"Obedience" was how it was referred to. Man, I was obedient. I pulled straight A's. I never missed prayers. I never missed Mass. I could and did everything that I was supposed to do. But, I was a young man with a zest and zeal for life in a program that made we react with the constant "I am obedient but I am too young to die!" Also, I spoke up. To this very day, speaking up and asking questions is seen as an act of disloyalty.

Okay. I'll admit that in 1973, when four out of five of the priests and eleven of the fourteen novices were sick with the flu in the novitiate friary (except the retired and aged Father Tim Joe, Brothers Paul, Fideus, and myself), we (no, it was totally me, I confess) convinced Father Tim Joe to break open the booze closet (a luxury/privilege only granted to and enjoyed by the good ordained fathers—*God's will!*) and enjoy a few belts at dinner. Now, it was bad enough that we were drinking some great cheap wine with an Italian dinner, but I could tell that Brother Fideus was getting a bit nervous. He was a squealer. So, we had to find a way to get him out of the picture before he blew it. Surely, he would have spilled the beans during a bout of scrupulousness.

"Hey, Fideus, you look a little pale. Are you okay?" was my question put to him. Brother Fideus had just admitted that he was okay and actually feeling great. (Shame on him! You never admitted happiness or good fortune in Irish religious life. This would be in direct confrontation with the "no pain, no gain" spirituality of the Jansenist Catholic Church). Upon further query regarding his health, the statement finally come forth: "Why do you ask?"

"Hey buddy," I continued, "you look a little pale. Let me take your temperature."

His response was, "Thank you and God bless you, dear brother." *I know he hated my guts.*

"Good God, Fideus," I exclaimed with the same genuine sympathetic concern that an owner of a Jack in the Box would have towards the owner of a neighboring McDonald's going out of business. "You have a 103 degree temperature! You better go to bed!" I confess that his temp was normal, 98.6 degrees, but it put him to bed and out of my hair for three days. He was mad as a hornet when Brother Paul, mad at me about something else, spilled the beans.

Anyway, the night of the great flu plague was great: laughter, good wine, *Kung Fu* at 9:00 p.m., then time for bed. Ah, a good night's sleep with a buzz on! That night I recall awakening on the hallway floor of the friary right in front of Father Superior's room. I had passed out cold after having one too many glasses of that rot-gut wine with the rest of the guys in good health. This would surely be grounds for the "instant adios." There would surely be another "Grand Inquisition." No way would I admit it. Thank God, Brother Paul who also caught a good buzz, dragged me into my room laughing all the while. He literally saved my life.

How Father Superior found out, I'll never know. But he did. I still think it was Brother Fideus. I mean, I was only eighteen and a novice. I was out for the count and, thus, about to be banished from the friary with two charges on my ecclesiastical record: being a novice with no canonical rights (scriptural justice and Christ-like mercy never enters) and believing that I had become a being who is nothing.

You're nothing! You're nothing! You're nothing! No matter what I did.

I'm nothing? This was and is the continuing shock of my young religious life and I still surrender to it at times—not being enough. Now the threat only appears on a very rare occasion. *Thank God!* When I was not "in the robe/collar" everyone with a robe/collar was so good to me. They were so kind to me, so compassionate. The experience of having them be so WONDERFUL to a poor guy who was struggling with living with the "marriage from hell" initially made me feel like I was something. I entered feeling like nothing could stop me and that I had everything to contribute to the family. By the time I left, I was nothing. Sucked dry.

Now in formation, where were the guys who smiled at me (during a time when padres did not smile) and helped me carry my cross? (during a time when padres were the cross. It's all cross, baby!) Where were my male role models, godsends, baseball card-type heroes, who were still my heroes, who led me into this life? Of course, as I mentioned earlier, a lot of them had already left and gotten married, divorced, arrested, addicted, and successfully relocated in another career.

I was determined, and still am, to be the characters they were to me and to cherish as my most valuable jewel the experience they afforded me. Call it timing, call it being ready to be implanted with some good seed, but they not only gave me a feeling that I was okay, but they also gave me that burning desire for more. Who wouldn't want it? Call it what you will—the need for God, family, male bonding, and escape. This was and is a positive stepping stone for me today. I have been living this life with the hopes of sharing, caring, and loving the same way that I experienced my "beginning" when I said yes to a spiritual faith life. This was my motivation before entering formation (seminary) and, thus, religious life.

So, I left my life experience of La Canada (a little city nestled in the foothills of the Angeles Crest Mountains directly bordering Pasadena) and entered the novitiate and became a friar, now under the watchful eye of a bunch of new and different friars. They weren't like the guys that I met "on the outs." So, after entering the Order I was so jazzed because now, I'm in. I'm part of the family. I'm one of the guys. I am a part of a gang that I loved and who loved me. I am Brother Ken and part of the family.

Wrong.

To make a very, very long story short, while in formation (seminary process) I can say quite emphatically and with certainty, that I was never affirmed once of having been called by God to be in the Order or even, now that I think about it, that I was even going to get to heaven. I was cursed with the "BUT" demon I talked about earlier. "God loves you, BUT . . ." All I'm hearing and all that I am feeling from the guys in the friary is that I am nothing. But everyone else loves me. Why am I so terrible to you guys, and only you guys? Because I guess I'm not easy to live with. I say it's because I gave so much. I was more into my human-ness and had lived life more than the majority. I'm not bragging. But it became very apparent that I was about to become the black sheep among the membership. Go figure.

I entered the religious life continuing to avail myself of the experience of love, care, and kindness, i.e., God—that I was so blessed to have experienced from the Order before entering. Before and up to that time of my entering the Order in July 1972, I was just thriving with considerable progress and achievements after only seventeen years of living, struggling, and having accom-plished what I thought was some huge stuff for a kid my age. I had paid my own tuition making the necessary dough by cleaning classrooms and cutting hair at my high school and helping my mom (a single, divorced mother of five working full time at Robin-sons in Pasadena for four dollars an hour). How the hell she did that has been a constant source of meditation for me ever since.

I was a master cook; I could arrange and organize anything. Man, I couldn't hit a ball for the life of me. But I could pay bills, buy liquor (I sold fake IDs), throw a dinner for 250, supervise extracurricular activities, and stage music concerts at my high school. To my amazement, in 1972, everyone loved Kenny Deasy, aka Betty's kid. This was a newfound revelation for me. I assure you, I didn't know why and I continue to be a little miffed by it all. Hello! I'm not in therapy because every day I'm skipping through the tulips with the joy of Sandy Duncan eating Wheat Thins!

As I hope you can tell by now, I really needed a meditation spot (to put this all back into context) to sort out all the feelings, aspirations, and disappointments/confusions that come with being me. So, back to the journey that led me to the discovery of my meditation spot and my not being comfortable with claiming with certainty that I had been given a special calling. The place: the novitiate in the Santa Ynez Mountains.

Again, as a novice you were beginning your process of "discerning a vocation" to the religious life and, specifically, discerning the choice of this particular way of life in following Christ in community (e.g., Franciscan, Dominican, or even a brother of St. Francis of the baby Jesus of Nazareth. Or, the one I wanted to start—the OML's—Order of Mere Laypeople). Discerning a vocation is good. It is filled with doubt, confusion, aloneness, and uncertainty. (And they wonder why folks aren't lined up around the block to enter religious life these days.) Seemingly, when "discerning a vocation" you are only supported in this process with dignity when you are in the seminary formation process. When you are still discerning after final vows, and/or ordination to the priesthood, it's a "vocation crisis." (A crisis? What could be better than discerning with the Lord the quest to be happy and at peace? "God would never like that"? I don't think so.)

To this day, I don't know what's worse: trying to get into the priesthood and stay there or undergoing what one goes through— shame, failure, guilt, shunning, disengagement—when you leave the unhealthy demands of religious life in order to better yourself and be healthy. There was so much opposition to me in my formation. I often wonder if my excitement for ordination was because I was giving my life to God and his people, or if I just didn't want "those guys" to screw around with me anymore. *God's will!*

God has been good.

So, in practice, a novice goes through a quarterly votation when the solemnly professed community decides on your fitness as a candidate for profession into the Order. A votation was when the padres are assigned the task of assigning "God's will for us all" by passing around a basket. In front of each friar would be an assortment of black and white beans. With each candidate they would drop a white bean indicating, "He's a solemnity" (no problem: a kiss-ass, dependent, doesn't ask questions, etc.) or a black bean for "He's probably the Antichrist" (i.e., emotional, sensitive, independent, sneaks out of the friary all the time, drinks cheap wine with Father Tim Joe, etc). I was never a solemnity. I was a black bean.

So after barely surviving the votation (thanks to my good friends, Father Columban, Tim Joe, and Cyprian, as mentioned) I needed to get to MY meditation spot. So there I was, thinking, praying and discerning my vocation to the Order and religious life (if you didn't it meant you were conceited). *God's will!* This place, this spot that I discovered, was the womb for me (and this declaration is coming from a guy who's been accused that when he was born he popped out of his mother's *whooziefudge* and, after taking one look around, tried to crawl right back in); my safety place; my security; my place away from *them*.

Oh my God—this place, this spot, was gorgeous. I was totally into it. I constructed a cross (without permission, of course) in the valley in which no one ventured but me and the beasts, the German short-haireds Carlotta and Max. The valley was green with towering oak trees, older and obviously wiser than any other living thing around. The sun was shining. Again, I was totally into it. There in my spot, I was thinking about what the hell I was doing in the novitiate. I felt so saved, thanks again, to Father Columban, Father Cyprian, and Tim Joe, the latter being a partner in crime previously during the "Italian Fest" we enjoyed while the plague hit the seminary. I also knew that there was one more votation to go before I was to make my first vows and, consequently, begin the scholarly college process of formation in San Francisco.

I hated being weak and afraid. I knew these experiences as a kid witnessing his mother getting beaten up by her husband. I should have never told my superior that one. He was never the same to me after that. This came at a time when he had just finished reading his first book on psychiatry and concluded now that he was an expert psychoanalyst. The Novice Master, who now felt he was Drs. Freud, Jung, and Maslow all in one, felt compelled to make me his first guinea pig. He insisted on my dealing with the feelings that I never had experienced up until then. He insisted on going back to those memories of the past which I thought I had put in place. He entered into a place where he was not invited in my life and how dare he force his way in. He destroyed my dignity.

In my meditation spot, I kept thinking about St. Francis Assisi and his being rejected by his family and Church leadership for seeking a life of and with God. I recalled the huge figures that helped me discover who I was and the fact that it wouldn't kill me to actually like my self. Here, in this place, I was really at peace. I knew I wasn't alone. I knew I was screwed, though, and didn't have a chance. It would take a miracle. I wasn't sure I wanted to stick around for the pain that any miracle of "you better stay" would bring. All of a sudden in my little newfound womb, my paradise, the wind really started to blow. Then the clouds opened up to the point where a beam of light from the sun tore through the branching life of nature and focused itself right on my illegally constructed cross. Then the two dogs ran to my side and kept close. Then two deer came down and started to graze around the cross. Then a large owl circled around the cross and landed itself on one of the tiers. I ran like hell. The Lord answers prayer but I wasn't going to stick around to find out what his answer was.

Moving on . . .

It's thirty years later. I am forty-nine; ordained sixteen years at this writing. I had just recently asked the Lord for my never expressed or experienced adolescence back. I prayed the assuredly midlife cry for the fountain of youth. I have worked hard to keep healthy (healthier) and keep in shape. I actually come as close as I ever have to that place where I think that someone could actually love me. AND . . . here comes the clincher . . . love me for who I am and not what I can do. That someone could love me for even the things I tell the shrink and spiritual director (whom I wouldn't need as much if I could share myself with someone who would want to hold me and who would allow me to hold them, mutually). I also quit the Prozac three weeks ago. The feelings are back!

The good Lord granted my wish. I received a return to my adolescence. Now I'm praying for him to take it back.

GET OFF THE CROSS.
SOMEONE ELSE NEEDS THE WOOD!

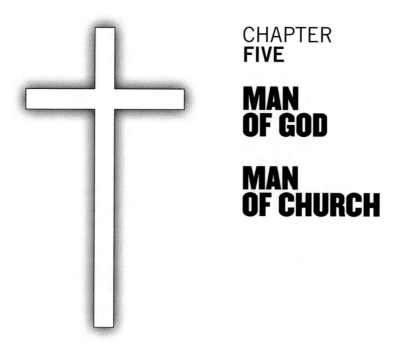

CHAPTER FIVE

MAN OF GOD

MAN OF CHURCH

Am I a man of God?

Wow. That's a tough one to answer because that has all the stereotypes and connotations that come with it: Perfect. Otherworldly. Hypocritical. You know. Am I "Church man"? Man, that one I can answer most assuredly.

NO. Am I church? YES!

I am a family man who is into community, accessibility, and care. I don't find myself connected with the business of church that "Church man" brings to it. I am just a guy given a life by God who is a Christian (a Roman Catholic) and who has decided to respond to his Christian faith (urgings) by being a priest—a Roman Catholic priest.

I don't know if I am holy as it is presumed to mean by churchmen, those dear souls who believe that they are entrusted to make faith in God understandable to poor schmucks like you and me.

They present the Lord as a left brain puzzle to be thought about and not felt. *Love is a thought?* Frankly, I believe that most of these churchmen fail miserably in this when they seek a place of rank and prominence rather than seek to help bring the tender and powerful Christ to others. So, as you can also deduce I am not very "Roman" (i.e., antiquated, irrelevant, arrogant, sterile, suffering from denial because they actually think that what they present as theology is taken by the laity as par excellence.)

This Roman methodology is outdated, long-winded, and irrelevant. Everything is historically based and scholastically presented. Their methodology is contrary to my experience of faith rooted in Jesus, his mission, and his manner of teaching. There are very few people (alas, those in the real church) I know who sit and read (or who could even possibly understand) their long theological treatises on God, scripture, and morality. In the seminary, though, you have to. As a matter of fact, my years of reading this stuff haven't proved to be very helpful. Why? Again, the average Christian doesn't read it or need it. This method of teaching and preaching theology tries to present the faith by feeding us endless, long run-on sentences (like I oftentimes do) with footnotes dating back to the Middle Ages (which I don't). It seemingly ignores as insignificant the innate urgings of us mere humans for a life of spirituality without having to enter a cloister, a monastery, a friary, a life of celibacy, a convent, or a hermitage.

To me, the most relevant theologians are the nonclerical and noncelibate spiritual theologians who are married or, at least, involved in a relationship. I would presume that the treasures of the married "lay" theologians don't even get attention from an academic clerical church. They should. They have relationships. They're comfortable with being human. How can the nonrelational celibates tell us how to have a relationship with the ultimate love? For them ultimate love is cognitive, solving an equation in the abstract. Whoop-de-do! Hooray for them! I hope they enjoy it. None of us really do, because we don't get it. Most of us need a lot more feeling and need to not be made to feel bad about having feelings anymore.

I am sure that my "loyalty" to the Church is being questioned, and that I should be very careful here. I often feel that I have been called to clean up her mess for many a year on the local level by giving a refreshing approach to life, love, God, and being totally Catholic—just not Roman. Sometimes I feel that loyalty to the magisterial Church is synonymous with being loyal to Amway Corporation. Hey, a corporation is a corporation! These "people of religion," degreed and ordained people "in the know," can present themselves to be nonrelational: otherworldly intellectuals who still believe that God and love are far and distant; non-embraceable, unattainable, because of his infinitude and omnipotence (but also because if they were to present God intimately, sensually, and affectively, they would be called in by corporate Rome). If the pope ever calls me in, he is going to have to spring for the ticket: first class, baby. *I am not significant enough though. I am safe.*

The magisterium of the Church as a corporate identity obviously seeks to imitate that which either their superiors demand or their need for superiority demonstrates: distance, unapproachability, and the self-made arrogance that comes with their acting out with pomp, lack of credibility, and lack of touch with the real world. It's about being correct more than true; historical more than experiential. It's not about being real. It's about being number one. It's about being male. Faith is a life that needs excitement! Faith is a life that needs to be invigorated! Faith is a power that needs to be put into action. Faith is about being connected. Faith is about growth. Faith is about overcoming hurt. Faith is confessing with the hope of growth.

Have you ever been to Rome? I dig Rome. There is love, wine, walking around, beautiful museums, and fantastic church structures of art so fine—walking around at night amongst the ruins, the people, and the piazzas—ahhhhh. Viva Roma! But, if there is any action, life, zest, and energy going on in the church there, you could have fooled me. Frankly, there ain't any action in the local churches or the "Big Daddy of Churches" in Rome. I first went to Rome in 1986, my last free summer in my whole life (i.e., the last before ordination). I've always wanted to visit the Vatican, a building that for me has only been on postcards and in history books. I am a big fan of the documents of Vatican II held in the 1960s and '70s—what a fine, Spirit-filled document. When I got to Rome for the first time, though, man, did I know that there was a Holy Spirit. No such document with such loving clarity and charity could have come out of this crowd of prelates minus the Holy Spirit.

Rome, as the hub of the Roman Catholic Church, an institution that is commissioned by the Holy Spirit to continue to lead us along the ways of Jesus Christ, is so antiquated, big, stale, and dusty. But could I throw a bash in the papal palace? (And think of the yard sale!) For me it is puzzling and hard to reconcile that the churches of Rome, those places that are to lead us around the world as Christ's primary instrument, have become museum pieces for tourists. Among the Romans, any respect for the clergy is nonevident (except that they are patrons of the local fare) and few of the religious walking around in habits and cassocks look very happy or at ease. The poor habit-clad sisters walk a million miles an hour with a smirk I would imagine one would have if they were wearing hair-shirt panty hose. The pale-faced, prancing padres/seminarians in their flowing cassocks walk around with such an air of superiority and smug self-respect. They, like most young clergy, scare me to death. What they really need is to get . . . well . . . never mind. No, I'm not going to say it, but they do need it (something under serious question today), and they need to get the candle wax out of their ears!

Why do we of religion have to act like we're so painfully and lifelessly miserable, emotionless, and otherworldly? In Rome, where directives and admonishments about church are communicated there is constant fear of being excommunicated. The churches are empty. The "home of the chair of St. Peter," where the love and joy of God is communicated by demeanors of academia and pain, does not communicate a zeal for life and a subsequent spiritual conduit of the love of Jesus Christ and love for the poor. The way the Church of Rome presents itself is so dull, dusty, and cold. It is hard to get all "papal-whipped" over an institution wherein its own churches are empty. Empty three-hour liturgies. Empty clerics. Empty leaders. But they act like they don't get to be a bunch of swell guys and gals. They certainly must have a burning love for God and his people! Why else do this, to live in Rome? Why don't they just loosen up and have a good time? Ambition? Ambition for what, rank? Swell. Getting a promotion without a raise—how fulfilling is that?

Oh, yes, I forgot. The cross. No pain, no gain. Oh please. Don't get me wrong. It's not that I am ungrateful for these people who really do sacrifice. But if *they* don't even act excited, alive, and grateful, how can I be excited, alive, and grateful? If they exude pain, hell, death, and passivity—I can't date that! I truly wish the institutional church that everyone gets so excited about, or is fearful of, would look at itself from the eyes and standpoint of the people it is called to serve. I wish they could see that, from the point of view of anyone who is really in touch with themselves, that what they claim to be important is just not important at all. This is true especially for those of us who have finally weaned ourselves from the age-old condemnations from the institution and have found solace in the community of the faithful—and in their own selves.

"I Confess to Almighty God for what I have done and for what I have failed to do." I don't want to live in Rome. I don't want to go to hell either. Frankly, I would prefer someone to hold me at night *without a fresco on my bedroom ceiling of the Blessed Mother looking down upon me.* I prefer to hang around the real people of God and of the world. I choose to hang around the poor not because I am a saint but because they are so much more fun! *Ever been to the slums in Rio de Janeiro? Best views and celebrations in the world!* I choose to hang around those whom I am told that I shouldn't really be hanging around with, the sinners—these dear people who really are loving, risky, vulnerable, crazy, and exciting, who are drawn to be themselves, to be different. I prefer to hang around those people who love me but who don't push me into the priesthood corner all the time. People I prefer to be around are those who will touch me and not stalk me. I am so blessed to have a few people who will allow me to be mutual and with whom I want to be mutual. The fun people—people who are in touch, silly, different, searching, and imperfect. In short, I prefer to hang around the real Church, the real people of God, the real "kingdom"—"On earth as it is in heaven."

Having entered into the formal ranks of church as one of its ordained ministers in 1987, I have held on to and have tried my very best to share the experience that God has given to me—that "I am beloved"—even when I didn't quite believe that my life, like everyone else's, is a total gift that I have yet to fully understand, appreciate, and celebrate. That you are beloved, also! This is my passion. This is my joyfully intensive cause, mission, calling, and platform, while having quite a life in the process. The office of priesthood within the institution of the Church has been key in helping me become myself in this regard. To (1) take the crud of my past which I have been resurrected from, and (2) to joyously lead people who have felt condemned by the Church (that church, parish, which still maintains in appearance, manner, and method to have that exclusive line to discern who is of the living and who is of the damned) to a new experience of God, self, and Catholic community, (3) to help people believe that they are so beloved and beloved by God, whom we depend on to help us try to love in the manner (intention, mission, and hope) of himself in Jesus of

Nazareth, who is alive and dynamically present to us through the Holy Spirit, and (4) to help people experience the Jesus in the present moment, in the present person.

The Church has been my family. Yet, I am tired of picking up for Mommy and Daddy. Truly, Christ hurt in the past. And more truly, Christ hurts today. Though the institution of the Church writes about the hurt, it also writes checks contributing to the hurts *(that's our money, by the way)* and it has even had to apologize for ignoring and/or contributing to the hurt. It's apologized to Jews, non-Catholic Christians, gays, women, Muslims, and more. But, where is the sacrifice as evidence of remorse? Where is the hurt and vulnerability as indications of sincerity? See, this is the problem. We "official people of church" don't appear as sensitive to those who sacrifice every day. We act imperialistic and don't appear to be one with their sacrifices.

Sacrifice is important. Is not sacrificing for others the true test of any love? To continue to love even when it hurts; to continue to give even though you are wanting? To not just say, "I'm sorry," but to really try to afford whatever reparation is necessary in order for the real experience of reconciliation to happen? See, if priests were married they would never get away with saying, "I'm sorry," without some sort of reparation. Isn't that why God, again, gives us Jesus? God, who is love, was not known by his adorers to be vulnerable, personable, relational, and touchable. In other words, God was not real to us then and many times is not real to us now because we rely totally on how the magisterium presents him to us.

Distant. Hooray for the Father being God! But while our Father art in heaven, we poor schmucks on earth are suffering, struggling, wanting, dying, vomiting, dying of AIDS, open to ridicule, open to bigotry, etc. Remember Atticus Finch in *To Kill a Mockingbird*?—"You don't know a man until you get in his skin and live in it a while." That's exactly why God gave himself to us in Jesus. God, in Jesus, hurt then. God, in us the Body of Christ, hurts now. The question now is will Christ hurt alone? Will Christ hurt alone, again? As I am writing this on the ten-year anniversary of the Los Angeles riots, I will soon be leading my people in Mid City (known as South Central where the riots took place) in prayer on the Catholic Feast of Corpus Christi: the Feast of the Body and Blood of Christ then; the Body and Blood of Christ now. This celebration is huge to the Catholic celebration of the Holy Eucharist—when you say AMEN (i.e., I believe) to the minister's proclamation of "The Body, Blood of Christ" when the Lord God is put into your person.

This amen is not just "say the secret password." It is saying amen to yes, that is Jesus. Yes, I am Christ today. Yes, we are Christ today—all of us in the same boat though each of us has a different seat assignment. This is Jesus Christ, the Lamb of God who takes away the sins of the world. "Happy are we who strive to become what we receive." As I am reflecting on this great Feast of Corpus Christi, the Feast of the Body and Blood of Christ, I find myself drawn and comforted in my weak faith by the truth that throughout the history of our human race there has been no one person (and known deity) who has captivated as much interest and human response as the person and story of Jesus whom Catholic, Protestant, Orthodox and nondenominational Christians, like myself, refer to as our Christ.

Think about it. The motion picture industry has sought to capture this Jesus in such Academy Award-winning films as *The Greatest Story Ever Told,* and in many more like this one. In the world of art, I don't think there is any one story that has been captured so much in paintings, sculptures, frescos, and architecture as that of Jesus, or so influenced the lives of the many who have devoted their lives to him throughout the Christian tradition. In the literary world and music world, over and above the best-selling New Testament, I don't think there has been more attention given to any subject than to this captivating Jesus—how to model his love as a true purpose for living and respond to his call to love. And, of course, in the course of world history, there has been no one human figure that has attracted as much human response and attraction. Today, not only do millions of Catholics throughout the world daily and weekly celebrate the Body of Christ in the Eucharist, but there are one billion people who call themselves Christians. Multiply that by the total human response over the last two thousand years. No one person throughout human history has drawn so much interest or has caused such a human response to the cause of love, or any other cause, as the Jesus we celebrate today on this Feast of Corpus Christi.

Why? Because it's an old story with many paintings, songs, books, edifices, etc? There are many other great stories. So why has one man's story drawn the most attention? I believe there are two explanations: (1) Jesus hurt. That our God, in Jesus Christ, has shown us how much we can love and be loved, until it hurts! That true intimacy in life comes from the cause of compassion, to carry the burden of others, which Jesus not only talked about but also personally sacrificed for upon the cross. (2) Jesus heals. That the *experience* of this love and ability to be loved has been convincingly given to us through one other when we have hurt—when we, either directly hurting or seeing the hurts of others, have seen no greater human response than that given in the name of Jesus. If we really think about it, not only has the experience of Christ's love come to us through prayer and spirituality; for a lot of us, the direct and most convincing experience of Christ's love has been experienced in how we love one another, especially the poor, the sick, the ignored, the mistreated, and the forgotten.

Today, as we celebrate the Body and Blood of Christ, we focus not just on the object or person of Christ in the Eucharist, art, storytelling, or architecture. We focus on the living, breathing Body and Blood of Christ which is all of us: how we take the Body and Blood of Christ and live it as we "go forth to love the Lord, Our God, and *one another.*" These true stories of our Catholic community helping the sick, the dying, and the estranged, are endless and inspiring.

On the other hand, though, we cannot celebrate how today the Body and Blood of Christ is *hurting.* Specifically, the Body of Christ is hurting when the poor, children, families, the elderly, and those labeled by society, politics, prejudice, and economics are not being treated with dignity. Whether they are Catholic or not, old or young, Democrat or Republican, gay or straight, rich or poor, legal or illegal, is not an issue when the needy come to the Body of Christ. Christ lived, died, and rose for all, and the poor need to be loved as Christ loved. This is our mission, our purpose, and our joy in response as Christians, people who bear the name and continue the mission of Christ.

Recently, our Body of Christ has been greatly and catastrophically affected by the recent legislature cutting welfare support for Americans and legal immigrants who we judge not to contribute sufficiently to the state and county. Today, the Body of Christ is hurting in the way that our brothers and sisters who are the poorest of the poor—the elderly, families, children, the sick, and the immigrant—are being greatly and immorally affected by the recent legislative changes in our state and country's welfare and immigrant *"reform,"* for lack of a better word. As the laws governing our state and national welfare system are changing they, and those who create these laws, impose extreme hardships on the working poor and on those seeking work. Though these laws invite a transition from welfare to work, they do not take into account the smaller number of dignified jobs, training, and childcare that make this transition reasonably possible. Recent cuts inflict a danger to the human family resulting in mothers and fathers being unable to meet the social, economic, educational, and moral needs of their children. Additionally, after all the new programs which have been designed to limit if not eliminate benefits (Social Security benefits, Medicare, food stamps, etc.), state and county governments must work collaboratively to ensure that general relief, food, health care, and security and genuine care are available to sustain the most vulnerable.

I am so proud to say that my cardinal and a whole bunch of good pastors in Los Angeles whose parish members are directly affected by these new hardships have met to discuss, discern, and challenge our Catholic membership on how we are going to respond as Christs to our poor who will come to us for aid and protection. At the same time, pastors from those areas whose members are not largely affected are being asked to support our poorest members of the Body of Christ through prayer and communicating to their elected representatives of the true hardships that present legislation is inflicting on us.

From such powerful meetings the cardinal, the bishops, and these pastors wish to assure the poor that we stand in solidarity with them as we will continue: (1) To meet the rise of fear, hopelessness, and desperation among our poor by educating and updating our pastors and their parish ministries on the recent laws and upcoming legislation regarding welfare and the rites of legal immigrants; (2) to monitor legislation through the California Catholic Conference as well as having our own pastors walk the halls of the State Capitol to assure that basic legitimate services are assured for our poor; (3) to help our legal immigrants to become full citizens, for example, but continuing to sponsor citizenship classes and ESL classes; (4) to provide legal assistance, referrals, and resources through our Office of Catholic Charities, Regional Offices, and the Cardinal McIntyre Fund for Charity; and (5) to provide moral and spiritual support to those affected parishes and their pastoral leadership as we continue to join in solidarity in opting for the care of our poor. This is only a beginning. With God's help more specific support measures and resources will be determined and made available.

The Body of Christ subscribes ultimately to love, not man's law; to mercy and not condemnation; to giving and not taking as the truths and mission given to us by our Lord. Contained within this Ultimate Truth is that we are all one body of Christ, though many members, and that when one of our members is mistreated, impaired, hungry, ill, or abandoned—when even one of our brothers and sisters is hurting—the whole body is affected and experiences the hurt. For those hurting directly they need to know that the Body of Christ will be there for them and protect them. When those who are not hurting directly hear of this they need to know that they, the Body of Christ, must respond as Christ to our brothers and sisters by helping and protecting them. We must assure our poor brothers and sisters that we are with them, and, like our Lord did and does for all of us, will sacrifice for them. So, I think it is perfectly normal to say that the Church is not perfect. It should not act like it is, especially when it gets caught. Whether the hungry rich or the hungry poor, we still hunger.

On one hand my experience in my relationship with the church has been the number one key instrument and guide of God to me in my life, love, and sense of beingness. Then at the same time, I don't know any force or any institution in the history of my world and of modern-day western civilization that has inflicted more shame on me and countless others than the Roman Catholic Church. Like any relationship, there is always the tension of what is good and what is not so good. So, as I roam along and confront those angry questions, I've got to say, as I have said and as I've heard many men say about their wives and mothers and girl friends after experiencing total disappointment: "You still can't help but love the battle-axe!" My old man sought after the Church for the only safe and whole and empowering connection that he had in life. That's why with guitar masses and English being the new liturgical language, he felt betrayed and abandoned. That's why he left the Church, the same Church that condoned by its silence his constant and abusive behavior towards himself and, thus, his family. He left. The new Church was challenging him to grow, and not allowing and enabling his behavior anymore. He was being forced to try to understand, and no longer allowed to go to church every Sunday then go home and beat up his wife and son. If he was alive today, I am sure that I would be his number one disappointment, with the rest of the religious zealots of our time.

But, alas, the good times—oh my God, there have been so many wonderful good times. The best ever! I will surely get to those later.

CHAPTER SIX

THE NEW GROUND ZERO

June 2001

"Father Ken? This is Jennifer from Celebrity Cruises. Would you ever like to be a chaplain on one of our ships? You take care of your air travel and we'll pick up the rest. You can even bring a friend with you."

Now, that's what I call the "If today you hear His voice, harden not your heart," in response to a divine calling. Though there may not be a whole lot of certainty these days, this calling is the perfect revelation of the Lord's will for me especially when it is conveyed through the person of one of his children, Jennifer: You've got to love that. I picked a week cruise to the Bahamas leaving New York on September 16, 2001. I invited my buddy Joe to come with me. We arranged to fly to New York on September 12, 2001 to visit my sister and brother-in-law in Manhattan. What better way to begin a week on the ocean than first tearing it up around the Big Apple? I always wanted to have a drink on top of the World Trade Center.

6:30 a.m., September 11, 2001
The Beginning of Ground Zero Momentum

"Joe?" I called. "This is Ken. Sorry to wake you. We're not going anywhere. Turn on your TV." So the cruise from heaven was dropped because of someone's decision to take a trip "in the name of God" to hell, causing terror, murder, and destruction in New York, at the Pentagon, and in Pennsylvania.

My God.

This would be one of many other disasters reducing pillars of strength, prosperity, and arrogance into the "ground zeroes" of our day: the City of New York; American security; the ongoing Middle East crisis; and the growing accounts and scandals of sexual abuse by the clergy and other public servants on children—as well as the scandal of how the magisterium of the Church is being exposed in its historical refusal to protect its people, and its hand in contributing to the abuse. The Church does not acknowledge that we are still in the process of learning whether we choose to recognize it or not. And, as we are learning, the teachers need to be taught and should want to be taught.

April 13, 2002

So here I am finally on the ship, the Celebrity *Century,* having rescheduled my cruise since the 9/11 trauma. As I am beginning this, I just got out of a wonderful hot-tub experience wherein I, amongst the bubbles and seven newfound friends of a whole fifteen-minute duration, had been drinking Bahama Mommas (a sissy la-la cocktail) and laughing and just enjoying the freedom from home, the papers, the news, cell phones, and the scandals.

"So, Bob? What do you do for a living"?

"Ah, Bambi, my name is Ken," I responded to this beautiful, blonde woman of life and beauty products while becoming frightfully aware that I have not seen this many white people in over six years—and just when I thought it was safe to be Ken and not Father Ken. Ever hear of wanting to escape a hot tub? Because I was there on an official capacity, I didn't hem and haw that I was a shrink, a schoolteacher, or a social worker in the inner city of Los Angeles, like I normally would.

"I work with the people of Mid-City Los Angeles as a Catholic priest."

"Oh really, how wonderful," the remaining four in the tub say politely (while the other three instantly make their escape).

"These must be rough times for you." Wow. These are strangers and they have been the only ones that have had the decency to extend an empathetic gesture of care. They were Jewish. There were probably only a handful of brother and sister Gentiles back home that even approached me to extend genuine care during a time that totally sucked for a priest.

Interesting.

Priests are not monsters. Actually, not *some* of the greatest, caring people but all of the greatest caring people in my life have been priests. But, I can understand why someone who hasn't had the experience of a personable priest would hide their children from us. *Hey, they come clinging to me!* Through the media, the entertainment industry, and literature, priests are usually portrayed as intellectual, wimpy nonrelationals who robotically exercise the will of the present pontiff and/or local ordinary (a bishop, archbishop, or cardinal). Though we appear very much like intellectual weenies of protocol and parliamentary procedure at, especially, priest meetings, we are all over the board (and this usually comes out during the happy hour immediately following these official meetings when we join together as a presbyterate).

This is quite a painful time in a Church that has shown its corporate leadership to be high on their horses, and now, like the rest of us schmucks, high on their crosses. This means that resurrection will come, but only when the magisterium of the Church and the real Church learn, listen, and reevaluate themselves. We priests need to act more relational, available, and lovable, without getting our total humanness sucked out of us. The laity can be brutal, especially if you're a revolutionary priest who has decided to show his humanness. Surely, the leadership of the Church of Rome by all appearances acts, communicates, and still spends as the Church of the Middle Ages. The authority of the Church is being questioned now as the padres who have turned abused children into another chapter in our faith have made the slaughter of the Holy Innocents prove salvific. I, personally, have to think, pray, and discern how my actions, my humanness, and my weaknesses contribute to this tragedy of Church indifference that existed way before this crisis. I can only hope and pray that all of us are being sensitized to this situation as to how we deal with each other at church, and at home, work, the freeways, the supermarkets, the voting booths, and with the daily choices that we make.

At this writing, what I just expressed above is very real, painful, and conflicting. Yet, conflict is not bad. Whether I am the abused, the abuser, the victim, or the victimizer in any situation, I have to think. I have to pray. Anyone can react. To be fully a priest is to be fully human. To be of the Spirit must include a discussion of that which houses the Spirit: my flesh, my story, my history, my urgings, and my own need for a Savior. It ain't just the authority of the church that suppresses the humanity of the priesthood by ignoring and not dealing with issues of "healthy and intimate priestly lifestyles." It's also the people. Particularly, it's those people who were raised: (1) Knowing the religion, (2) knowing the historical details of the development of the religious traditions, and (3) knowing the biographical details of the characters of the tradition while never taking the time to know, share, integrate, and apply the salvific meaning and relevance of such spiritual gems today in everyday life. In short, these dear people know of their religion as a sacred cow and strongly feel it under attack and reduced to a "white elephant" when lovingly challenged to move ahead. It's like being challenged to remember the "I do's" of a marriage that began twenty years ago, reapplied, renewed, and reevaluated so as to deepen the relationship.

For a lot them, I say sadly for me and all the good priests who profess this dimension of their priesthood as the "sacrifice behind the love," that celibacy means that we are the 7-Eleven of God—a twenty-four-hour convenience store for "God things" and quick fixes. (The other night at two in the morning the phone rang with the caller saying, "Father. I heard the pope died. What are you going to do?" My response: "Go back to bed and I suggest you do the same.") *Whoa—GET A LIFE AND LEAVE ME ALONE!* Yep, we're "Open All Night." And when that's working, terrific. And if it is not because of a padre's illness, limitations, depression, family death, or just because he's bloody tired, hungry, or horny, we're treated with the same disappointment that one experiences when they have a flat tire. Getting a flat tire is never convenient. It failed me at the wrong time. (When is the right time for a flat tire anyway?)

Unfortunately, with the Roman magisterium, any questioning for discussion of how to further the relationship of God, of how to be Church to the people of today, is sensed as an attack or non-Catholic if it is in any way passionate or full of expressions of humanity. To look for some relevant and sensitive rationale to the older doctrines of Church tradition (celibacy, women, women priests, married priests, gay love, ecumenism, allowing ex-priests to serve in the church, etc.) is perceived as an attack, and the Church in Rome is usually unwilling to even discuss it. The resistance one receives in these matters from Church magisterium is because they have felt the need to always have the answers (sign of strength) and not have to ask the questions (sign of weakness)—that their authority to be the "answermen" is what we stupid people need. Still, the institution of the Church has bought into the secular claim that the real power is in being right—to claim that it must always appear as the model *par excellence* of liturgy, evangelism, leadership, morality, and truth. But in fact, what the people strive to hold on to in faith is that "it's our weaknesses that make us strong."

If you look at Christ, what made him credible (remember, he didn't travel around with the authoritative title of MESSIAH on his driver's license) was the way he presented himself as a vulnerable human being living, identifying with, and serving people whose life situations (being lepers, ill, in material and spiritual poverty—the confused, rejected, full of doubt, despair, wonder, thirsts, hungers, and urgings) caused them to ask some questions about a loving God and the feeling of aloneness that came with their getting through the day, in contrast to the thing about getting to heaven after you die. Jesus asked and listened to the same questions, and even if he knew the answers, he knew it was being present with the questioners that was important.

He did not make the questioners feel demeaned, unheard, offensive, and small. He saved that treatment for the religious zealots who claimed to have the answers and suppressed the people with them. Jesus wanted to be inclusive, to draw people to not so much believe in him as God but to believe in the mission and the One who sent him on the mission—to, again, offer them a newer, clearer, and more honest and sensitive face of God, world, and self.

The persons of established religion at the time, and the political powers of Jesus' day, the Roman bureaucracy, attempted to destroy him and the growing, extraordinary power of his love. The local religious figureheads and Roman powers of the Holy Land were threatened that Jesus was fueling a new quest, a new drive to find their own God in a very dramatic way—that God, the Truth, their Truth, was not exclusively found above and beyond, BUT within and among—a way they suspected would fly directly in the face of their coveted power. And the rigidity and refusal to bend that the powers of Jesus' day exhibited presented the same problem that the church's leaders oftentimes appear to possess now—that need to be right, to always be in control, sitting at the head of the table, can continue to cause the same alienation now as two thousand years ago. The need for people to discover their own truths, purposes, and dignity was more important than convincing them of an outer power (political or religious) to surrender to. Jesus, I believe, was not attempting to start a religion as much as to help people discover their own dignity, power, and spirit—to help them discover the power of God within their own persons and each other.

Alas, this is the reason why he dined and commissioned the sinner, the hungry rich, the hungry poor, and the social and cultural outcasts. Because these classes were more open to allow and accept the Truth as much as a vacant lot has more ability to allow the possibility of grass to grow on it as opposed to a lot that is littered with broken glass, old tires, and litter. Catholics have been taught to have the answers and know all the formulas. We've been taught to memorize and claim to be the first and the right, always connected directly to Christ. Thus questioning is seen as a sign of stupidity and disrespect. We Catholics have not only been taught not to ask questions, I'm not sure we even know how to ask the questions. Catholics don't know what questions to ask or what questions we can feel comfortable asking without bowing and scraping! Ughhh! Seemingly, we have been taught how to "argue" the religion, but know little about having a relationship with God and Christ. We were not taught how to "share" our faith. We were not taught how to own our faith, how to feel the love of our God especially when the religion has let us down. We were taught to KNOW and memorize. We were not taught to explore the "So what?" Know religion?! Know God? Hmmm.

The present scandal involving the sexual abuse by clerics of children has been referred to as the 9/11 of the Catholic Church. The present Church authority is being criticized for not asking the questions in reference to the issues that brought on the 9/11 of our Church, but also for not being sensitive to a credibility problem that has existed for a very long time. They will never take the blame; they appear to simply say "sorry" with no or little retribution, and when they even come close it makes headline news. Taking responsibility for this mess would be a sign of weakness and, God forbid, sin. Excuse me! Those two jets have been coming at us for a long time (and there are many more out there that don't take sophisticated radar to detect, by the way) and they were then and now not given concern, importance, or proper attention. They were noticed but ignored as irrelevant by the corporate authority of the Church of Rome, the Roman Curia—including the pontiff, I suppose. OR, they were easily and conveniently categorized as an attack by the devil and the sinner of the present time. All things lead back to Rome and I'm not the one who devised that flowchart! And where were the people, the real church, during all of this? Still in the complacency and certainty of the Middle Ages and the Holy Roman Empire. We are the select. We are "the chosen."

If this is to be a 9/11 of our church, then it should be associated not just with a disaster, but to a lesson learned—a new genesis of how we are to appear to live and love each other, giving witness to faith and not religious tenets. If nothing else, 9/11 taught us to rethink and reweigh a lot of things. This sure happened to me. But it was a strange and wonderful phone call from a person in New York during that awful time immediately following the terrorist attack that put it all in perspective for me. It wasn't until about three days after the 9/11 attack that I realized I wasn't running or working out like I normally do. I wasn't even praying. Instead, I just needed to take "solemn high naps." It was then I realized that the depression and anxiety that had already hit everyone else had finally gotten to me, a diocesan priest in Los Angeles' inner city. At first, I was holding everyone up, trying to answer the unanswerable questions my parishioners kept throwing at me: "Father Ken, why does God let things like this happen? Father, how can there be such evil in the world? Father Ken, why aren't there any jelly doughnuts? Father, my son works in New York, please pray for him, and did you know we're out of toilet paper in the ladies' room again?" I knew they wanted me to make sense of it all, to hold them. But after watching the endless news, trying to reach my own family in Manhattan, imagining what it must have been like to have been there, the truth was that I just wanted someone to hold *me*. I knew I was supposed to lead my flock. I wanted to empower them. But I couldn't have felt more powerless.

Then on Thursday, the phone rang. There was an unidentified male caller on the line. "Father Deasy?" he inquired. "Father Deasy?" Oh, no. No one ever calls me "Father Deasy," unless it is some right-wing Catholic bells-and-smells nutcase, probably from Back East. "Yesss . . ." I said hesitantly, like one slowly approaching a land mine. "I'm calling from New York," was his response. See? I knew it! Cardinal Egan?

He continued. "I was at your parish, St. Agatha's, about three years ago and I had to call you. I haven't slept in two days!" He calls now, after three years? Here it comes. What possible waxy, yellow Catholic buildup did this guy want to be finally freed from? What, in this time of national tragedy, was he losing sleep over? A sin he had confessed a hundred times before, but wanted to do again just to be sure? The Host touched his teeth? A dirty thought? Or . . . even worse . . . he touched himself?! The sinner! If he says he slept through my homily, I'm not giving absolution. Speaking of sleep, isn't it time for a high holy nap? He continued. "When I was at your place, I felt so good when I came to church." *Felt good,* I thought to myself. Don't let that get around town! You felt so good, that you never came back? Heck, dude, if you want to go to church and feel like dirt before, during, and afterwards, there are plenty of churches you can attend. "And your community was so welcoming! I had to call you and let you know what has happened to me!"

"I would love to hear it," I lied. Be careful, dude. I am a celibate man who hasn't had his eight cups of coffee yet. He continued.

"I live in Manhattan, and I felt the urge on Tuesday to go down to Ground Zero to lend a hand. I just had to help. I had to be there. But when I got there, there was an old, beer-bellied fireman guarding the area. One look and I knew: retired, angry, probably a bigot. He was everyone I'd ever been pushed aside by. He was all those who didn't call me back when I was auditioning. I'm an actor." *What restaurant?* I wondered.

"He was my dad. The disapproving monsignor when I was a teen. The Church. He was my former boss. He was my former self. He was scary as hell! I said to him, 'I want to help!' Mr. New York Fireman Bigot reprimanded me and said, 'You can't go down there.' But I said it again which is not my style. 'I must go down to help!' Needless to say, I wasn't the only one wanting to go down there. And every time I pleaded to help, I received the same gruff, official response: 'You are not allowed to go there. You cannot help. You will only get in the way.'" What do you expect, dude? Security? Liability? Danger. I'm glad I wasn't there, though. I felt powerless a continent away—being that close, and still not able to do anything. He continued.

"I gave it one last shot and asked, 'Well, sir, what can I do?'"

"'You can give blood at the Red Cross like everyone else!' the fireman snapped back. Father Deasy—I looked at him with a zeal for honesty and pride I've struggled my whole life to maintain. And even though I feared he'd shun me, I confessed. I told him: 'I can't give blood. I am infected with the AIDS virus.'" *You didn't tell him that! What were you thinking?* He continued.

"The fireman paused and stared right through my soul. He just silently stared for a few seconds which to me, felt like a year. Said nothing. Then, it seemed to me like in slow motion, he lifted the yellow 'Danger: Stay Away' plastic ribbon that bordered off the area, found me a hard hat, got me one of those name tag badges, and said, 'Son . . . have a ball!'"

I'm crying now. It feels so good to cry. It's been a while—at least an hour. He continued. "For the last two days, I had been working side by side with people who would have normally condemned me for who I was, how I got the virus, my life. But, then and there, it didn't matter. I was a giver. I was a man. I got dirty. I sweated. I hungered. I had thirst. I was with the dying. I am dying. My dying hands were needed and valued. For the first time, I believed that I was one of them, the rescuers, and the rescued. I was . . . I was . . . I WAS!"

I'm dehydrated from crying. *Where the heck are the tissues? And my coffee?* He continued. "You there, Fadda?" *You mean what's left of me? You're killing me!*

"Yes. Of course, I am," I answered.

"I am sooooooo tired," he said, "and I am so alive. I am so alive. I am so normal!" *Oh, baby, if only you knew.* I had to ask, though.

"So why the call? And why me? Why us, the parish?" I was so flattered and humbled and begged the question, as my coffee was cold and invisible to me now. He continued.

"Because your Catholic community was the first that had blessed me with what I had felt was unusual for Catholics. I felt accepted by Christ, and the acceptance and the welcome of your place was at first as surprising as the fireman's." He continues. And so will I.

As the Good Witch said to the Wicked Witch, "Be gone! You have no power here! And be careful, because a house might just fall on you!"

In other words, I'm not sure that even the people, the real Church by the way, ask the questions that are needed since this supposed 9/11. Actually, with the present "hierarchal structure" of the "Holy Roman Corporate," these questions wouldn't be given any attention anyway. The people's cry is oftentimes "What about me, God? What about me, Church?" The Church has taught Father will fix it! Well, what happens when Father needs fixing? Now I am the pastor of a great parish. I arrived here eight years ago, dead. They gave me life. I have been lucky to share this Spirit that they gave me back to them. We're a church of recovering Catholics: ex-priests, gays, straights, illegals, whites, blacks, pinks, purples, gangsters; in other words, PEOPLE. It hasn't always been easy. *You think I like seeing my own two feet on the coffee table every night?*

Last year alone, some members of my congregation (a small number with a mixed bag of agendas) thought that I was "bashing the religion" because I had raised such issues as "using homilies to vent my displeasure"—credibility over authority. Why celibacy?—is it about religion or is it about spirituality? What was really behind it was that I welcomed gays, whites, illegals from Mexico and Central America, mixed relationships, non-Catholics, public sinners, crying babies, and single-parent families with kids born "out of wedlock," whom I will baptize.

These people, the Sanhedrin of the present day, were people I had loved and confess not loving as much as I should anymore. It hurt like hell. In their cry to "fire his ass" and be right, they were inconsiderate of my person, my home, and my life, and of their own goodness, spirituality, and hypocrisy. I admit I bring it on myself a lot of the times. Once during a talk I can remember saying, "You love me, right?" Their response, "Oh yeah!" My response, "Thanks. Would you still love me if I, claiming my honesty and not wanting to hide, walked in the room with a woman on my arm?

How about a man on my arm? How about an illegal immigrant on my arm?" I interpreted the silent response as "No. You're alone. We would still love you, but you would have to go."

"But I am the same person who you just said you loved. I still buried your parents. Baptized your kids, fed you when you were hungry, got up at two in the morning to be with you in the hospital, fought for you at Immigration Services, visited you in jail, and tolerated your stoning me with your own scrupulousness and complacency. I'm still the same person I thought I heard you say that you loved."

The silent response meant "We do, but you don't have what it takes to be a Catholic priest, at least. Bye-bye. You are the weakest link. But thank you." I am not a crybaby, though feeling appreciated by these people would work. I am a grown-up man not being suppressed by Cardinal Mahony (who will return my calls), or John Paul II (he never returns my calls, by the way)—just myself when I don't have the courage to live with the freedoms that come with being a man who is a Christian, and feels fulfilled as a "human doing," and a "human being" in being a priest.

Now, ask me about tomorrow and you may get another story. Is this restlessness? Am I leaning toward infidelity and unfaithfulness to my vows? No. I can only live in the present. The past and the future do not exist. It is about being a man who seeks to be rooted and who is not stuck but often feels that way, and who, if told he has to defend himself because he simply questions the "boys in red or the man in white" as much as he questions his own self, will respond with *Whatever! By the way, I'm not important enough to be inquisitioned.* Like anyone, we all have to own and live our own Truths and not the truths assigned to us (the capitalization of "Truth" intended). No man, woman, and/or organization should distract us from that. Unfortunately, just like in marriage, we don't exercise the option to explore this Truth until we are overcommitted legally with responsibilities to family, spouse, and work.

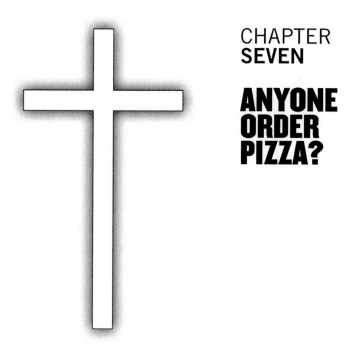

CHAPTER SEVEN

ANYONE ORDER PIZZA?

This is the church, this is the steeple, open the doors and let in the people!

About twelve years ago I was serving as a priest in my second parish assignment, on the Westside. By far, it is one of the most beautiful churches in Los Angeles. This is and was a very popular Catholic parish. Very ornate, traditional—a bunch of statues, pillars—very nice to look at. As a worship space I would have preferred to celebrate the Mass in a gymnasium though. From the worshipper's point of view, the building was a picture of beauty with its highly adorned sanctuary and grandiosity. From my point of view, as a celebrant presiding on the very same sanctuary, the nave of the church was long, far away, and not much for connecting with the worshipper. At the same time, though, the church was really trying to be a church. The parish leadership was really bent on being a community among a tough crowd: yuppies; homeless; looky-loos who only registered so they could get married there someday, or get their kids enrolled in the elementary school; die-hard traditionalists, a parochially ignored Spanish-speaking population; rich liberals; celebrities; and peons.

It was church to me at that time. Though it was located in a very exclusive beach town, it had all the components of inner-city life. It was there that I developed not only a more intense desire to celebrate joyful and youth-filled liturgies, it was also a place where my desire to serve the poor was realized and actualized more and more. In the area were poverty, homelessness, loneliness, and potential for great ministry. At the time, it was the best for me "ministry-wise" though living there was . . . well, that's another discussion. I remember one day about eleven years ago just after Christmastime preaching amongst the throngs and asking, "If this building collapsed, would we still be church"? Here I was trying to get to the point that over and above the statues, the building and the stained glass windows, "church" was an experience, a community, and a revelation of God's love to us in the present.

Two days later, while I was in Big Bear, California, enjoying my Christmas break, a major earthquake rocked Southern California and the church was damaged to the point that it could not be used with safety. The frescoes had fallen, some of the ceiling had collapsed, and it was in danger of being demolished. The building of the church was destroyed. The "people of church" were empowered. I remembered calling the monsignor inquiring how things were. He told me about the destruction. I asked if he wanted me to come down the mountain and help. He said no. I came anyway, gladly.

The monsignor and I had a struggling relationship that is quite typical in rectory life in which you live where you work. I thought this would be a good opportunity to offer him fraternal support, and try again to attempt to correct his view that I was a threat to his empire. I could tell that, though surrounded by many supporters, he felt the burden of rebuilding his church was his alone. I totally understand that today, now that I am a pastor. Then I was rebellious, in denial, and transferring my final intolerance of feeling rejected, accused, and not enough for anybody onto him. Like with my dad, I suppose, the pastor was also just like me. What I resented in him, I resented in myself . . . and he was getting away with it!

What the monsignor has become today I appreciate more as I continue to come into my own person, calling, and sense of self. Today, he appears to me to be a man who has grown, been humbled, and whom I truly see and respect as a man of God and a "man of church." I strive to be the same, taking into account our different talents, stories, and divine summoning. If I am a "man of Church," though, it will be on the margins which is where I like it.

Upon returning to the rectory, there was a loud noise caused by the sweeping up of cracked Waterford crystal and Lladró figurines that were shattered across the hardwood floors of the monsignor's and the other associate priest's quarters. They took a huge loss. As for me, there was no destruction in my quarters.

I can remember them asking me, "Didn't you lose anything, Ken?" I said, "I lost nothing." "Why didn't you lose anything?" they both inquired. "Because I don't have anything!" Well, at least I don't have a lot of things, though the things I do have are not of an easily destructible nature. My assistance was not needed. Again, my lack of loss was a threat. So, I helped a few of the old folks put their things back on their shelves and returned to the mountains. For the following two years while the church was being rebuilt I really enjoyed saying Mass in the new gymnasium. For me, I was so glad that I did not have to be burdened with rebuilding the building of the church. For me, I was just glad to be able to help people be church, feel church, and be Christ. I never knew I had it in me. I never knew that the Lord would want to be "enchurched" in the likes of me.

"Francis, my Church is in ruins," was the divine voice spoken to a wild playboy Italian in the fourteenth century. There's a city named San Francisco in homage to him. It wasn't a building of the Church that was in ruins. It was the experience of Church that was destroyed by arrogance, wealth, and exclusion of the "different." Francis rebuilt not only a small chapel named San Damiano, but began to cause a reconstruction of the Holy Roman Catholic Church by reminding it of its poor and its need to be vulnerable to the same poverty of life and spirit to which we all are susceptible. It ain't about the buildings. And if people don't get it, it's because we don't live it. God, through Francis, uploaded new software in the machinery of the Church.

On the occasion of celebrating a daily Mass nine years later at St. Agatha's, with a huge attendance of six people in the congregation, a young kid walked up in the middle of the Eucharist and said with no fear or apprehension, "Did anyone order pizza"? The congregation gasped and then laughed. They realized that the pizza was to be delivered to St. Agatha's Church and he presumed from his own experience that the "church" was simply a building in which services were received. It needs to return to being the opposite: a community where services are given; and if the services are limited to being a house of ritual, it better be a ritual that conveys a reality. Herein lies the mission and the real challenge.

A few years ago I was invited to New York by a dear, long-haired, hippie-looking friend of mine, Dr. Rick Montz (a wonderful friend who died in his forties of a heart attack while jogging in Baltimore), who you would have thought by appearance would be the last person to be admitted into a papal organization of the Church called the Knights of Malta. Basically, this is an organization of men (papal knights) and woman (*ladies of the knight?*) who hold one or all of the following qualities: big bucks, career prominence, a lot of business/social connections, a devotion to being Catholic, and a dedication to the poor. I know a lot of Knights of Malta, Knights of the Holy Sepulcher, and Knights of St. Gregory, and they are basically very good people. They are politically conservative and highly traditional. In addition, and most admirable to me, is that it would not be a rare occurrence for a knight or a unit of knights to financially stake an entire family who has a sick member to a full-expenses-paid trip to Lourdes, France, in hopes of a cure for mind, body, and/or soul. Again, though these folks would be more traditional than myself, they are wonderful and generous people. As I always say, "There's room for everyone! Just be nice!"

Rick was a prominent doctor, surgeon, and oncology researcher from UCLA and Johns Hopkins Medical University. Though Rick surely did not look the part, by appearances a total hippie, he was a huge guy in science, faith, family, and friendship. I couldn't wait to see him sit among the gray-haired, tuxedoed, baby-knights who were waiting to be dubbed by Cardinal O'Connor in Saint Patrick's Cathedral. Rick, on the other hand, couldn't wait to see me, a young blonde, blue-eyed, long-haired, obviously California-looking progressive sitting among my brother elder priests who would also attend this most high liturgy. On the day of the investiture of the knights, I arrived thirty minutes before the ceremony to the beautiful and most stuffy St. Patrick's Cathedral. I approached the sacristy to vest and I was surprised to discover that this was where only the bishops would doll up for the ritual. *I got out of there as quickly as I could.* I proceeded to the lower sacristy, where us lowly priests of the people would put on our albs and show off either our tailor-made stoles or mere "off the rack" stoles purchased through a catalog. *You think we get this stuff at Macy's?*

As I entered the sacristy I was immediately caught with the realization that I was the youngest one in the room by at least three hundred years, and much more excited about the after-party than the two-and-a-half-hour ritual that awaited us. *You think you are the only one who gets bored at church sometimes? You* should see how exciting YOU ALL look sometimes when we're trying to zap you with a little joy and celebration! I, being a courteous fellow who despises being in a room of peers who don't have a thing to say to each other, made my rounds and introduced myself to the awaiting clergy, *my brother priests.* I thought I was convincing that I really cared and wanted to make a connection. They, in turn, were rather convincing that they could care less about me and what was about to happen upstairs in the magnificent cathedral, truly a beautiful piece of architecture. Tourists love it—a place of liturgies par excellence, according to the liturgy police. Totally lifeless, though, according to the common coroner. If any of the boys were invited to any one of the after-parties, I was invited to three. It would be a waste of good French champagne. Yet, I continued to make my rounds with no luck of discovering any signs of life or vibrancy.

Then, the Lord sent me an olive branch.

"Good Father from California," a voice said to me as I felt his hand on my shoulder, "you must realize that the more east you go the more unfriendly we are." This priest happened to be one that worked side by side with the late and great Cardinal Joseph Bernadine of Chicago. "Oh my God," I whispered, "thanks for the validation that I wasn't transported to the wrong world!" He responded, "Stay with me, my friend. You ain't seen nothing yet."

Suddenly, an elderly, pasty, white-faced man, who was dragged out in purple and black (I was jealous that he was dressier than me) walked down to us and clapped his hands three times to get our attention, I presume. An ecclesiastical pacemaker? Jump start? The announcement came forth: "Please gather yourselves in groups of eight and proceed upstairs to reverence the Cardinal." Say what? Reverence whom? My face showed utter shock as I immediately prayed a prayer of thanksgiving for my situation in Los Angeles with Cardinal Mahony. I turned to my priest angel from heaven and said, "What the hell is he talking about?" The response was a simple, "You'll see."

As we walked upstairs and as I looked ahead, there was the cardinal archbishop of New York, leaning against the statue of Saint Patrick, totally preoccupied with other matters and dignitaries. As he was standing there not noticing any of us, groups of eight priests would bow before him. NO WAY! He's not my bishop. That's okay. He isn't watching anyway. As my group came to our turn to pay our respects, our "reverence," the remaining seven in my group bowed oh so slowly with their elderly backs cracking with the deep bend. I remained erect. Standing straight is what I meant! And, of course, he had to look only at our group. I was busted.

His cold stare looked into mine—a standoff. He was curious to see who I, this strange-looking, sun-tanned padre was, as I stood in contrast to the gray, lifeless, ministry-beaten others. I moved on feeling comfortable that I would not have to notice him any more even though he was about to be the main celebrant of the high liturgy of Saint Patrick's Cathedral! Go figure. Fate would have it, though, that his throne was directly across from where I was sitting. I kept hearing Betty Davis saying, *"Fasten your seat belt, this is going to be a bumpy flight."* I offered up more thanks for my very own Cardinal Roger Mahony. He is a such a good man to me! Though I am not on his A-list, I know him well enough that he must struggle with being "professional" and with being "personal," though I do not expect him to admit it. He is progressive. He is and has been totally square with me and allows me to be creative and flippant. Though I lose water when my secretary says, "Cardinal Mahony on line one!" I still respect him and am at ease with him. I often hope that the cardinal will survive all the crud he has to take. I would be sad to see him replaced with some guy needing to get us back to "the good old days" of leadership, liturgy, ministerial authority, priestly living, and all manners of pontificating.

Before long, I was out like a light though my eyes were totally opened and focused. This surely is my greatest talent achieved after four years of philosophy and four years of theology. I can look at someone during a meeting, a conference, a class and be totally in another world. This is great. Without anyone ever noticing that I am clearly unconscious I can look so attentive. But, to this day, I remember this clash of the word "reverence" and the reality of "how to reverence." To revere is to hold dear, I firmly hold. To revere someone does not mean that you lose equality with him/her. It does not mean that you put them up on a pedestal. To revere someone does not mean that you approach that person with, "Lord, I am not worthy." How many times did I hear in religious life, "If you don't revere the man, revere the office"? I suppose this is true if you are looking at a plumber, a mechanic, or a baker. But this certainly does not apply to politicians, doctors, and clergy—people whom other people entrust their lives and livelihoods to.

I can often appear and rightly be called irreverent. I am called this because I get caught up with people rather than offices. I get excited about mutuality rather than pomp. I certainly don't take myself as seriously as others presume me to because of my office of being a priest and a pastor. I certainly do not sit on a pedestal *though those who I have disappointed with my humanness would disagree with this self-disclosure.* I like to laugh, and I don't kiss rings or ass! At the same time, I am not demanding anyone to do the same with me. I call them as I see them though my timing is not always that great and my choice of words is not always that prudent. But this freshness makes my parish in Los Angeles, where many recovering Catholics, Jews, and Protestants, from traditions that promote our lack more than our worth, find a good place to come for new life—for a genuine and affectionate experience of God in the Eucharist, the Word, the priest, and, especially, the community.

One of the many groups being victimized by religious exclusion are the good and wonderful folks who come to our parish who are many things: God's children, smart, brave, generous, Spirit-filled . . . and homosexual. One Sunday, after a marvelous liturgy which focused on how the inclusion of the Gentile among the Jewish Christians of the early Church was still very much a challenge today, I tried to connect a problem of the early Church with being a relevant point of discussion of life in our present day. I was especially trying to target the racism, bigotry, rash judgments, sexism, and social casting that still very much exist in our world, cities, and churches which is contrary to the teaching of the good news.

Pretty simple to equate and understand, right? Wrong!

Earlier, I started the story about the African American lady who came up to me after this Spirit-filled liturgy and said, "What are you going to do about those homosexuals that come to Mass?" My response to her: "So, now we're going to put them in the back of the bus?" Ouch! Take that you sanctimonious religious zealot. Quit reading the Bible and live the thing, will ya? Even the devil can quote scripture! Herein she was attempting to theologize on how the Church has claimed this "grouping" to be disordered behaviorally. Sinners! She forgot how in the early history of our country, worshipping congregations and even religious orders discriminated and placed their brothers and sisters of color in the back of the church. She forgot how many of the cultural needs of her African American sisters and brothers were ignored by a Roman Catholic Church that demanded Latin and no spontaneity or charismatic expression. I can actually remember quite a few pastors of the past and present referring to charismatics as "charismaniacs"! This church did not revere or respect her culture or her sisters. So why was she revering it?

Big Brother? An Oedipus complex? Fear? Fear? The fear of being underestimated more than you need to be? Like being swatted on the butt at a college fraternity initiation: "Thank you sir, may I have another?" SWAT! No pain, no gain. Look like you're suffering and Jesus will love you! Oh Lord, I am not worthy! I can't respect that.

Another story really drives this point home, this question about how relevant reverence and respect are in today's church. Once during my five-and-a-half-year term at the church in Santa Monica, we were having a rehearsal for the monthly high school Mass. The kids were very comfortable in church and it was a friendly place for them. There was laughter as they were rehearsing their skit that was being organized to act out the gospel reading for the day. There were characters in the class and it was loud and joyous and I am sure that Jesus in the tabernacle was really digging sharing his home with them. God's house? A man in his early sixties came up to me furious because the kids weren't genuflecting in front of the tabernacle when they crossed it.

"These kids don't have respect these days like we use to," he yelled.

My reply, "Sir, they just aren't as afraid as we were!"

When respect is gained by fear it is surely not respect. It is intimidation. AND IT WORKS! Sad to say, it really works much better and quicker than positive reinforcement, empowerment, and invitations of collaboration based on compassion, appreciation, and tapping into one's own sense of decency and Christian spirituality. Screaming and yelling and threatening the flock with threats of plagues and inevitable condemnation gets quicker and more quantitative results than reminding people of Jesus' calling and commissioning us to discipleship. I hate to say it, and I will hate myself if I ever deliberately use it, but fear and intimidation are the best tools for getting control and making people do or believe a certain thing. Why do you think that fundamentalists of

all religions are so popular and forceful today? I have tried inviting people to minister to the parish out of joy and not fear of hell.
It doesn't work as well as "If you don't do this you're going to hell,
you'll go blind, God will kick your butt. *And Toto, too? "And that
goes for your little dog, too!"* So, to those coercive leaders who
demand control through intimidation: *"You better do this or a house
just may fall on you!"* I say, *"No! Be gone, you have no power here!"*

Last week in my parish in Los Angeles, we had a second collection for a great charity sponsored in the archdiocese, The Cardinal McIntyre Fund for Charity. While the collection was being
combined into one basket in the back of the church, I proceeded
to invite the faithful to further become the Eucharist that they
just received, by becoming involved in a particular ministry. While
I was pushing our Gospel Brunch at the House of Blues to promote our summer camp, CAMP GOOD IN THE HOOD, a little
girl in a sparkling white dress, skipped up the aisle and gave me
the basket of offerings. She then gave me a hug and skipped back
up the aisle to her awaiting and now mortified mother who felt
she would be shot for raising a girl who would actually be allowed
to hug me, a priest. Is she crazy? The community applauded and
was ecstatic at the little girl's freedom and joy. Good God, can you
imagine her doing that in St. Peter's Basilica in Vatican City,
Rome? *"Swiss Guards!" I can hear it now, "Arrest that little tramp and
bring her here to me!"* Shame. Shame.

I have to confess that I am suffering at this point in the text
from my age-old fear of not being understood. Many of you are
now probably thinking that I am a total schmuck and smart
aleck, that I am totally degrading to the level of WHITE ELE-
PHANT the sacred cows of our religion. If that is true, it is only
because of my lack of writing skills and my, again, being a
searcher, an adventurer, a hopeless romantic trying to carve out a
life in this church whose methodology and approaches to continuing the mission of Jesus as entrusted to Peter are becoming

seemingly irrelevant and in much need of reorganizing, reevaluating, and reassigning, in order to clean house.

Do I have a problem with the authority of the Church? I definitely have problems with certain factions of the authority of the Church. As world ambassador? Right on! As a promoter of social awareness to those areas of our world that are in need of our prayers, defense, and resources? Right on! As an entity that has apologized to those groups whom it has even victimized in the past: Jews, gays, women, non-Catholics, non-Christians? Right on! But the Church as loving, forgiving, approachable, compassionate, and sensitive Christlike instrument of God's empowerment? There we have some problems.

But, since "CHURCH" usually refers to its corporate leadership, I wouldn't count on it to be the gentle, healing touch of Christ. Most definitely not. That's our job and we need to focus more on exactly what that means.

I am not saying that the hierarchical church doesn't try. What I am saying, though, is that the Church as a corporate body of leadership, collectively, does not always come off as a Spirit-filled vulnerable Body of Christ as it should; as it must. It certainly does not appear to invite or encourage discussion of making the Catholic community a viable and affective tool of bringing slices of heaven to those of us in the world who are seeking it. It certainly seems negligent to the spiritual needs of its people, its clergy, and the world on which it exists. It still maintains uniformity and unity as synonymous. Sadly, it still needs to assert its superiority as the main way to God. It still asserts its authority, taking the divine gift of infallibility that was entrusted by Jesus to Peter the Apostle, and acting like an overbearing dad who controls his kids with threats of "As long as you're under my roof you will do as I say." But who's hearing this? Who wants to hear it?

In my years of being a Catholic in California, mainly in Los Angeles where I was raised and where I love to live, I have to say that we have some awesome bishops. As mentioned, the cardinal Roger Mahony I serve under is a good man who has views that I AM SURE are contrary to the present magisterium's scope or attention. Though I would never want to work under him directly, and neither would he welcome it, I respect him very much. He is fun, though his personality is not warm. He's got a terrific sense of humor, and he's as sharp as a tack.

I can remember once at a priest conference where I asked him afterward if he ever lost any sleep at night due to worry and stress. Without batting an eyelid he said, "The only time I lose sleep at night, Deasy, is when I am awakened wondering what YOU'RE doing next!" He is in no way suppressive. He has respected my need and everyone's need to grow to be themselves, for me to grow to become Ken and Father Ken. But because of his office and the history of such an office, everyone walks around him as if on rice paper. I know that if I really screw up he's got to call my butt in on the carpet. He doesn't make the big rules, you know. He is smart not to interfere with the Holy Spirit and God's plan for each and every one of us.

I am lucky to have a bishop who knows me and respects me even when he knows of the many struggles I have within, with the tensions that I deal with in people's own inner quest and with feeling helpless when standing side by side with incredible authority. He knows of my basic goodness as a man even when I get flippant, emotional, and all caught up in trying to convey my frustrations with a church that should be more frustrated as well. He knows of my need to be creative and engaging. He knows that I'm crazy, that priests think that I am crazy. But, he also knows that I am a lovable crazy. He really knows and respects me, and he also knows that I know where to draw the line. Well, most times.

He needs to be in charge, though. And man, oh man, is he good at it. What he has done to ensure proper benefits/salaries for those in education, for example, is huge. He has worked hard to provide assistance for those members of the clergy who are in need of psychological and emotional help by providing the fraternal assistance, funding, and permissions for us to take advantage of it. *Unfortunately, many of us chose not to, though.* He has championed along the lines of being a social advocate for the poor, the marginalized in society and Church. He has ensured that religious sisters and their communities be properly compensated for their ministry when in service and while in retirement. He has ensured that seminarians not have a financial hardship while in formation for a life of priestly service. He has empowered and connected as much as he has led women, laity, and ex-clergy to lives of dignity in the Church they love. He has connected peoples of other faiths and religions to feel included in a common mission of God, Yahweh, Allah, Buddha, and Shiva. He has seen that the laity not only be invited to participate in liturgy but also be trained to be affective ministers. He has influenced more affluent parishes to be more connected financially and fraternally to the poorer parishes. He has grown as a man. He has cried in public. He is hurting now with the present scandal of sexual abuse of children among the clergy.

I feel I can call him "friend." And though I wouldn't want to work directly under him, I am his friend. I fear that someday some nutcase Catholic Nazi will shoot him down. I fear who will replace him when he dies, gets transferred, or becomes a CEO for UNICEF. *I want that job! The UNICEF job, not the bishop's job.*

On the West Coast we have more awesome bishops: Syl Ryan in Monterey, Stephen Blaire in Stockton, George Niederauer in Utah, and, especially, most of our regional bishops who assist the cardinal in Los Angeles. These are good bishops because they are good men. They are men who are struggling with their own ministry, relevancy, and the confines placed on them as a bishop. I often wonder how they are doing during all of this stuff with Church scandals and papal suppression. They look so tired and powerless oftentimes. Whether this is because they find themselves more under the gun as a bishop, because they have become more involved than they would prefer in the business of the Church, or because they know that Mahony calls the shots and any other collaborative efforts on their part may seem futile (that is the Roman papal system, you know) . . . they look soooo tired. They'll never tell me though. They can't and shouldn't trust anyone.

Again, we have to recall that the doctrinal Church can be said to have historically appeared to have been preoccupied with its assertion and claims of sacramental and moral authority. Presently it is being rocked with not only scandals of immorality among its clergy, but more alarmingly by the way in which they have failed to appear to respond to the age-old accusations with genuine sensitivity and remorse. Therefore, with the focus of attention showing how Church authority has engaged its clerics and lawyers to respond to the accusations, the assault on its credibility and relation to its flock has further increased the Church's problems. It's unfortunate that it has taken this shock, which has been likened to the "Twin Tower Destruction of Church Credibility" to grab and engage the attention of the Church's current local leaders. As a result, I know that many of the American bishops are discussing informally and formally (out of Rome's earshot, of course) who is ordainable. How do the ordainable live, love, and allow themselves to be loved? Who do we listen to: God? Accountants? Lawyers? Victims? Who is accountable? Who is to blame? Who is liable? What is admissible? What is confidential and/or privileged information? How can further black eyes like this be prevented?

Now, I know that we have to look at the Church, and life, as both/and, and not just either/or. Now, this is a major point. We white folk love to look at life as either/or. *Latinos and African Americans culturally look at the "both/and" of life.* Church today is both a business and a service (not either a business or a service); it is both an institutional force and as vulnerable as a lamb; it's both a leader and a servant. But the bottom line is that with all the hoopla that it has demanded from the people, with all the hoopla that has been given to it/them by the people, and all the pomp and ritual that generates this hoopla in the first place, the boys in red need to learn one basic business door-to-door salesman technique: You can have the best vacuum (i.e., product) in the world, but if the salesman is a schmuck, so is that vacuum.

Conversion is about sales. Sales do not just focus on the quality of the product. What also must be considered is service, support, guarantees, and warranties. When choosing, purchasing, selecting, and investing, you can't just rest on the quality of the product. It is very possible that the product, the Church, may be the best! It sure may be what is needed. But, better choices by the consumer are made in light of other options. As the phenomenon of religion decreases in necessity and the growth of the phenomenon of spirituality increases in vitality, with this spirituality comes the need for support, direction, and connection. The Church on the local and national and international level better get on the ball if it is going to sell it, to evangelize us! The Truth is held dear in the Church. But you better know how to sell it to shepherds, farmers, fisherman, men, women, girls, boys, poor, the rich, saints, hookers, taxpayers, tax-collectors, black sheep, white sheep, Asian sheep, non-Catholic sheep, and ugly sheep. *Does virgin wool come from ugly sheep? Along that line, does extra virgin olive oil come from extra ugly olives?*

Alas, the true questions of life one ponders when living alone and not having wife and kids hounding you—I've had the ability (luxury) of thinking way too much about absolutely nothing of real importance, dreaming of ambitions of little relevance, addicting oneself to ideas and/or plans that are anything but liberating of the human and the Holy Spirit. It is usually when I am not alone, not being ambitious about my rank, and when I am not feeding the demons within, that I have my "freedom moments";

i.e., moments when it all (life, studies, history, all of it) seems to come together. *These freedom moments are dangerous because they change your compass forever on one hand, and they can make you mad as hell because it took this long to actually get it. Why didn't I get this earlier?*

I was noticing more keenly then ever while reading the Creation passage from Genesis in preparation for the Holy Saturday Easter Vigil Service, that when God created the world during its respective days that at each step along, the creation was affirmed as "AND IT WAS GOOD." God created the heavens and it was good. God created the Earth, and it was good. God created the waters and it was good. God created the little birdies and the animals, and it was good. God created man and, and, he took a nap. Well, the question can be posed: Did he screw up when he made us? One can think so by the way we behave. But this is not the case. The "good" is more of a metaphysical term denoting "complete." The world was the best he could make it, complete in itself. Yet, for the human, we are not complete. That is the whole deal. Though catechism class taught us that we are here to know, love, and serve God—*in other words, KEEP OUT OF HELL*—we are here to be completed, to have our potential as individuals and as individuals in a community realized more and more, and to allow love to drive the hell out of us. We are here to have our potential affirmed and celebrated the more we become loving and affirming, celebrating others, especially the "non-celebrity."

To grow in the image and likeness of God, the fullness of Love, is to be completed in the image and likeness of the nature assigned to us. The love of God in Bob is going to be a different expression of the love of God in Maria. We are called to a life of fulfillment and enrichment as we proceed deliberately and openly to being the best apple we can be if we are called to actually be an apple. The challenge (temptation?) is that while we're actively striving to be the best apple we can be, we are often trying to be an orange, because somewhere along the journey that's what we're convinced would make us happier. Being more. And the want for more is usually confused with the want for more stuff that is so unimportant and unessential.

And as I have always held, the discovery of who we are as Church and churched, as evangelists and the evangelized, as the converted and the converting, is a delightful surprise. The places, people, time, and situations change the plans in your life. *If you ever want to crack up the Lord just tell him what you think your plans are!* Ten years ago at this writing when, again, I was serving in Santa Monica, the Los Angeles riots took place. Up to this point, I was only a year or so there and was immediately immersed in hundreds of white weddings of which I would say seven out of ten could have given a hoot in hell about marriage preparation! *Just give me the wedding of my dreams, please!* And I was immediately acquainted with infinite demands for funerals, house blessings, confessions, and meetings. *In the old days the saints wore hair shirts.* Now they go to meetings. Just as annoying and torturous—Sunday masses, daily masses, school masses, more masses in honor of new buildings, the pope's birthday *(he never showed),* and Monsignor's "Welcome Back from the Holy Land" (again!) Mass! *With the high number of times that he has been to Jerusalem, I'd swear he'd put more days in Jerusalem than Jesus ever did!* My priest friends would commonly refer to this type of parish that caters endlessly to the sacrament demands of the wealthy clientele as a "sacrament factory." And what type of padre usually would want to be in a sacrament factory in a wealthy area? A son of the Church? A champion for Jesus? Perhaps. And perhaps a guy who wants lots of stipends. That is, $$TIPS$$.

At that time, I wanted to be in Santa Monica because I enjoyed being close to the beach and was attracted to the social outreaches that it afforded. I wanted this situation enough to believe the pastor's pitch that he was in search of a minister who would collaborate with him and co-pastor the parish, together with the laity.

But, I enjoyed this parish immensely even though there were always masses! *I swear there would be days when after my fourth Mass I would want to say, "And Jesus took the bread, AGAIN!"* What saved me?

Some who insist that they're "in the know," but who I say "know everything about nothing and nothing about everything" would rumor that it was my Hollywood "connections," that put my ministry on the map. That is so off the mark! Sure, when I've been invited to be creative and contribute to media endeavors, I enjoy it. A recent joy was when I was invited by "Brother Tom" Shadyac to contribute some "theologizing" to the directing and writing of his movie *Bruce Almighty*. Outside of having the great power of prayer that I continue to discover, I have just been blessed with good friends and life-giving relationships and experiences. Still, the greatest relational experiences have been within my own universe away from the bright lights of Hollywood. From bowling, dining, and skiing with buddies to visiting jail cells and the sick and elderly in hospital hallways and bedrooms, I have discovered God's real love. In short, what had saved me from the burden of ritual was allowing me to discover the beauty of relationships.

Having real relationships are like receiving prized possessions and saviors from God. I feel relational, both socially and spiritually, while not claiming to have perfected an ease in maintaining them. Another major blessing, outside of being close to the beach in Santa Monica, was the power of relationships that I made at the gym, in prayer, and with some good folks who really knew how to enjoy a good party thrown by myself in the rectory *(which would begin to be planned immediately upon becoming aware that the monsignor was planning to be out of town)*.

And, of course, there are the Westside restaurants: Valentino's, the most delicious and expensive wines in the world; *i Cugini*, free booze for the padre; and Anna Maria's, more free food for the padre. Remember: Father is America's Favorite Guest! The "food" that saved me, though, was a renewed love that drew me into the priesthood in the first place: the incredible amount of social outreach to the poor in the parish and the resultant love that poured back from these poor.

For example, El Hogar in Tijuana. El Hogar is an orphanage (a home for homeless kids) that I adopted upon my arrival at St. Mo's. We would have these huge food drives, and massive shopping sprees at Smart & Final in preparing to deliver all sorts of stuff to the kids. Then we would pack them all in three or four rented vans and haul them to Rosarita Beach for a huge barbecue. God, I loved doing this ministry. I couldn't speak a lick of Spanish but always had either Ester Cabanban or Joe Galvan (kids would call this Apache Navajo man "Indio") around to help me out. I would always go away feeling great! Needed. Appreciated. I *always* left Tijuana, the jails, the juvenile detention camps, or the outings to help people out feeling swell. I did something for someone. Ah, those faces! And, of course, all of us upon arriving would feast on pizza and beer. "Anyone order a pizza?!"

It was Thanksgiving at St. Monica. Every Thanksgiving, assisted by the leadership of Michael Bandoni and, eventually, Rick McGeagh, I would organize and cook over thirty of the ninety turkeys myself for our Thanksgiving Day dinner for the homeless of the area. The high school kids would help me cook. Carlos, a high school senior, when helping me gut the birds, grabbed a turkey neck and inquired what it was. I told him that it was the turkey's "Johnson." *(Forgive me, Carlos—but the look on his face was priceless!)* They would help me serve, clean, then sit down and visit with our brother and sister poor.

I hated those demeaning, buffet-line feedings of the poor where the slop was dished out to our guests, and I, consequently, insisted that our event would be a "meal" and not a "feeding." Ours was a sit-down affair where our "guests" would be visited by one of our "hosts" (i.e., the high school kids); placemats would be drawn up by the kids in the elementary school on 8½ x 11 inch paper; there was valet parking for our guests' shopping carts (their homes on wheels); every oven in the plant would be fired up; people would bring in cooked turkey meals from their homes; and an army of carvers would be on hand slicing the turkeys with age-old, unsharpened knives. *Show me a church that has sharp knives and I'll show you a pastor that has dated.* Jean Guelpa would be hidden away opening and warming up the hundreds of donated cans of string beans.

It would be a gas watching many good people get involved and do what they're supposed to do as Christians—minister! While Jeanette would annually supply stocking caps, parkas, knit gloves, etc., for the winter that lay ahead, there would also be more volunteers than guests. What I really came to enjoy, though, was watching our guests go to the "boutique" after their meal. The homosexual community would take over a large class-room and open what is known today as the Boutique—a clothing boutique. This originally was taking rummaged clothing that we once literally just threw out on the floor for our guests to scavenge through until these guys came in and took over the place. This ministry became a place where donated used clothing and shoes were tastefully displayed, while the aroma of rose-scented incense, coffee-while-you-shop, and chamber music would fill the room. Our guests would be assisted by a "shopper" as any elite would enjoy at Barneys, Bergdorf Goodman, or Saks Fifth Avenue. These guys would treat our homeless "guests" with such dignity and respect—*they knowing all too well what it is like to be labeled*—as they would hurriedly pick and choose their wardrobe for the upcoming winter.

Afterward, we would all meet in the faculty lounge of the high school. Before you knew it, the beer would be flowing, we would all anxiously await that messenger from God—"Anyone order pizza?" The surprises of endless graced moments in serving the poor *(when*

I wasn't preparing the hundreds of Binkys and Buffys for marriage, I mean, their wedding) abounded there while I was at St. Monica's. While the area property owners wanted to rid the neighborhood of the homeless, I was just trying to make sure that they were warm. Not because I was a hero but because I felt the "urging" to take a different initiative. While I was trying to help the homeless feel dignified, one of the other priests was trying to scare these "bums" away. When a priest was on their DUTY DAY he would be assigned to care for the homeless who came to the door. When I was ON DUTY they knew it. Dagwood-type sandwiches would be plentiful—*that is if I had time between marriage (I mean, wedding) preparations.*

But, in all of this, I was still living in the comfort of a nice house in Santa Monica with all the creature comforts and perks that come with living in a progressive parish in a nice area. I sure wasn't complaining about the plusses of being in a beach community that also had the typical "poor" and "not so good areas" that any city has. Frankly, like most white English-speaking-only priests, I wanted to be a pastor but was fearing the day because according to Los Angeles Archdiocesan policy, a padre's first pastorship can only occur once he has served in the inner city; i.e., with the poor. This means Spanish—I was terrified of this. Me? Mr. White Boy living in the hood? I couldn't speak Spanish. I was afraid of leaving the good life. I felt loved by the people of the parish of St. Monica's. But, again, the Lord had plans for me. My end was beginning. My beginning was beginning.

Which takes us to the Los Angeles riots, the civil action on the wake of the Rodney King verdict: Finally, I get you to the riots. *I told you I was a roamer!* The pastor was in the Holy Land *again,* the senior associate pastor was in Palm Springs *again,* and there was a visiting theologian from New York who literally hid under the bed during the entire ordeal. From Santa Monica, you could see the smoke and the flames. It was so close. I felt so far away, though I was manning the ship as much as I was allowed to.

Shortly after, and upon the return of the other associate pastor after the flames had subsided, the idea arose to gather food and clothing from Santa Monica to bring to the people of South Central Los Angeles, a place named St. Peter Claver Center, off of Crenshaw and Jefferson. Needless to say, while the associate "acting pastor" announced it at all the masses, I did all the footwork in organizing this project, and I dug it. *This will be awesome and I will drive the big old truck all the way down there, all the way to South Central Los Angeles. All the way to Crenshaw and Jefferson!*

So much food, money, and good clothing came pouring in from the good folks of St. Monica. On the day we were loaded up and heading out, a priest friend of mine came by to offer assistance, once learning about our little project. He brought the stuff that every priest acquires during Christmas and Easter: martini olives, martini onions, pate, anchovies, assorted teas, cheeses, and sausages. I said to him, "Hey, Buddy! You can do better than that! I know you have lots of weddings. You got a hundred bucks on you?" He, feeling busted, surrendered one of the few hundred dollar bills that he had received the previous week. I placed the bill in my upper pocket and victoriously drove off into the sunset *all the way* to South Central Los Angeles.

I probably was more excited about driving the big old bobtail truck that I had rented. *I used to drive armored trucks and dug it the most!* (Mr. White Boy is driving *all* the way down to the hood!) I loaded up a big thermos of hot coffee as I prepared to lead the caravan of good people *all* the way. I couldn't believe it took us only fifteen minutes to get there! South La Brea was just off the Santa Monica Freeway and I was shocked, stunned, and humbled by my stupidity and apparent ignorance of my local surroundings and of my local poor brothers and sisters living so close to the extravagant Santa Monica beach area.

When we arrived, people from the area were responding to the pleas of the local preachers to return the stolen goods that were looted from the surrounding markets and retail stores. The stereos, VCRs, household furnishings and appliances, etc., were coming in. Coming up the walkway of the Center was a senora with a thousand kids hanging from her. She was responding to the pleas of her parish priest and returning goods that she had acquired from the looting—three bundles of Pampers.

My heart was just breaking. When she came up to me I wasn't wearing my priestly duds, mind you. She just thought I was some normal dude. She handed me the Pampers and said, *"Lo siento, senor. Senor, por favor, perdoname!"* ("I'm sorry, sir. Sir, please forgive me.") Her brown eyes were so sincere and shame-filled. I took her Pampers and then, WOW, remembered that I had a one hundred dollar bill in my pocket.

I gave it to her. The look—the shock on her face was spiritually orgasmic for me! A reward? A gift? She sure wasn't expecting a gift of a hundred dollar bill in exchange for returning twenty-five dollars in stolen Pampers! Her face; ah, her lovely, weather-beaten face. She was amazed at being awarded for her humility, for her honesty, for her wanting to regain her dignity. She was from a parish called St. Agatha's. *Ain't that a mindblower!* Small world. If she recognizes me it must really be a mindblower for her. I wouldn't remember her at all! In the spiritual business we don't call this a coincidence. We call this connection "providential"! I, now the pastor of the place where she was from, was on the board of directors of the St. Peter Claver Center where she and I had met, and I live in the same neighborhood! *Which I can't say is the case for the numerous other ministers who have big, traditional-looking churches and storefront churches here in the neighborhood.* Again, it's like an angel from God surprising us with a stranger announcing: "Anyone order pizza?"

So, to me, this has been "church"—allowing myself to be surprised; allowing people to be surprised; surprising people with a new face of God, church, and self; bringing their antiquated and shame-laced experiences of God and church to a level of freedom, joy, and even humor. So, while everyone seems to be preoccupied with the High Church, I prefer to be and to remain the lowest form of church possible. Besides, it's lonely at the top. It's wonderful down here. No wonder Jesus chose to stay away from the higher-ups of religion. No wedge could open those doors.

Call it shocking! Call it attention-getting! Call it me "acting out" past angers and suppressions. All I know is that in a church where it's the same old thing every day (*And Jesus took the bread, AGAIN*) it works! It makes people think. It expands their borders and horizons that they were taught to believe were never to be broadened. My first real dose of just trying to add a "right brain" dimension to a "left brain" ritual of the Eucharist came spontaneously and instantly upon ordination and receiving my first assignment. After years and years of watching the seminary priests "do Mass," looking absolutely miserable during the process, I was ready to jazz up the "celebration" of the Eucharist.

It didn't take long after I arrived at my first assignment as a priest. Though I was excited, raring to go, wanting to use my personal charisma the way I thought I was ordained to do, I knew I was in big trouble. I knew almost immediately that there was going to be an eternal fight to make this church and its sacraments relevant to the people AND to make my priesthood relevant to me! For example, being tortured with life-sucking sermons all my life, I had taken on the habit that before I ever preach I, first of all, actually prepare for my homily. In so doing, I always ask, "So what?" when prayerfully and quietly preparing each gospel passage that is ordered to be proclaimed with another scriptural passage from the Old Testament (the Hebrew Scriptures).

"Today Jesus is born" . . . *so what?* Today we celebrate the resurrection of Jesus on this Easter Sunday . . . *so what?!* Today we celebrate Christ's Ascension into heaven" . . . *so what?!*" In other words, what do these "events celebrating Jesus" have to do with me? It is imperative that I be creative and intuitive to my surrounding reality and where I stand in it. It has to be personal while not being exhibitionist. Therefore I have to know what is going on in the world. I have to know my audience and know what is going on in their worlds of sixty-plus-hour work weeks, mortgage payments, infidelities, overextendedness—what it is like being not appreciated, being this but doing that.

Especially central to my ways, within my own personal agenda when preaching or ministering, is the idea that life is hard enough as it is. When preaching, don't make it any harder for people. In other words, BE INTERESTING! So, if they want hellfire and brimstone; if they want to have the life sucked out of them and be bored as hell with the mass, the ritual, or whatever, THERE ARE PLENTY OF CHURCHES THAT SEEMINGLY SPECIALIZE IN GRANTING THE EFFECT! I don't get around much but when I go to church on vacation, disguised as a human being, it seems that these Spirit-sucking communities of fear and "no touching, please" are the majority.

I can especially remember my second Christmas as a priest in Woodland Hills, California, under the pastorship of the great monsignor Richard "Dick" Murray. *I used to love greeting him every morning with, "Good morning, DICK." His usual jovial response: "I don't like the way you're saying that!"* As I was beginning my priestly ministry at the age of thirty-three, he was about to retire from his at the age of seventy-five. I was young and sassy; he was older and sassy, and "one of the good old boys" in the old church. *I like to say during this time that "I brought him along slowly!" He certainly says that about me!*

Now, the first Christmas Mass the year before, my first Christmas season as a priest, was dead and boring with no flash! Then, I remember vowing that I was going to jazz it up! God bless Monsignor Murray, he allowed me to do this stuff though I know he thought I was totally off the wall! It was Midnight Mass. Instead of a dead little tree, I had obtained three twenty-foot Douglas firs, about six small Nobles, and more lights in that church than Chevy Chase had in *Christmas Vacation.*

Everything went off without a hitch. The music was different. There was dancing. There was laughter. It was so non-Catholic. All during the Mass, Monsignor Murray was taking it extremely well, though I knew he was uneasy (only because it was different) with all this nontraditional and nonritualized joy and Christmas cheer.

He was and is a great man! He was just not exactly comfortable with the feelings, joys, and "right-brained stuff" with which I was growing comfortable. Jesus, I'd hug anyone! But, I also knew that I would never be anyone in this church if I wasn't introverted, formal, and "official." Finally, the blood rushed out of my head and I thought I was going to faint. "I forgot to tell Monsignor about Santa Claus!" The idea was that Santa Claus, who was being played by the late and wonderful Wally, would come down the aisle after Communion and kneel in front of the baby Jesus and say some prayers. Cute, huh? Well, at the conclusion of Mass all I could think was, I am not only going to experience a fate worse than death, but by the time he is through with me, I would have preferred to have died and gone straight to hell!

Good Golly, Miss Molly, I prayed. I promised Wally who was sitting in the confessional the whole time during Mass that I would check it out with him. Wally was also a dear friend of the "Monz" and I promised him I would get it all okayed beforehand. I forgot. We were all going to die. As the Monz began to conclude the Mass with a "Let us pray," I held him back. "What are we waiting for?" he growled.

"Santa Claus!"

You should have seen the look on his face. Down the aisle of the church comes Santa Claus (staggering just a little) with his HO HO HO's. The expression of the good monsignor was one of "What the hell is next?" Santa, upon approaching the manger scene, knelt down and made the sign of the cross in such an exaggerated way that I'm sure if a plane were flying overhead it would have mistaken Santa's gesture as a signal to land. The Monz was speechless. Then, God saved me. A little girl came down the aisle. *Swiss Guard! Arrest that girl! She left the pew! Executioner!* She hesitated as she approached the kneeling Santa Claus. Then, so slight and reverently, she surrenders and kneels right next him. Oh my God! Is that a tear in the monsignor's eye? To this day, he denies it.

You're a hell of a good man, Monz. In today's priesthood you got to love any priest that loves saying the 6:30 a.m. Mass every morning—such happy faces that hour in the morning. I have just never understood how people can worship and celebrate and look like they're in pain. Why do we have to act so uptight!? Ironically, it seems that Europeans think that Americans are the most uptight, stupid, ugly, and arrogant people in the world. They're right! We are, when we travel to Europe. But they sure like our money. On the other hand, the European Church is so lifeless and boring and traditional. Nothing changes. Do they think that the Lord really gets off on all that stuff, the bells and the smells?

Now, if a banker cannot count, he's got a problem. If a cook can't cook, he's got a problem. If a teacher can't teach, *he writes a book on teaching!* He's got a problem. If the Church cannot connect to people in the manner of Christ, it's not only got a problem, it's a car without an engine. In today's time, I hope the managers of the store (Church leadership including myself) are hearing that their customers want to feel connected, served, and not denied the goods. But, if the managers aren't with their customers and only hang out with other managers, how are they to know? If the customers don't complain and communicate to the managers, how are they to know?

Corporate Rome has been relevant in the realm of being a world ambassador: bringing down communism, and anti-Semitism; being ambassadors of social justice when it comes to the poor, education, and providing advocacy for the undignified. BUT, as for being a relevant "connection" for the people of God to God, it isn't, it shouldn't, and it couldn't. But, as an instrument ordaining priests with the sign saying, "Men Only, Please," and "Heterosexuals Only, Please," it has lost its relevance and awareness of what people need in order to be ministered to, and to be empowered as ministers. Imagine, having to go to classes to be a "greeter" (i.e., usher) in the church! Geez, Louise—if you're not nice or pleasant YOU NEED NOT APPLY!

I have been told that I don't act very priestly because I am more "front and center" and "live on the edge" than most. What is that supposed to mean? That because I have passions and feeling and doubts and fear and questions, that because I'm human and free, I am not adequate to be a good and holy priest? Well, yeah! I can remember taking the Myers-Briggs personality inventory. I answered the questions with the motivation of "this is how I WANT to be seen" rather than "this is who I am." As a result, I came out on paper as a raging introvert! Actually, I am a raging extrovert who is more introverted than most extroverts. I felt at this very outset of my priestly formation that I was to be quiet, academic, reserved, proper, and correct. That I had to be a left-brained introvert who was supposed to hide his feelings, passions and needs.

I'm a sinner! I'm not perfect. I also have needs. I am NOT the one with a closer connection to God than the laity. Sometimes, my only escape is my nap (which I really try to take every afternoon as "religiously" as I can. "Dear God," I pray before each slip into unconsciousness, "Lord, send me a good dream!" For me, dreams are free vacations. And I also realize that naps are gifts. I don't know how you mothers with infants do it! You are the unsung heroes. No one dreams like a celibate—I mean, no one! Medicated or nonmedicated, a good hardworking padre sleeps like a baby and dreams like no other man. Though, I have to admit, my dreams are very therapeutic, they are also very reveal-ing. My recurring nightmare is one that I receive all the time, espe-cially when I've had a day of feeling inadequate as if I am, again, stepping on the hem of the skirt of holy Mother Church. *The big breasted (domed) mother that she is!*

The nightmare usually takes place in a classroom where, after studying and fighting for a million years to get ordained a priest, I have finally finished my last class and final examination neces-sary for ordination. All that is left is the final interview and vote by the faculty.

I am rejected.

This "nightmare" was a release from past failures to be approved for vows, acceptance and affirmation, as well as tapping into the want of being accepted by my peers, by the ranks of church—in short, to be affirmed by Mother Church as a good boy. To be told otherwise was, and is, huge. I think I am a good guy. I know that I am little different. I give until it hurts, I think. Why so much rejection, especially when all I ever wanted to do was be "one of the guys?" One of the most painful decisions I had ever had to make was leaving the Capuchin order. They were family to me. I mean, really, there was nothing more that I wanted in life than to be one of the guys!

The Capuchins truly saved my life. In high school the "Caps" were truly the ones who exemplified to me that I was good, that I'll be okay, and that I am worthwhile. It is truly while being a product of the ministry of the Capuchin Franciscans that I am alive and here. Whether my desire to be included by them was healthy or not is a matter for me and "the couch." Whether I was emotionally healthy or not (and I probably was not) pains me when I think of my immaturity—I was only seventeen when I entered. All I knew at that time was that the Capuchin experience made me feel wanted, invited, included, and had been the necessary male support in my life. I felt I was a success, a leader, a contributor, a man. Ironically, when I entered the Order's formation program, I became a battery being discharged of all its previous power. Though I entered with energy and the belief that I had something to offer the Order, Church, and God, it did not take long before they discharged all the life from me. For the first five years of being a Cap in the seminary, I was taught to believe that I was nothing. This was more indicative of the Irish approach to religious life of thirty years ago than a "Capuchin" thing. No matter what I did, I was never enough. For an adult child of an alcoholic, this was my death, my cross, and, yes, the cause of the resurrection I now enjoy and share. These first five years were my cross that I was about to be resurrected from after another cross was endured.

This C high school student who earned a 3.9 GPA in college while getting a BA in philosophy was banished by the superiors of the Capuchin priestly formation program (along with Brother Gregory) in September 1977. Without any discussion, and under Holy Obedience, I was informed that I had to leave the seminary in Berkeley. Though this was another blow to me, it ended up being the biggest blessing of my life. I was exiled home to St. Francis High School in La Canada, California. Brother Greg got sent to Fresno, California. I obviously got the better end of the deal! I was about to be resurrected. The provincial Father Enda, who had been instrumental in my childhood development and who also saw the good in me (when visiting padres from Ireland, for example, would visit San Francisco, Enda would give me the credit card with the decree "show them a good time!") had to listen to the superiors entrusted to run the program.

I could see in his eye that he was powerless, but he was also a man who didn't believe in the NO-WIN scenario. There was always resurrection to every cross. He knew that I wanted to minister at St. Francis, so I was exiled there. Oh my God! This apostolate was the greatest lifegiver and lifesaver ever afforded me. ALLELUIA! RESURRECTION! I was returning home as "one of the guys," just as I had always wanted. The first year was great. I worked hard. I was living with some great guys, friars, some of whom had been my childhood heroes. I dressed like them—I wore the habit, that is. I ate with them. I drank with them. I partied with them. I worked side by side with them. I prayed with them. I would do anything to be included. I was home.

The first year was so great that I asked Father Enda if I could stay another year and not return to the seminary.

He said sure. The guy always cared for me though he would never say it.

The second year was also great. I was free! I was a man! I was working! I was successful. I was home. NO WAY WAS I GOING TO GO BACK TO THE SEMINARY! When I told Enda this and asked if I could instead discontinue priestly formation and remain "just a brother" (in other words, not return to the certain death of the seminary where I was nothing but assured that I was a pantywaist), I was told that this was not going to swing. If I wanted to stay in the Order, I had to continue priestly formation in Berkeley. This was what the seminary superiors insisted—truly a control issue on their part, invoking the vow of Holy Obedience. As a result, during the happiest time in my life when I was most glad of being a Capuchin, where I felt spiritually alive and was one of the guys—I had to leave.

Though I had shown that I would pay any price to be one of the guys, I finally got enough dignity returned to me to say that there was no bloody way that I was returning to the cross—seminary—when I didn't have to. Of course, I was told by the superior in Berkeley that I should be ashamed of myself and that I should be more grateful. *Thanks, Father. Keep the change.* I left in June 1979. I had been moonlighting every night after teaching a full day for the last six months because I had no bucks. I had no family to go home to, no car, and no place to live after I left. I would leave the friary at 2:00 p.m. wearing my full habit. I would drive to the local gas station and change into my suit, anticipating being a personnel director for the retail shops at Los Angeles International Airport. I was ashamed to be discovered. Brother Ken was leaving the Order.

Funny, I didn't miss it as much as I thought I would. Though I missed the guys, I realized that I missed the ministry more. Eventually, I would be invited back to St. Francis High, this time as "Mr. Deasy" and not "Brother Ken"—after a year of doing everything from supervising gift shops at Los Angeles International Airport (making sure that the customers had enough gum, smokes, and dirty magazines to keep them occupied while in flight) to being an armored-truck driver and vault clerk (from being an instrument of peace to carrying a piece). Wouldn't you know it, though, that the padre that also encouraged me to take on the role of being the first non-Capuchin director of development would eventually also plot to have me removed because of his own jealousies. Some things never change. My personality still gets me in trouble because it is so non-Roman: it's human, joyous, explosive, and touchable.

To this very day, though, I am very close in sentiment and appreciation to the Order and to the Franciscan spirituality. They have been and continue to be a huge part of my life (having played a huge role in my resurrection, after being a huge cross of pain that I deal with therapeutically). These guys have helped me out here in the hood. They were present at my ordination. They hosted the reception after my ordination to diocesan priesthood (which, by the way, was a total blast). Father Matt Elshoff (who was one year behind me in the seminary) has enhanced a great ministry there at the high school. I am proud to have been a product of their goodness. It is still tough for me to return there, though. Is it so bad to want to be included? This is all I have ever wanted. I am embarrassed how, at times, I have gone to extremes to get this immature but needed affirmation. I not only left the

Order. I left the Church. While discounting all the good things that had been done for me through my relationship with the Church, I had chosen (like many do today) to leave it all because of a few bad apples. I was sick of priests and their authority. I could only see the dirt on the windows; the glass was always half empty, and I had to blame someone! So I blamed the religion that preached invitation but from which I experienced "all are welcome but the likes of you."

While I was a fund-raiser at St. Francis I had to compete for the almighty dollar with the guy across the street, Monsignor Boyer, the pastor of my home parish, St. Bede's. Though the parish was directly across the street from the high school, many of its families were sending its kids to a Jesuit high school in the inner city of Los Angeles. I felt this was treason because, again, the Church was following the dollar and not the poor little guy across the street. This cross was about to be my resurrection and my eventual return to the Church and the faith.

I had just experienced a three-martini lunch and it was Good Friday, the day in which we remember the three hours of Jesus on the cross. Historically, for me, this was a period (as taught by my mom, God rest her) that you did not watch TV, you did not play, and you just did nothing (unless you wanted to go to church).

So, having an experience of a three-martini buzz, I decided to go to church (I had not gone in three years) a pay a quick visit. This was the church where I buried my mother in 1974 and received the sacrament of Confirmation, from which I graduated elementary school, and in which I was an altar server. As I floated into the front pew I felt totally at peace. I thought it was just the buzz. After about a twenty-minute visit I had to reluctantly go back to work. As I turned around to go I had noticed that behind me was a totally packed church of childhood familiar faces anticipating the beginning of the solemn Good Friday service. I was stuck! The ancient saying, *Never leave a service early or you'll turn into a pillar of salt* arose within my twenty-eight-year-old person. Needless to say, I stuck out like a sore thumb because of my fancy suit and youth, and got many looks that said, "Kenny Deasy is back." I sat there alone and silent in the front pew for the entire service being celebrated by guess who? My competitor, Monsignor Boyer.

I was totally at peace just sitting there while being oblivious to the ritual. The martini bliss had long gone and I continued to sit there for two hours following the conclusion of the service. I had missed God, my mom, and my Church. Finally, from behind, a hand was gently placed on my shoulder. It was Monsignor Boyer. "Hey Ken," he said. "How are you, my friend?" I felt his words as sincere and kind. All the angers, hatreds, and crosses seemed like they had never existed. "Would you like to come in for dinner and a drink?" On Good Friday? What about the fast, the abstinence, and all that stuff?!

I joined the Monz for dinner and a shot. I rejoined the parish. I reentered the faith. After a few months came the affirmation of "You know, Ken, would you ever think of being a parish priest?"

Yes.

I felt invited, wanted, and included. All it has ever taken is, again, go where you feel connected. I entered the seminary in 1983. I was ordained a parish priest when I was thirty-three years old, in 1987. I celebrated my first Mass at St. Bede's with Monsignor Boyer at my side. He was like me: different, a family man. Though he was as traditional as they come when it came to viewing Church, Church authority, etc., his personality was totally unorthodox. He loved to set a table and preside at a meal. He loved to celebrate. He loved to invite. He loved to give presents. It was these traits, alone, that made him a fine priest who was especially affective while presiding over the Mass.

He had all the gifts and all the education. He had all the success within his career as a priest. But what made him so awesome as a shepherd of souls was that he was a fine man. His candor and accessibility would eventually get him into some trouble. He was accused and gossiped about. Soon after he retired, he lost his sight, was totally reliant on people to help him, and had the burden of having to wear a colostomy bag. Worse than his illness and dependence on others were accusations of fondling a young person years back. He was removed from the parish during his retirement and refused convalescent housing due to his love for his dog, Trudy. He died accused and confused.

His funeral was packed with over one hundred priests there to honor him. I was one of them, but regret to this day that I was wasn't around more during his dying days. Father Lawrence Signey and I went to visit him in the hospital in Orange County. As he lay there hooked up to life support with eyes wide open I said to him, "Leland, I pray that I could be as happy a priest as you are. I pray that I could be as faithful as you are and love the priesthood as much. I pray that I could be as obedient and forgiving as you, and am so sorry that I have not been there for you during your most wanting times. Please forgive me and trust that even though I had taken you for granted, I love you."

One of my profoundest dreams (and alas, nightmares) which I hope to God never, ever comes true is that I am made pope. But believe me when I say that there are many guys who really dream this one over and over whether they are asleep or not—and they hope to God it does happen! For those who love "the power" and love to doll up in the flowing Roman attire this would be a clerical wet dream or, as we were taught to call it in moral theology classes, *"a nocturnal emission"*!

The square of St. Peter's Basilica is packed with millions of people, while they and billions of people elsewhere are awaiting the announcement of the new pontiff to succeed John Paul II who finally went home to God at the age of 134. *No comment.* After a long and arduous process of trying to elect a pope, the white smoke from the chimney signifying that "we have a pope" is made apparent to the world. The scene is set. The eyes of the world are focused on the top balcony of St. Peter's Basilica overlooking the throngs. The cardinals position themselves in their cardinal garb (in the dream they look like bowling shirts) flanking the left and the right of the center balcony draped with the seal of the Church, two keys noting the temporal and spiritual wealth of this instrument ordained to protect the poor and the less worldly and otherworldly. *Go figure.*

The bells are silenced. Everyone is just standing there waiting and wondering not only who the new pope is going to be but also "WHERE THE HELL IS HE?!" Finally, the bells start ringing and ring and ring, louder and louder. Though everyone's eyes are fixed to the center of the upper balcony, all of a sudden the huge center door at the bottom center of the basilica, on level with the people, opens its massive self. There stands a little guy, in contrast, dressed in white, with sandals, walking slowly and humbly to the step that is level with the people. The place is going wild.

I announce my name. Pope Jordan ("Jordan" being the scene of God's wanting us to feel beloved and the Jordan being the place where there is so much religious violence and religious hatred that it stands as a present day mockery of the will of God. I look up at the cardinals looking down at me. On the same level with the people, I look up at the guys who are to be serving with me—together. They want to come down. They don't know if they should come down. They don't look like they are happy up there. They are scared to come down. They're too tired to come down. They're too exhausted and spiritually dry to come down.

"Hey guys. Please come down and join me and the family, will ya?" Some see this as an invitation of freedom. Some see this as a challenge and a threat. At the same time, the moving trucks owned and operated by the "Starving Jewish Students Moving Service" hired to move the Vatican to Carmel, California, arrive.

Then, BLAM, I'm shot and killed by some white right-winger. The thirty-second pope!

Now, there's a dream!

So I'm a fun-loving guy with an edge. *Actually, if I was made pope I would have the mother of all yard sales! Imagine the art auction! No deals!* This edge makes me appear irreverent and willing to take on authority. *My only intent is to highlight the greatest dimension of Christ's Church which is empowerment of the people, and disciples.* I have never believed that "uniformity" and "unity" are synonymous. This is one of the most inherent tenets of liturgical worship—we all must do the same thing, say the same thing, and quote the same thing at the exact same time.

No way.

Harmonious diversity is the greatest plan of God though it is typically the greatest threat to Church authority. Harmonious union, as opposed to uniformed union, is the greatest challenge to a Church that insists on their own respective pledge of allegiance to the status quo. As a result, the greatest gift of a loving and ultimate God, self, and world, is missed.

Atheism and agnosticism are so easily understandable these days. I am convinced today that when I meet someone who initially claims to be an atheist that they are spiritual people who are simply claiming that they don't believe in the God who is presented to them by institutional religion. Sometimes I don't either, only because I don't buy that institutional model—as ultimate, exclusive, better, and perfect—and believe that the best ways to teach about God are not demonstrated in religion class. When I was asked to teach an elective of my choice at the local elementary school where our Capuchin house of formation was, the authorities expected me to teach a religion class of rambling creeds and memorizing dates of Holy Days of Obligation. Instead, I wanted to convey an experience of joy that comes from someone "of the religion." I taught a cooking class called "Baking with Brother." I taught them everything from making pizza, cakes, and meat loaf to the subject of the final exam: cream puffs. Hey, so I love cream puffs—something so delicate, fragile, and sweet while being so easy to make. *Just like faith!* I just think it must be a hoot to have kids who are now adults saying, "I remember this teacher we had who was a brother. He taught us to cook!"

For me, the seminary was like living in an institutional surrounding such as *Hogan's Heroes*. I had a party system in check that was tremendous. When in the seminary, it wasn't a rare occasion for one of the dear brothers to come to me sick as a dog with a cold, and I would heat them up a hot toddy of scotch and lemon juice since I was the only one who had a full bar, wine cellar, microwave, and refrigerator in my thirty-nine-by-nine-foot room. I also had a cable-TV line that I spliced from the cable that went to the bishop's television. There wasn't a place in the seminary that I did not throw a party. There was St. Mary's Dorm (a two-story structure where we'd meet every night downstairs in the room called "Mary's Bottom" where we would have a shot or two. We threw parties in the bishop's house, the bell tower, the basement of St. Joseph's Dorm, the convent (with the nuns present, by the way), and even the Grotto Garden which held the image of Our Lady of Lourdes. I was in my thirties for God's sake! Why can't men give themselves to the Lord and have a good time too?!

When they put me in charge of entertainment we had the best parties in the seminary and I was proud of it. Friday night would be Television Night with *Dallas* and *Falcon Crest.* Then, afterward, it was off to the Denny's in Camarillo (the only local spot where you could get a drink in those days) to order chicken strips and sissy la-las (Long Island Ice Teas). When we had our monthly "community nights" I upgraded the tradition of "ice cream sundaes" to Bass Ale and little chicken wings (we called them "chicken dicks"). I seemed to unintentionally shake and move institutional Church borders and I seem to have gotten away with it. No one complained—well not to my face. But, life was to be enjoyed and I still believe it is meant to be. *If you are really living life, you don't have to look for the cross during Lent! It'll find you quite easily on its own.*

But, it's all about bringing people to the table in order to connect. Amongst all the lofty requirements for priesthood, if you can't cook; if you don't know the price of toothpaste; if you're afraid to love for fear of losing control; if you're afraid to be loved because it might make you want more; if you can't laugh, cry, and, especially, wash your own damn dishes, I seriously don't know what right you have to be a parish priest.

Anyone order pizza?

So why did I become a priest, and even more important—why did I stay a priest?

Because I wanted that "pizza." I enjoyed the pizza I had experienced before, and wanted the pizza that many of the people I looked up to seemed to be enjoying. I wanted to explore the many other pizzas that must surely exist! And there is something within me that drives me to want to share my pizza. In the process, I have learned that there are many types of pizza—we all enjoy our particular favorites. And, many of us don't like to share—we don't like to try new things. *I remember shuttering at the thought of even trying pineapple on pizza! Today, it remains my favorite topping (accompanied by ham).*

So along the way, I have learned that we really do need to invite others to share in the joy of our abundance—to share our "pizzas." We must be patient with those people who see their pizza as "the same old thing," and feel stuck with it.

In America, the priesthood is in obvious disorder and trouble. A state of crisis might be obvious, but what's the answer? Renewal? Readjustment? Attack? These "issues" have been the topic of discussion, officially and quietly, for hundreds of years. It doesn't take a divine apparition to suggest that the issue of diocesan priestly purpose and lifestyle must be analyzed and confronted, and the purpose of the priesthood, vis-à-vis the public, must enter a period of reevaluation. Among many things, the Church especially needs to change its focus from asserting authority to repairing its credibility.

How to recapture its essential spiritual charisma and mission with attention being paid to its health, affectiveness, and effectiveness is going to cause some necessary and painful rethinking. Particularly, with the shortage of priests today and the understandable reluctance of good people to respond to God's calling to participate in Christ's ministry as an ordained priest, the Church as we know it needs to enter a process of reexamination, which, for the "safeguarders" of the religion, is called a crisis.

Of course, the priesthood is now being seen through the prism of the recent sex abuse scandal which actually only involves a small percentage of priests. And with the leadership of the Church appearing to respond to this issue as a "corporate matter" rather than with accessible, imperfect, sensitive, and compassionate support for our brother and sister victims, I sure wouldn't want to be a bishop/archbishop, let alone a vocation director for the priesthood! I say "appearing" because I also know that bishops have gone out of their way to meet personally with the victims, as well as the accused, but no one prints it, airs it, or reveals it. Why? Though a corporate scandal, it still is a very personal, private, and pastoral matter not to be used for grandstanding. *And since when does anyone want to hear good news anyway?*

Though many higher-ups will cry that the shortage of priests is a crisis, I'm not sure it is. There are many pastors who hate the thought of losing control and still want to get things done their way (which often means not getting done at all). It is time for the "baptismal priesthoods of the laity" to be affirmed, empowered, prioritized, and activated—just like Jesus did. Though many will cry out that the shortage of priests is assuredly a sign of the "devil in our midst" or people choosing "a life of sin" rather than grace, people are well aware that there are healthier and more personal ways to commit oneself to ministry than to be a priest. Though "clerics" are entrusted to the care of the Church, there is plenty of expertise, talent, ability, and health that can be offered in a leadership capacity from those who are not in the clerical state. While the problem is getting good guys to apply to the seminary in the first place, another problem is that many of the new diocesan priests who persevered through the seminary are leaving within a few years after their ordinations. There have been hundreds of papers, books, studies, and lectures dedicated to this topic. Everything from sin to America capitalism and individualism has been pointed out as the culprit. Anyone with common sense saying that celibacy is not a hindrance to good men joining the priesthood needs serious help. *Well, if it worked in the sixteenth century it should work today, right?*

But of course we all know that it's just *celibacy* to blame, right? Wrong.

But, when it is all said and done, while theologians and psychologists write and write about intimacy in celibacy, if the people who actually feel called to priesthood are not responding, it's because of the one thing that is missing in how we priests appear to live our lives:

Joy.

Where's the joy? Where is life lived with a sense of zest and observable feeling?

Now, who's joyful today anyway? There are probably more ex-lawyers than there are ex-priests. Especially in our good old U.S. of A., where one's lovability is seemingly synonymous to one's perfection, it is hard to find joy. Everyone is trying so hard to be "correct," whatever that means at any particular moment, that there is truly a hesitation in living a joyful existence. Will the "real me" please step forward? We're ambitious, we're scared, we're threatened, we demand warranties, we demand insurance, we demand assurance, we want backups—we're so scared of losing what we have rather than pursuing the real truths of life. It is also painful to be "giving until it hurts" to a family/spouse/community that constantly confronts you with a "Well, but what have you done for me, lately?" attitude.

"Yeah, it's nice to pursue *your* real truth, Father, but I have a wife, three kids, and a social status to maintain." This is the same in priesthood. Unless you're a good preacher, any disclosure of who a padre really is not only remains a mystery, it's really something people don't want to know but love to fantasize about. How about that TV series *The Thorn Birds*? Expressions such as "We love you, Father" indicate the same affection you have for your water heater WHEN IT IS WORKING! If you're being fed, if we are working, we are wonderful in your eyes. If we're imperfect, vulnerable, tired, and "can't be all things to all people," we're a disappointment. It isn't just that we don't appear to be happy campers, but we are only individual men who don't always feel that we have permission from you to be human. Of course, because every parish priest has different levels and degrees of "needs" we will all respond differently to your issues and questions.

But, let us be human, will you? More and more, as priests become aware that they experience the same boundaries and levels of aspiration/achievement that any man does, they also realize that if we're not able to meet the needs of the people, it's not because we're jerks. It could be just because we're tired, unable, or just lonely. Or it could be because we're having a toothache. We're just as human as the Jesus whose humanity you seem to want to ignore. *The apologetic defense, "I'm ONLY human" is such a cop-out. Jesus' miracles and impact are evidence of the power of his humanness—of our humanness—and not just a sign of his divinity/of our divine self.*

Please folks, don't take us so damn seriously! If we're not as "on" as you want us to be, don't take it personally. The "clerical priest days" are over in which "Father is always right and he has chosen the highest calling!" *Sadly, that isn't always true. There are still a lot of diehards out there who apparently want "the good old days" of wearing cassocks, Latin Masses, Go-to-Hell Theology, etc.* As we're accused oftentimes of the need to "get over ourselves," so do you need to see that we're as loving and caring and accessible as you allow us to be. If you're with a padre that you truly just can't deal with, get over it and finally open up to understand that the Church is not about the priest! And, if you truly can't look beyond the imperfections and inadequacies of a pastor and don't ever sit down and discuss it with him (especially because of unwillingness on your part or his part) then go where you are fed. We are spiritual, loving, feeling people who are striving also, I assume, for a relationship with God in our lives. And, yes, there are those who are just trying to survive—to maintain their ministries, feed their flock, and be at peace with it all.

Some of us are just plain tired. Just like you.

Truly, the demands and expectations you place on us can be incredible yet we can't get you to show up any other day than Sunday! Sadly, we priests—like many corporate figureheads, doctors, lawyers, auditors, DMV workers, cops, and waitresses at the diner—seem to actually be working hard not to appear as human. There's an expectation that we must be some "otherworldly" religious eunuchs—intellectual nonrelationals—who are passionless answer men to the mysteries of the physical, spiritual, social, and relational human condition. Again—like you. Though the film industry often portrays us as wimpy sterile cuckoos—like a clan of robotic "Stepford Husbands" of the "Vatican Wife" who wants more babies but doesn't want to stay home and take care of them—we aren't portrayed like we're engaged in the normal realities of life. We are not portrayed as humans but as men who are "kept"—not having to deal with the day-to-day realities of our flocks. We appear arrogant and uninformed of the normal goings-on of the normal Joe (or Josephine). Believe me, we priests are as diverse as any other social grouping, and are no easier to pin down:

We are able and we are incapable; we are human and we are robots; we have a clue and we don't have a clue; we are retired and we are active, old and young, gay and straight, or maybe both. We are introvert and extroverts, conservatives and liberals, traditionalists and progressives. We are people who preach that "hell is around the corner" and that "the kingdom is at hand!" We are virgins and nonvirgins (my God, some of us have kids, either hidden under the covers or have been widowed and had children). Some of us have had good childhoods, and some, childhoods from hell; some of us are loved, and some have had the emotional crap knocked out of us.

Hey—just like you. Okay?

It's not like I expect every priest to tiptoe through the tulips with a passionate love for everything that moves, but when can people get a chance to see us laugh, cry, and reveal our humanness? It's not that we have to be major touchy-feely extroverts (which I am), but we oftentimes appear as brainiacs who deny feelings of passion and view dealing with basic human emotions and needs as weaknesses in our priestly role. But, hear me on this one, if you're an accessible, vulnerable, and delightfully human padre, you can get swallowed up alive. You have to be careful and not become the ATM of salvation that people want you to become—the 7-Eleven of salvation.

NOTE WELL: I ain't going to climb on that cross here. Okay?

We padres have difficulty describing our joys in priesthood. Maybe it's because we're men, but we hesitate in expressing our passions, wants, and joys in God, service, and ministry. Regrettably, for me, official priests' meetings are an incredible draining experience. Don't even show feelings. Be totally in your head. These affairs are so sterile, the guys so guarded. Everyone acts totally different in meetings and don't even express what they REALLY WANT TO SAY until Happy Hour!

I don't know if it's just because I'm Irish, but it hasn't been until recently that I have come to positive grips with my passionate ways of expression through words and actions. I have finally become free from the many years I had been ashamed of being sensitive and emotional, much to the chagrin of my religious superiors. I remember saying to a fellow priest, "I know you all think I'm crazy!" His response, "But, Deas, you're a lovable crazy." He, in a lovingly honest way, also said to me when I tearfully confessed that I'm not sure that I can live this lifestyle much longer because of a lack of passionate connection, sex, and mutuality: "Deas, if you don't have what it takes, you should leave." Sadly, this guy has also gone through some painful soul-searching due to feeling drop-kicked by the boys upstairs. He is no longer saying, "If you don't have what it takes, leave." He, like me, has to truly and prayerfully examine and believe in why we do this thing called priesthood.

Yet, while the ranks of diocesan priests are on the decline, the parishes wherein there is collaborative empowerment with the church membership are thriving. Though the magisterial body of Christ suffers from deafness and the inability to have a discussion, the rise of membership in Catholic parishes throughout America and the revitalization of the laity on the local parish level are occurring. The parish leadership may boast of the brilliance and charm of their pastor, but they will surely also admit to being empowered as evidenced in their being and acting as co-pastors to the community which, as a result, attracts the new membership. Here, the priests are simply doing what Jesus had commissioned us to do in the first place by sending out the disciples out two by two to minister to each other, to be Christ to each other, and to experience ultimate joy in the process. The joy, life, and vitality of the parish community are what draw others to participate in the spiritual and ministerial and communal wonder of the particular parish.

Now, with the empowerment of the laity there comes a challenge to "priestly living" as we have known it: You don't have to be a priest to serve the Lord and his people. You don't have to be celibate to serve the Lord and his people. You don't have to live in a rectory, be tied to the apron strings of the local pastor/bishop, or be miserable to serve the Lord and his people. I thoroughly believe that though priests say they enjoy their priesthood, we corporately do not (1) appear to enjoy it, and (2) we certainly don't enthusiastically express why we find this life so delicious. Yet, I have given hundreds of vocation talks; I think I appear pretty joyous, fairly human, and am a fun-loving, vivacious guy.

Just because I'm a priest doesn't mean I'm dead—I'm not suffering; I feel vitalized, fired up! I am a screaming extrovert who also needs some strong introvert time. So I must also confess that when I am miserable I show it just as plainly. And when I am not smiling because I am lost in my introverted self, I look angry. I sure don't wear a poker face. Thank God I don't have a tail to further give evidence of what I am really feeling. And to the best of my knowledge, no one is flocking to priesthood because of me! There are hundreds of priests who I admire so much. "My God!" I often say to myself, "I wish I could be like him! There are so many good guys that are priests. No one laughs harder than when there are four or five priests out to dinner. They can be so cool. When they are doing their "priestly thing," though, they can appear to be totally different people.

The guys I admire as priests—and I really wish I knew more priests and had better relationships with the guys—are incredible male role models as well as being true imitators of Christ. They are so full of love and joy. They are so humble. They love their Jesus and their people so much and are so peaceful, not complacent. I have seen guys who have literally dived into the bowels of the hells of others and who generously carry the crosses of others silently, painfully, and heroically. There are so many priests and bishops who are examples to all of us of heroism, valor, and sacrifice. Their concern, especially for the poor, the imprisoned, the illegal, the religiously ostracized, women who have had abortions, and for those who have "fallen away," is huge. Their presence, availability, and accessibility to others are driven by a spiritual life like none other.

I feel especially bad for bishops who have gotten a bad rap simply by association to the corporate entity. The ones I have known on the West Coast have been terrific: the charismatic and total man's man Syl Ryan; the pastoral Gerry Wilkerson; the caring and sensitive-to-the-poor Gabino Zavala, the pastoral and human Joe Sortoris; the educated, fraternal, and tall Ed Clarke; and the spiritual while humorous George Neiderauer have all been good to me. They have been my true models of priesthood and one can see the Holy Spirit's work in their having been made bishops.

Yet, some of them look like battered oil drums. The job has aged them harshly. Even the "under the gun" Roger Mahony, cardinal of Los Angeles, has been a good pastoral mentor to me, as well as an advocate of empowering the laity and focusing our attention to the rites of women, the poor, outcasts, and others. But you see, I have a respect for them not because of their office but for their persons. I don't cling to them because of rank. There is nothing that they have that I want. Sadly, when you are a Catholic bishop you lose your humanness and freedom, you become the office. I'm afraid their episcopal office (which has become a total CEO-type of function, in appearance) has diverted these good pastoral men away from their people, their priesthoods, and their own joy. These poor guys have no community to hold them and talk to them as a parish priest does if the priest allows it in the first place. They seem to be removed from the pastoral dimension of their priesthood and have become swamped in the programmatic administrative world.

Heck, I don't know if they are happy or not. If they aren't, they're not going to tell me. But there definitely seems to be with a bishop, in contrast to a pastor or a parish, less freedom to "think or talk outside of Rome." In this office, more than any other in the Church, a hint of open disagreement or discussion of something that doesn't go down well with "the big guy" is seen as disloyal. Presently, the majority of bishops are appointed by the present pontiff. If you disagree with Rome, it's *"Hey, I have a lovely cathedral for you—in the South Pole!"* Once, when in Istanbul, Turkey, I, along with thirty other priests on a monthlong sabbatical, met the local bishop. He was an Italian man in a diocese where there were just as many Catholics in his largely Islamic domain as there were in my parish. Because he was a total fish out of water, you could hear the other priests whisper, "I wonder what he did wrong?" There are some topics that simply are not allowed to be discussed at all. Women priesthood is one of them. Optional celibacy is another. Of course, topics like these are simply suburban topics for those who have a lot of time on their hands. When you live in the hood, child, there are other matters that are more important! Unfortunately, people don't want to know their bishops as "persons." They are known for their high office and celebrity status in the religion.

So these are some really great guys, and if some pastor in Los Angeles feels that his creativity and freedom are being suppressed because of the local bishop, he is copping out! Totally. There is absolutely no "watchdog" pressure from the local bishops trying to keep their troops at bay. Oftentimes I hear that Bishop or Father So-and-So is such a watchdog when, in all actuality, I know him to be the opposite. The people who push their priests onto a pedestal do the priest and themselves a great disservice. The priests who demand the pedestal are simply afraid of disclosure, confrontation, and/or being discovered.

Yet, I know for a fact that there are a lot of priests today who do not demand the pedestal. It's too damn lonely! And the priests who are totally off the pedestal are constantly being thrown back on the pedestal. It's called, "Father will do it!" My experience of priests, in general, is that we're a lot of fun, great storytellers, passionate, affectionate, and sensitive; yet we seem to be driven to act the complete opposite when in the public eye that expects the Roman way. There seems to be an expectation and a "waiting for permission" to convey humanness, weakness, surrender, and tenderness. And it's safer to hide your heart and hold your cards close to your ches; believe me, being openly loving and living your own truth is never safe. But to live otherwise is exhausting, unhealthy, and grounds for acting out.

Hey! We are all guilty of this and not just Father. Thankfully, I have become more at ease with showing my passion for love and joy in my life as a Christian man living his faith in the Catholic context of priesthood. But, like marriage, you have to live it through your own story, experience, and person. As there is no defined way to be married, there can't be a defined way to live out your priesthood. It is acting out your faith. The goal here is to follow the Christ, God, Yahweh, Brahman, Allah, etc., of your experience, of your own story.

So why does anyone want to be a priest anyway? And why would they stay on as one? In wanting to become a priest, I was one of the fortunate ones who had way more positive experiences of church than negative ones. All I know is this: from my very earliest childhood experiences to the very present, I have never experienced such joy, connection, and vitality than with the many Catholic sisters, Capuchin Franciscan priests, brothers, and parish priests. Has there ever been a bunch of schmucks who were nuns, friars, and padres? Yes. Are there many doctors, lawyers, mothers, fathers, or presidents who have been cause for pain and disappointments in our life? Yes. Are there people who we have *allowed* to let us down because we have placed unreal expectations on them?

Yes.

I fully realize that my reactions to the harsh realities that I have experienced in life have been largely influenced by my own imbalance and immaturity when it comes to having expectations of others. In looking back, I am embarrassed when I see how I had behaved largely due to my own neediness. I am humbled when I recall the forgiveness and understanding of those I offended or accused. I am so blessed in having grown through it and having had the grace, support, and balls to do the work. Though the journey was long and painful, I can totally empathize with those who would rather live in denial than in actually dealing with it. But, on the other hand, I am free!

I have two journals. In one, I write all the bad stuff. This is my venting journal. In this one, I blow out all the anxieties over feelings of disappointment, being misunderstood, or being unappreciated—WAH! I never, ever, refer back to this book—the book is not for feeding the pity pot. Just recalling some of the disappointments in this writing, though, and going through the feelings of reliving some of the negative stuff have been therapeutic, painful, and the best confession I have ever made. *And I ask you, my brothers and sisters, to pray to the Lord, our God, for me!*

The other journal is the "Book of Ken." In this journal I write about all the positive experiences of life: the really empowering experiences that range from personal successes to overhearing a begging homeless person wish upon a reluctant donor, "Have a promising day." I always refer back to the "Good Journal" because it reminds me, when I get totally distracted, that God has visited me, that God has visited us. This journal reminds me in my moments of despair that in the eyes of God I am okay and will be okay. It is my own personal book of my own personal bible. *Shouldn't we all recall our own personal stories of how the Lord of joy and peace has saved our butts?!* At the present, this is how I try to view life. I try not to respond reactively and childishly to the "poor Kenny Deasy" moments of life and focus more on the absolutely wonderful, kick ass, hysterical times of connection, achievement, and peace.

As I look back on priesthood, especially, I have come to see my life not so much as being a good priest as much as seeing how priestly life has ultimately blessed me. Why would I do this otherwise? Aren't we all supposed to get something out of our priesthoods, marriages, and missions? Yes, it is great to give. But there also has to be a return. It is good physics. Like all of us, if we don't take time to reflect upon, share, and attest to all the miraculous ways that we've been blessed in the process of helping others, we will surely die. So, I did not have any high spiritual ideals that compelled me to become a priest. There was not this burning passion for Jesus or love of the Father as portrayed on the ceiling of the Sistine Chapel in Rome! Again, going back to earliest childhood, I witnessed more joy, connection, courage, and laughter around the many Catholic religious sisters, Capuchin Franciscan priests, brothers, and parish priests than with any other group in my life.

And I wanted some of it.

I still want it and it is up to me, while participating with the love of God, to seek it. Believe it or not, with all the crap, I am still more influenced by the more positive, life-giving, and valuable experiences than by the negative ones. I received my initiative for compassion, generosity, and fun from them, and wanted to share the same with others in return. In other words, it has worked for me—compassion is cool. Carrying the crosses of some and lessening of the burdens of others has always been something that I am naturally, spiritually, and often dysfunctionally, drawn to. It's not because I am some Holy Joe. It raises my spirits and I can't get enough of it! To this very day, it has been the experiences and freedom from my own past crosses and resurrections blessed upon me that continue to ground me. All these experiences are directly connected to my current ministry, and it has been within the context of the Catholic Church that this intimate presence and experience of Christ has been so present and real.

"There is no better love in life than to give one's life for one's friends."

Well, I do want love in my life. And for me there has been no greater love for me than when others have given their life for me, and when I have had the honor of contributing to the life of another. Period. This is my experience. I know there are other experiences out there that I could give a "good go" to. But until they show themselves to me, if it ain't broke, why fix it? Alas, there are the natural questions and cravings that make me think there are other pastures to graze. Some call these "greener pastures" temptations. I have learned by now that if I yearn for purely selfish gains, worldly wealth, fame, and power, then I screw myself. If other quests present themselves that cause me to consider splitting, then I have to discern whether these are temptations of the Evil One or, rather, summons sent by the Holy Spirit to "share the good news" in a different and/or more profound way. *Humbly, I have had to do this many times.*

Do I want to be alone in life? No. Do I want to live a life of not being touched and not have another enjoy my touch? No. Do I think celibacy is a positive contribution to the mental, emotional, and sensual dimensions of my life? Nope, but I don't think at this stage marriage would work for me. Up to now there has never been more life-giving and lifesaving experiences of intimacy and empowerment in my life than those I experienced in priesthood. I will hold these as divine and resist swapping them at a whim with the hopes of something greater. I have been blessed.

I still have many fears; my lifelong feelings of separation, abandonment, and rejection are huge. My spiritual director suggests that I ask God to allow old fears to remain "if it be for his glory." Funny. There was a time I would have said to this spiritual mentor, "Are you nuts? You got to love God and know that he/she loves you before you're going to pray that prayer of surrender!" Well, I have to confess, that I have been given slices of heaven—an experience of the goodness of God in so many ways because of my Catholicism and priesthood. So, I do pray "let it happen, Lord, but just don't let me be alone in it all!" But I am really not totally there yet, but I am on my way. Sure, there are imperfections with everything in life. I try not to start admitting to my needs with such phrases as "I don't have . . ." and "I can't have . . ." Instead, I try to begin the process with, "What I really need to do is . . ." while knowing that I have the freedom to do it because with God all things are possible. And with the world of Church ambition, politics, and money, all things are not necessarily possible and rosy.

Show me a perfect life, will you? Show me some one person or philosophy more historically popular and more attuned than that of Jesus and his mission, and I'll worship it. If I think of it, I know my life has been hard at times, but as a result, it is probably fuller than most. As long as I am getting something out of it, I stay. In the process of feeding, as long as I am also getting fed, I stay. And for me to be fed is simply experiencing that it works! As long as when I serve the ball, for the most part, I feel that the ball is being returned, I stay. I do not stay because I made a promise to the Church and feel obligated under pain of serious sin to be obedient to the bishop. These are important, but, mind you, my motivation to get up in the morning is not because the bishop needs me to. I am a single man and make sure the bills are paid in allegiance to the office of the bishop. That's plenty enough for me, and him, I am sure. God and I are totally cool on this.

In hindsight, my vows to the Church were in order for THEM to allow me to live my calling to be a priest and to be in a life of joy that I had experienced earlier. I wanted to be one of the guys, to be one of the family. Since then, I have gratefully grown with a faith in my self and my baptism. I actually and finally believe in a loving God. I oftentimes say, "If I am a successful priest it's because of my living out my 'baptismal priesthood' rather than my 'ordained priesthood.'" When I think about whether I want to continue living this lifestyle for the next five or ten years (and most likely die alone when my ticket is up) I want to cash in my whopping six thousand dollar IRA Keogh, take the money, and run! I sure won't be able to run far, though. But it is exactly in the NOW, my NOW connected with the NOWS of others, that I feel enlivened, empowered, and fulfilled. While also having the clouds of fear, rejection and betrayal oftentimes making it difficult for my resurrections to shine, history has shown that everything will be all right when I allow it. When I don't, I just keep myself on the cross. This is what I confess always. It is only me who keeps me on the cross and it is my lack of faith in me, in others, and in God's will that prevents it. This is my greatest sin. This is the rock that I roll on my own tomb and with which I only hurt myself. Of course, since I'm confessing, I will blame my own self-condemnation on everyone else!

You see, all I know is the NOW.

As I have said before, I know there are seven sacraments of the Catholic Church (sacraments being ritually "present encounters of Christ"). All things being equal, with the growing shortage of the ordained priesthood there are fewer "dispensers" of these ritual-based encounters. The greatest sacrament for me to celebrate is not one of the seven—the greatest sacrament is that of the NOW and not of the THEN—to empower you in the NOW. In hindsight, my motivations and aspirations for entering the seminary and pursuing a priestly calling were not because I was passionately in love with Jesus and passionately in love with the Church. I was passionately drawn and attracted to the liberating experiences that those good people in religious life achieved for me and my family.

I wanted that life of joy. I wanted to give witness to their joy, their Christ. And it wasn't until later that these experiences and wants of joy came to become known to me as experiencing the actual blessings of Christ. But alas, when I am asked, "Why did you become a priest?" I avoid the question because the answer would be way more intimate and personal than the "quickie answer" that is being expected.

So, the real question is why do I stay a priest?

Hey—there are a ton of you married folks I would love to ask, "Why on earth do you stay married?" You, too, don't always look so swell! I know, I know, "because of the kids." Let's not even go there, please! But I can honestly confess and say, that for many years I have stayed "because of the kids." I had stayed because I had a puffed up ego and a codependence on my friends who I had thought would leave me upon my departure. I've seen too many times when, once a priest was transferred after six-plus years in the parish, all his dear friends stay behind. Plus, I invested my blood and time and life in so many people and programs that I felt compelled to remain. I am constantly taunted by the historical promise of God set forth in the Jewish and Christian traditions, that the best is yet to come. This was my gift, my calling. Who am I kidding? Then, it was pride. It was control. It was being smart. I have totally learned how to use the powers of the priesthood, prestige, wealth, authority, and freedom of accessibility as a tool to enhance what I felt was my own personal calling and assigned mission. *God! I know that sounds arrogant and I so apologize. I'm really not!* We all should talk about our own personal callings and platforms on which we base our decisions. I can tell you most assuredly, I use the powers of the Church way more than they think they use me. I have the privilege of really helping people in what really matters: to walk side by side with people to the frontiers of grace.

I am also "America's Favorite Guest." Being America's Favorite Guest comes not only because of the false conception that "Father gives up so much for his people" but because I am a "Timex/Taco Bell" priest who not only "takes a lickin' and keeps on tickin'," but one who "thinks outside of the bun." Like us all, I instinctively act out my creative, affectionate self while still trying to manage the academic, theological, and doctrinal side of priesthood. *Talk about a personality clash.* I chose to live not waiting to experience heaven after I croak. I live to experience heaven in the present. If Jesus of Nazareth were to walk into my church I would say, "Hey! Cool! Great to see you! But you can leave now, because as long as we are gazing upon you, we are ignoring the lasting experience of you within ourselves and among others." Much of the Catholic tradition (and much of the Jewish tradition, I suppose) is preoccupied with teachings of a historical God. This is what God did THEN. This is what people did THEN. It was because of the "then" sins of our forefathers and foremothers that we are in this predicament today.

The Holy Land is "Religion Land." The Holy City is "Religion City." They are honored because of what they represented and signified in the past. The root of salvific beginnings was of course, THEN. The phenomenon of religion presents its doctrines footnoted by ancient historical traditions from which we are seemingly supposed to never sway. As I experience it, this is exactly the reorientation that Jesus was trying to achieve with people, not to keep looking at the PAST. It's time to grow up, quit feeling stuck because of the "sins the past," and realize that "the best is yet to come" when we allow ourselves to believe in a more loving face of God, self, and each other. There is a TRUTH still to be had! It ain't over 'til it's over! The Holy Spirit will make sure of that.

Needless to say, this new personality and dimension that Jesus affectively delivered about "God" did not go well with the political and religious zealots of his day. And not surprisingly, this will not go well with today's religious and political zealots. Sadly, many of the faithful continue to seek apparitions and "signs and wonders" while missing the very affirmations of God in the simplest of life experiences. We offer prayers for extraordinary miracles from heaven when, unfortunately, people don't realize that they are the miracles.

Sadly, there are prayers being offered to cure every malady and negative reality on the earth. FIX IT GOD! Fact is, we have been given his power and love to fix ourselves and others. We're just afraid to use it because we will have to change, or, God forbid, might miss something cooler.

And I am just as guilty as anyone else. I am just realizing all of this in my forty-ninth year of life. So, that was then, this is now. With all the bumps and bruises along the way for which I silently react with *"I don't need this crap!"* I can still say with all honesty, sincerity, and integrity I am fulfilled as a man and as a person who really digs the message of the good news of my Lord, Jesus Christ, in being a priest. I really believe in the good news, the Gospels, message, hope, and God that it brings to everyone no matter their religion, gender, sexuality, creed, culture, and history. For me, my experience of Jesus is as one who, with a burning passion for all people who wrestle with living life fully and authentically, brought a more intimate and positive face of God, self, and world to those who believed THEN that they were separated from God. A faithful Jew, he taught that we are not doomed to endless diaspora or an accusing cross.

Surely, today, diasporas are experienced with the inevitable losses of jobs, love, dignity, money, life, homes, and self-esteem. Jesus takes on the crosses of all worldly and human failures and transforms them into opportunities, for "the best is yet to come out of it all." Look at how at one time a patch of cloth in the shape of a Star of David worn by prisoners in the Nazi camps was a label of fatality, and is now a trophy of survival, restored dignity, and deserved pride. Look at how the diamond-studded crosses worn around the necks of so many were once a means of execution and judicial condemnation.

Remember, I am just like you. I am nothing special. I am weak and a sinner—someone who still needs to grow in imitating the love, patience, and surrender of the Jesus portrayed in the Christian Gospels—while still being joyous. Knowing this all too well, through the life of the Gospels then and the continuing affirmation of the love of God through the Holy Spirit now, I become something special—just like you. So, though many Christians proclaim with high-and-mighty, pie-in-the-sky arrogance that "JESUS IS MY LORD!" for me, the Lord God is behind all my down-to-earth innate hunger and thirst for the best of life as offered by the Jesus of the Gospels, and as lived through good people: the community. What totally turns me on about the Jesus in the Gospels are his human experiences that allow us to look at our present times—where God is coming at us—when we are responding to his incentives outside the temple, synagogue, mosque, or church.

His Surrender

Jesus was truly the ultimate victim who did not act like a victim. He is believed by Christians to be God in the flesh, a god who gets under our skin in order to make us more intimate, accessible, and vulnerable. He truly dignifies the word "surrender" which is commonly used today to describe an action associated with defeat. Jesus' plan was to dignify our humanness by allowing us to experience it to its fullness—love, want, rejection, and abandonment—and to make all experiences in life opportunities of being resurrected. Remember the '80s film *The Last Temptation of Christ*? All of the religious zealots of that year came forward (most not even having seen the movie) and reacted to Jesus having "feelings" for Mary Magdalene. They couldn't tolerate a God with human feelings and they reacted—with anger, cursing, and finger-pointing. As a result, they missed the whole message. The last temptation of Christ was, while on the cross, not responding to the invitation "If you are the Messiah, save yourself!" Now, here's God being crucified on the cross: the Ultimate Lover allowing himself to be seen as a loser condemned by politics and religious fanaticism; God being murdered by his lovers—stripped naked, spat upon, and mocked—Ultimate Love surrendering to Ultimate Rejection.

Save yourself, Jesus! Now, there's a temptation: Save your own butt, Messiah! He could of, you know, but he didn't. He takes us mere mortals at our worst—threatened, afraid, plotting, stuck, complacent—and saves us through our common tendencies to be ugly. I love that because I can relate to that! Can't you? I can recognize this great incentive in wanting to give a gift. I can also relate to the utter disappointment of the gift being rejected or not appreciated. There is no greater joy in giving a gift than when the gesture behind the gift, no matter how great or small, is recognized and celebrated by the recipient. The greatest joy in giving a gift is how it is received! Seemingly, as portrayed through the Gospels, the only ones who really recognized the gift that God was surrendering to give on Calvary was the repentant thief; his mom and his buddy John; and the woman known as Veronica who tradition holds as being the one who came forward to wash the blood, sweat, and saliva off his torn face.

Though he prayed, "Father, let this cup pass by me," *Father, I am scared as hell. I am hurting! What did I do to deserve this?* and though he prayed during his last breath, "My God! My God! Why have you abandoned me?" *No wonder why you have so few friends!,* he surrendered to the experience of love that he felt from God—experienced solitarily and communally within the poor, and the politically and religiously rejected.

Why?

Because in so doing, he demonstrates with his own flesh that the best is yet to come. God convincingly shows us that he is not just words, that faith is not just "reading the book" and "following the rules." It is choosing not to value the false powers of the world while surrendering to a greater love. The option is, though, believing that his love is greater than ambitions for wealth, fame, and power. The choice cannot be made until one has experienced this love either coming from them or coming at them. There is hope beyond the crosses of life. Resurrection becomes not just a physical resurrection after we're dead but is an experience in the NOW of our healings, attempts for solace and comfort.

His Perseverance

I am often amazed at this word "perseverance." It's a word we don't hear much about anymore. In a world of quick fixes, car-pool lanes, quick microwave magic, and drive-throughs, we want to go through life with ease, rapidity, and a lack of pain. Isn't it sad when people simply choose to wait, survive, and maintain through life without "going for the ring" when opportunities avail themselves? The resistance is largely due to this sense of unworthiness, an underestimated level of achievement, and a history of "You can't go there." What makes it even worse is that in a medicated world we often don't want to persevere through the irritating frustration that one must endure in order to get there. You can't fool around with Mother Nature. Where there is motion, there is resistance, one way or the other.

As Jesus quietly perseveres in his belief, person, and particular mission, he identifies with the inevitable reality of our humanness which is that of a bridge builder who always gets stuck in the middle. As a result, there is a "Come on over" message on one side and a "We don't want any" on the other. When I think of God carrying our crosses on the road to his death, I especially think of his stumbling and falling along the way. As the WAY OF THE CROSS/STATIONS OF THE CROSS Catholic devotion goes . . .

Jesus falls the first time, a second time, and a third time. I see, I receive, I take in. But he also gets up! He gets up the first time, the second time, and a third time. Why? In order to establish the Christian religion? No. In order to destroy Judaism? No. In order to make a political statement against Caesar? No. Then why? Because he loves us and knew that in persevering we would receive this gift like no other—a gift you can't buy at Macy's or Bloomingdale's and that has nothing to do with Valentine's Day—a gift of real love. How many good couples have destroyed their marriages because of a lack of awareness, reverence, and faith in their relationship and history that, when put to the test by the harsh realities and doldrums of life, are totally forgotten as an anchor? How many wonderful good souls who, because of tremendous cravings for love, connection, freedom, and fulfillment, sell themselves short by medicating this burning passion with booze, drugs, food, sex, and work? Too many of us still want to believe that "when you're down, you're out"! *Thank you, Jesus, for giving dignity to recovery!*

Alas the need for a flashy miracle! The present day miracles and miracle workers are those who enter processes of Alcoholics Anonymous, Al-Anon, Cocaine Anonymous, Gamblers Anonymous, and Sex Addicts Anonymous, even after falling off the wagon a few times along the way when persevering to sobriety, freedom, and dignity. These heroes keep going; they fall, they get up, sometimes alone, sometimes with others: When the going gets rough, only the tough keep going. Unfortunately, in our society the toughest are seen as the weakest—the single parent, the convicted criminal, and the addict. Fortunately, in faith, the weakest are seen as the toughest, as having an inner spirit to persevere with head held high because in all things we know our God is walking with us. He's been on this road before. There's been an experience of this "power" on the road. I am not alone.

His Humility

Is God humble? Religion often portrays God and gods as unforgiving, remote, and adorned with "might makes right" authority. Gods are power brokers! Now, here comes a God in Jesus who obviously is poor (the son of a carpenter who lived in a town that had no wood). Jesus was not from the higher levels of society. He sought out the neglected, the separated, the physical lepers (the sick), the social lepers (the poor), and the religious lepers (the unchurched) whom high society ignored or merely tolerated. As my Jewish friends say, "If Jesus were a doctor, everything would have been fine." As my political, suburban friends say, "If Jesus were a Republican everything would have been fine." Well, if you label and order your life according to your profession, politics, sexual identity, place of origin, or domicile (and I mean ultimately and solely), you are selling yourself short. Jesus made himself so humble and accessible by taking on a "regular type of guy" appearance, that everyone who was seeking to have his or her potential realized was given an example of how important it is to be TRUE to yourself and never ever feel ashamed.

Jesus the Jew, the Gentile, the Hindu, the carpenter, the next-door neighbor, the leper-loving, the nonpolitician, the Nazarene ("What good can come from Nazareth?"), the crucified criminal, and executed loser is now the Christ and accessible God who humbles himself obediently by accepting death on a cross. God humbles himself by not just reaching into our hells and pulling us out but by entering our hells and holding us during them. God does this. Jesus does this. Yahweh does this. Allah does this. Our Lord feels!

And we were given this gift of being saved for another reason: TO SAVE OTHERS! We still throw Jesus up on the throne and the pedestal and we still look up for the manna to fall down and hit us on the head.

We're the manna.

Jesus teaches us in humility NOT to value yourself as the Gucci or Versace of society (and there is nothing wrong with owning that stuff, but I wish to remind you that you don't see a U-Haul behind a hearse). God wants us to be happy by igniting and connecting our presence and availability into an awareness that we are all pretty damn lucky and should save others; that we should work our tails off and help those whose life situation prevents them from feeling blessed. It's hard to feel blessed when you're starving. Yet, it's not until we're starving that we will finally seek, get, and appreciate the nourishment that comes with grace.

His Invitation

Though the West and Western religions can often come off as exclusive, mirroring Groucho Marx's *You Bet Your Life:* "Say the magic words and win a thousand dollars"; the God in Jesus invites everyone. EVERYONE!—the sinner, the outsider, the rich, the poor, and those made in the image and likeness of God: which is all of us. I can't think of anyone whom Jesus ever rejected or condemned. So I am amazed today about how fundamentalists can be so condemning and use their respective scriptures as a tool of finger-pointing and labeling. Jesus never did; he invited everyone. The religious and political finger pointers condemned Jesus, and present-day zealots do the same.

This man and God, Jesus, had the ability to recognize people for who they are and for who they are not. He met people where they were without condemnation while certainly challenging the condemners. The person of Jesus empowers us all to be a light to move others forward to a life of peace during struggles, to hope during despairs, to acceptance during rejections, to wealth during poverty, to welcome while being ostracized. He looked beyond people's questionable actions and exteriors to show them their power, encouraging them to look beyond the rules and laws of the day to address their external actions. He encouraged people to reverence their stories, journeys, and intentions, and look beyond their computer hardware to get them to cherish their software, knowing full well that if it all gets munched and the backups are prevented, JESUS SAVES. *Get it?!*

His Generosity

In his poverty, Jesus was the wealthiest! The people who flocked to him were about to get more than just bread and a simple how-do-you-do. They would receive something more than money could buy—the Bread of Life. And we're still, two thousand years later, trying to get it! Giving out bread does not make one God. I remember in the '70s when thousands flocked to Randolph Hearst's food giveaway in San Francisco when he gave in following the ransom demands of the Symbionese Liberation Army in order to save his kidnapped daughter Patty. Literally, thousands attacked the shipments of food. But they didn't anoint him Randolph Christ, now, did they?

The people in the time of Jesus were fed by his presence, sensitivity, compassion, priorities, freedom, zeal, and mutuality. I don't know of any kind of Wonder Bread that can do that! They flocked to him in order to be in the presence of freedom, joy, and calm. They felt the power of his presence and in his invitation to "follow me." He continues to do now what the Lord did in Jesus Christ then: to resonate with all that lies potentially within us—the fullness of God. The invitation was for us all to receive and allow a Lord who until this day continues to entice us, and to share the experience of giving the Lord who, until this day, continues to entice us! He wanted to give us a gift, and for us to experience this gift. The price of this gift? He sent us a person, and though this person died, he did not lose himself in the process. I often ponder on the love behind this gift. *The gift that keeps on giving!*

Now, that's generosity! Yikes! And he didn't have to endure that cross. *"Lord, forgive me a sinner"* is the only reaction I can have when I put myself in comparison. His actions allowed people to feel like a million bucks without being given a million bucks. He gave more than money can buy: He shared his blood, sweat, and tears. He shared his experience of God with the credibility of his imperfect humanness.

Jesus Looked Outside of the Box

Jesus helped people see outside of the box or, again, as Taco Bell would say, "think outside the Bun." Jesus took the status quo of his day and stood it on its head—making this sojourn in life with God easier to bear. This is what Pope John XXIII sought in initiating the Second Vatican Council. As "Peter the Rock," this simple elderly Italian man sought to make our spiritual journey on earth less sad.

Ah, Peter. From this apostle I receive great inspiration. As the kids would say, "Peter is dope!" Simon Peter was made the chief shepherd to continue Jesus' attempts to lead the sheep. Surely, we would not have gone far on Donald Trump's TV show, *The Apprentice*. He was huge in not giving power to those things that were of this world, but to Christ's. Especially in his dialogues with Paul concerning ways to include the Gentile Christians with the Jewish Christians, we see Peter truly establishing openness to collaboration and discussion. I imagine him as a real hothead, though. He said, "Oh Jesus I would never betray you!" And he did. He said, "Oh, Jesus, I would give my life for you!" He eventually did. Peter is a great example of "It's not how you begin; it's how you finish!" Peter is so cool.

I often think of the gospel passage where Peter and the disciples were in the boat on the Sea of Galilee and the waves were tossing them all about. Then, all of a sudden, Peter notices Jesus walking on the water toward them. Peter, steps out of the security of the boat and starts walking on the water toward Jesus, and distracted by the waves, starts to sink. Jesus pulls him up and says, "Peter, you of little faith!" My response to this?

"Chill out, Jesus!" At least he got out of the boat. It was only a natural choice for Peter to have been selected by Jesus to continue his mission to get people "thinking outside the bun." Peter not only thought "outside of the bun," he "got outside of the boat!" When I am afraid, distracted, and complacent, I pray for trust, focus and conviction. I think of Peter and ask God for the grace to shoot me the same openness to grace that Peter possessed. Peter was appointed "the Rock" by Jesus not because he was the best. It is apparent to me that he was appointed the Rock because he was far from being a rock. Because of his own weaknesses, wants, story, and passions, Peter would have been more receptive to the good news and the freedom, affirmations, and challenges that it had for him. Remember in the Gospels that Peter, after Jesus was arrested, was away from the company of the other disciples and was sitting by himself around the campfire. People began questioning Peter about who he was, and three times Peter denied that he was one of Jesus' company. If Peter was away from the disciples, how do we know about it today?

He confessed it. He humbled himself before those he was charged to be an example to, and confessed his faults. He also must have confessed his need for God's mercy. He also must have confessed his need for the community's mercy! He obviously got it from them. But he got it originally from Jesus. When the resurrected Jesus meets Peter on the road, Jesus, instead of saying, "Where the hell were you when I needed you?" says, "Peace be with you. Let's eat!" For Peter to even stick around and continue to be in the company of Jesus' disciples took amazing faith and belief in the forgiveness of God and people. It took tremendous faith in his own power to forgive.

Poor Judas didn't have it.

I can't help but wonder if my pride would have prevented me from returning to the group and accusing myself before them. I also know darn well that it takes me a lot longer to get over betrayals than Jesus did. I would have been totally furious with Peter.

"Where the hell were you when I needed you?"

I really do pray to grow more loving and understanding. I will only be the better because of it. Can you imagine, on further reflection, what it was like when Peter met the apostle to the Gentiles, Paul. Paul, once a persecutor of the early and original "Christians," now, having had the experience of meeting the "glorified Jesus" on the road to Damascus, claims he is on a mission from Christ. He explains that the resurrected Messiah appeared before him on the road saying, "Saul, Saul, why are you persecuting me?" I can't even imagine hothead Peter's response when Paul approaches him with "Hey, I'm an apostle too!" To hear murderous Paul speak words that more or less convey "I also have had an experience and am commissioned by Jesus to be an apostle—just like you!" must have been too wild for Peter. *Later, of course, Paul writes in 1 Corinthians that he is the least and worst of the apostles.*

Peter obviously accepted this witness from Paul because they end up doing amazing things separately and together. Peter must have remembered his own betrayals and denials of Jesus by word, action and absence—the second, third, fourth, fifth, and seventy times seven chances in life that the Messiah had given him. Taking into account all the slack that Jesus had cut him, Peter had to accept the newly found Paul for who he was NOW, not for who he was back THEN. This is an amazing story of conversion, a fancy word for growth. And as evidenced in his writing, Paul never forgets it either. He spoke, wrote, and ministered always through the lenses of the "man who was totally off the mark" and who "now knows what really matters." Often, he confesses in his writing that "he didn't get it"—how the persecutor could become the resurrected, all the while preaching that his weakness is his strength. Paul, having all too much of the experiences of the religion of his time, takes it to another level once he responds to an actual experience of God.

The Damascus experience is only the beginning. Throughout his letters he writes and affirms that "the community" is the proof that God is with us in the NOW. For Paul, there is total identification between Jesus and humanity. Paul's great conversion was being confronted by a Christ querying the reason for persecuting HIM. Paul must have quietly reacted by saying, "I ain't hurting you. I'M out for them!" Following, Paul moves from viewing these people as "Jesus freaks" to "Oh my Jesus! THESE PEOPLE REALLY ARE YOU, JESUS!" Once having these experiences of God among the people, there is no longer the annoying "either/or" of religion which incurs an "us" versus "them" division.

In Paul, Jesus presents some of his best work—the possibilities of the miracle that anyone can be saved and transformed. He lays out the ultimate example of conversion and transformation—which shows that with God all transformation is possible—going from being the persecutor to the believer and preacher, from the strong and unbelieving to the weak in love and full belief. He's the ultimate example that complete lives can be lived in darkness, and that darkness is all-consuming until God's particular spark is applied; then all is possible. If Jesus could work a miracle with Paul, there is no lost cause, EVER.

For Paul, once you've had a taste of the love of God he could do nothing but accept it and share it. In so engaging in the presence of Christ he had a full engagement into his real self. Religion and politics tend to label everything on a dualistic level—the either/or model. Paul, on the other hand, begins to teach the joy of a unified, all-accepting way of spiritual thinking. His becomes a both/and, inclusive way of accepting the world: he would reach out and minister to the healthy and the sick; women and men; the accused and the admired; the free and the enslaved; the righteous and the merciful; the weak and the strong; the sinner and the saint. Today, in our EITHER/OR Western society, the light of Christ shines on the BOTH/AND. The goal of the Christian, the wants of our God as evidenced in Jesus and Paul, is to be who you REALLY are, to be who you were created to be. *Sounds easy, huh?* How many of us really take the time to be who we really are when we are stuck on who we thought we were supposed to be? How many of us take the time to even ponder on who we really are and who we are meant to be?

It's a big shift. I love my faith as I grow to understand and participate in it more. As I pray for an increase of faith, though, I still pray for help with my unbelief in an ever-loving God, others, and self. For me as a Christian man, what Jesus does for the Samaritan woman at the well is huge in my own common walk. Here's a person who not only was a woman (Strike one) but a Samaritan (Strike two). In the eyes of the male Judaic world she is out on two counts thus far. She also has been sleeping around (Strike three! You're out of there!). In the gospel story, she is drawing water from the well at noon. Jesus approaches her and asks for a cup of water. She is amazed at this man, a Jewish man at that, approaching her. As the story proceeds, Jesus offers her, instead, "a cup of salvation," the water of eternal life that will satisfy her forever. This cup of salvation becomes the knowledge of her true self. Here come those religious words again: "eternal life" and "salvation." And here's a woman who, like us all, sold her self short and lived a life of underestimation. This is why she went to the well at the dreaded high-noon hour instead of during the morning when it was cooler. The other women would be there. She would be seen and judged by her actions and reputation. She was ashamed. She no longer, if ever, liked herself. Jesus, instead of giving her the expected "Shame! Shame on you!" told her something absolutely loving and charming about herself that transformed her—a miracle not of raising the dead or curing a physically disabled person but a miracle available to anyone. Her disclosure about Jesus that "He told me everything about myself" is an affirmation that we should never judge someone by outward appearance—to her he was more than just a Jewish male with all that that entailed. *How would you react if someone came up to you and told you everything about yourself? Hmmm?*

The message of Christ and the mission of Paul is "Life is about being who you really are." All that is needed is to become "a new creation"; i.e., yourself. This is why it is called RENEW! Now, after giving a short glimpse of what totally turns me on about life and God, all I can say is that I want to share it, and have a good time in the process that doesn't distract from walking with other's pain.

There have been no more intimate times in my life than being at your loved ones' deathbeds. Did I like being awakened in the middle of night by the pager when a "sick call" came in at the local hospital or in a parishioner's home? No. But, once I got there (even when the sick person was in better physical shape than I), I always knew that there was a reason. That I was needed and that I felt honored to be there. Funny thing, though, is that as a kid, one the biggest detractors from even thinking of being a priest was that I was terrified of the idea of seeing people broken and bloodied in hospitals. Though I have surely seen things since that have turned my stomach, ALWAYS did the grace of God kick in and keep me from fainting.

There have been no more painful and yet gloriously intimate times in my life than when I have had the honor to hold you in your deaths. Though glorious, it doesn't mean that I enjoyed it, like I would rather witness your passing than go to Disneyland—but glorious in the sense that I had seen the strength of love in others and the grace that comes with living your truth enough to be present. I remember about ten years ago when I was called to the hospital to be with the family of a young infant born with a defective heart, brain, and other physical maladies. The infant was stable enough to leave the hospital and die at home. Needless to say, the parents were devastated by the prognosis but happy to go home. That very day, upon their return home, I was visiting with the family and cradling the precious child in my arms when he finally went into respiratory arrest. I can't even attempt to explain how I felt about this. But, I know that I immediately handed the baby over to the parents as the child was to expire in their arms.

Mom panicked and jumped up to grab the phone. "We got to call an ambulance!" she screamed. Of course, the natural response of any loving parent would be to call the paramedics if their baby stopped breathing and was turning purple before their very eyes. No matter how hopeless the situation was for a recovery, this good woman wanted to save her baby. Without even thinking, something snapped in me and I sprang up and made a dash to stop her. The look on her face, the hatred in her eyes for me—I was the enemy. "You're not going to stop me from saving my baby!" Her look made me feel like I was a "baby killer."

"If you call the paramedics they have to by law resuscitate your baby and you'll have to go through this again and again! I pleaded with her. "We can't prolong the dying," came out of my mouth. She stopped. She ran back to her baby. He died moments after returning to him. *A baby killer?* This returned me to memories of when my mother was dying of cancer in 1974. Then there was only radiation therapy which seemed to only prolong the agony of a dying person's final days. The teaching of the Church was "Prolong life with whatever means you can." Since my experience at the time was that radiation didn't seem to prolong life as I defined it (a school buddy of mine died from cancer in 1972, and I had experienced what radiation did to him), I asked Mom to decline it.

She did. I can remember a priest at the time telling me that since we declined radiation for Mom that I was killing her. Nice words to say to a kid whose mom was dying, huh?

"By the way, do you know that you're killing your own mother?"

Hard as it was, my experiences of life and the grace of the Holy Spirit allowed me to stand at the crosses of these poor people. We've all had a good cry together, and we've ended up having a good connection. I remember my mom's funeral. I also remember this little boy's funeral during which something compelled me to sing "Bring Him Home" from the Broadway show *Les Miserables*.

Funerals.

There have been no more intimate and challenging times in my life than when I have been called to provide some sort of solace and comfort to others when grieving their dead. Just last week I had the challenge and honor of burying a young man named Brandon Bennett. He was a nineteen-year-old African American man who was shot during the daytime while returning to his car after a trip to the ATM machine. Though I had only seen him at a couple of Sunday services when he was bringing his grandparents to Sunday Mass (I buried them also), I learned upon his death that he was quite a good guy.

Brandon was a leader, was pursuing education, was a loyal family member, and had dreams, goals, and ambition. Now he is dead, and what do you say to his family? People want you to represent God at this moment and "fix it"! I only pray that I could. For us in the inner city, burying another young person killed by violence is common. Such a waste and such potential destroyed. I remember presiding at Brandon's funeral. It was a thousand degrees inside this church packed with over eight hundred African American elders and youth, all in shock. The mood was so sad, and the mother requested that I make this event a celebration of his life for "now he is with his God and grandparents." I was not in a good mood. At the time, I was emotionally drained from the week and the impact of this kid's death. Common as it is, the shock over this taking of a life was unusually intense. To see so many people crying was heartbreaking, and I wanted to fix it for them. I could almost hear Martha tell Jesus, "If you were here my brother Lazarus would not have died." I also heard Jesus say "Lazarus come forth!" Though I did not even presume that I could raise the boy from the dead, I sure wanted to. I'm good but I ain't that good!

The sadness in the room endeared my heart to a higher than usual degree of pity and anger. I was really scraping for something to say as I stood among a mourning people wanting some answers and reassurance. Then, a surge of human empathy came over me: it's called the Holy Spirit. Then I said something like—

> *Family, I know that you have a lot of questions right now. Why Brandon? Why, God, did you take our son? What type of person would do such a thing? As you have said, "We give our son to God!" This is quite a generous gift! So, now, I am going to ask you for one more gift though you have surely already given enough. Surely, there are millions in Los Angeles who have heard about the goodness of your son. Through the media they have heard of the hopes and dreams that Brandon was actively pursuing in a town where "kids" are presumed to be in gangs, not having a chance of prosperity and dignity. Now, I am asking you, on behalf of God, to allow your son's death to be a factor in bettering others' lives. I am going to ask you to allow the tragic death of your son and his hope-filled life to be a miracle for others to allow and participate in.*
>
> *Because of your son's murder, I know that parents are holding their kids closer and that kids are cherishing their parents more. I know that people who don't live in the inner city are re-examining their prejudices and underestimations of us because of Brandon's goodness and prosperity. In short, everyone else is going to be bettered by your son's death! This is the ultimate gift anyone can give.*

Whether this hope was accepted or not, I don't know—I only plant seeds. But I felt in the process of this homily the touch of God and a once-wounded-but-now-healed Christ encouraging us all to "keep on keeping on!" Man, I do feel people's pain. It's a gift, and selfishly, it's a curse. Funerals and consoling people are truly tough. But I would prefer five funerals to one wedding, ANY DAY.

Weddings.

Like any priest, I have witnessed literally hundreds of weddings. More importantly, I have prepared hundreds of couples for "marriage." Annoyingly, but understandably, most couples only want to talk about the wedding. When that is the case, they've come to the wrong man. Having been involved in so many special event fund-raisers, I empathize with the stress that comes preparing an event such as the wedding reception. I don't really care about their wedding reception, but I assure people that in this church, weddings are always up, joyous, and personal. If they're not, it's because they and their guests are not up, joyous, and personal. Do you know how many times I hear, "Ugh! A Catholic wedding! Boorrring!"? Not here, baby! If my weddings are long and boring it is not my fault. Often wedding couples demand to have every syrupy song ever written (from "We've Only Just Begun" to "Baby We're Going to Make it Tonight") included in the ceremony. Aarrgghhh! Unless you have a General George Patton-like wedding coordinator, the wedding party is usually late and intoxicated, demanding a million extra wedding customs thrown in so their dream marriage will come true (i.e., flowers to Mary, the unity candle, exchange of coins, the lasso, jumping over a broom, etc). *Father, can our poodles Fifi and Pierre walk down the aisle with us? PLEASE?!*

I often hear the complaint that "the priest was so boring." Not me! It's usually the bride and groom who are wound up like a clock, and usually the guests are so tired of weddings already that their focus is to just get to the reception. So who gets blamed? The priest! Hopefully, by the time my brides and grooms walk down the aisle, I have sat down and visited with them for two or three appointments and have developed a friendly relationship with them. As I see it, after someone is dating for a good while (and one month, by the way, is not a good while), they fall in love (which is easy), and they have stayed in love. In the process of this courtship, I am presuming that the experiences of intimacy (and I don't mean just great sex) have already been experienced for better or for worse; for richer and for poorer; in sickness and in health. And I do know something about relationships. *Just because I'm a priest doesn't mean I was neutered at birth.*

After first acquainting myself with the engaged duo, I try to help them really see why they love each other while also telling them that they are no longer "just dating." Engagement is their seminary! It is the formal time to prepare for marriage, and not just the wedding. Honestly, though, if during the process all they continue to be concerned about is their wedding practicalities and continue to be closed to "marriage preparation," I advise they go to Reverend Bev down the street.

Minus my own personality defects, I don't deliberately turn people away. I have learned in any type of ministering it's about planting seeds. Hopefully, these seeds will take root and grow. Life has taught me to try and be open to giving everyone a shot and pray that during our meetings they will have grown closer to the Lord in each other. For me, marriage is a huge sacrament (another encounter of the love of God and his love for us). Married life says a lot about faith that continues to unwrap itself during the course of their life together. It is a lifestyle that demands a faith far greater than I believe priesthood does. *I can always close my door and wish to God that you'd go away!* I don't care if one is a professed Christian or not; if one is to stay married today (and if one is to be an affective priest today), you have got to have a reason, a spiritual grounding, a personal ultimate goal that you both share.

I believe that the manner of how Jesus lived is huge in this. Western society certainly does not encourage married life. In the eyes of the state it is simply a contractual agreement. Even the marriage certificate has CUSTOMER COPY shaded through the middle of it. Where in the world is the motivation to be forgiving, for example, going to come from? The world seemingly preaches revenge and litigation. Where is the motivation to be compassionate going to come from? The world seemingly prefers passion. If it feels good, it's "YEAH, BABYYEE!" If it hurts, it's "EXIT STAGE RIGHT!" Where in the world is the motivation necessary to sacrifice going to come from? The world only encourages sacrifice if it leads to an increase in personal wealth, fame, and power. Where is the motivation to put someone else first in your life going to come from? The world's motto is "Look out for number one"! Where in the world is the faith in the permanence of marriage going to come from? One sure as heck better have a motivation for staying married when the S—T hits the fan, which is inevitable.

There's got to be a larger picture; there's got to be a story. There's got to be something bigger than yourselves to believe in when "that certain feeling" subsides and the disappointments and disillusionments take hold. This is what faith is. To repeat, I believe and teach that as a Christian, the one major tenet of belief is that "there is no greater love in life than to give one's life for one's friends." We all want to be loved, to experience love, and share love. This is our nature. Jesus does this ultimately and tragically, by physically dying for us. We do this by living lives of compassion and "carrying the burdens of others; celebrating the resurrections of others."

God is love. We are made in his/her image, and God wants us to live in a loving world, and love in a world that is living. This is the covenant. God gives us the support of a spouse to minister to us according to the covenant of Abraham, Moses, and Jesus—permanently, faithfully, and for others. The bride is given by God to the groom. She is to minister to him and find happiness in this giving. Yes, believe it or not, one necessary prerequisite in order to be married is that they are happy. *You'd be surprised!* The groom is given by God to the bride to minister to her and find happiness in giving this gift.

So what I try to do in marriage preparation is help them discover: (1) Why they have chosen marriage as a lifestyle; (2) why they have picked each other for this lifestyle (*"Because we love each other" is not an acceptable answer*); and (3) though they intend to be married, a natural concern is whether they have the mental, emotional, and psychological capacity to be married in the first place. This entails discussions about such things like communication or whether they historically split up every time they have an argument or if one or both struggle with self-esteem issues; how they handle trust; and whether they have a history of permanence and longevity in work and relationships, etc. *Believe me, not everyone is right for marriage.*

Marriage preparation is really cool when the couple is cool. Many are not. I remember a couple, I'll call them Binky and Buffy. They were so cute it was repulsive. They couldn't keep their hands off each other and he had a glowing hickey on his neck. They were a whopping twenty years old and knew everything. I remember asking them, "Doesn't the idea of being married forever to one person at this early stage in your life scare you?" Her response: "Oh Father! Being married to Binky forever just isn't long enough!" I wanted to barf. You don't say stuff like that to a celibate who hasn't had his eight cups of coffee that day. They were in a hurry, and wanted the "Ride 'em in, let 'em out . . . Rawhide!" approach.

So if I am entrusted to be their priest during this process, it is an honor and I am going to do my best to assure them that they receive the fullest experience of God's love in the process. But, in all honesty, you'd be surprised at the total futility of some of these couples. You'd think that I was asking a stumper with, "So, why do you want to get married?" Like, this is a trick question? When I ask it, their reaction is unbelievably similar to the typical eight-year-old kid confessing his sins for the first time.

"So, why are you here?" He looks up in helpless wonder.

"Because my mommy told me I was personally responsible for killing Jesus at the ripe age of eight!" When I query the couple about their motivations for marriage, eight out of ten couples' pairs of eyes turn up into the air, and I've never figured out what the kids or the couples are looking up for! Why not just live together? It sure doesn't bother any of my friends. You want babies? You don't need to be married to have children.

"Oh Father, we couldn't have bastards, now, could we?" Ugh. Like, how is anyone going to know? If someone knows me as a bastard it's only because my old man called me one all the time.

"Oh Father, to live in sin for the rest of your life is not allowed by the Church." Church? Smurch! Without sounding conde- scending, I gently pursue with them that since they've been living together for three years how do they expect their "married experi- ence" to be different than their "we're just living together" experi- ence? If this is to be a transition to a more fulfilling way of living, then how will married life be different from the way you are living a "seemingly" married life now? Good God! How do I know this stuff anyway? I'm not married. *I could go on and on with wedding sto- ries, but I am trying to give up being cynical for Lent, and the rest of my life.* But with all the irritating paperwork, process, rehearsals, and nonsense that come with marriage preparation, I often wonder why the Church is sticking their noses in people's intimacies any- way. On the other hand, though, I totally dig the Church's rever- encing and enhancing marriage as Christ's sacrament. It truly is a ministry. It is what the bride and groom sacrifice for, and why they support each other—collaboratively. Now, if the apples try to make the orange an apple, *Divorce Court* here we come!

I totally enjoy preparing and celebrating weddings in inner- city Los Angeles. As a matter of fact, I have enjoyed my priesthood the most in the inner city. As I hope I've conveyed, the St. Agatha's assignment has changed my life forever. It is such a privilege and an honor to serve these wonderful people. My whole way of honoring and loving God, faith, church, people, and self has been a total miracle in the midst of this parish's wonderful ordinariness. The simplicity, spirituality, and generosity of a people living quite complicated lives in unimaginable living conditions are miracles to me. Their ease with expressing affection, want, dignity, and family is a major key to my own freedom as a man and priest.

Equally miraculous for me is how people who felt either a friendship with me or felt that I had touched their lives in some way generously journeyed with me to support my new parish family. My business friends, celebrity friends, and good old friends came to help me clean the place, set up the office, organize the files, while at the same time providing funds to facilitate "WE ARE OPEN FOR BUSINESS!" For a right-brained, progressive, relational, defeated, and vulnerable man, I had finally found a home while experiencing church as a predominantly left-brained, historically stuck, impersonal, and righteous religious institution.

The kids on the streets; the people in the markets; people saying "*Hola,* Padre!" as I walk my dog, Spirit; the fruit trucks rolling up and down the street; the vendors selling *elotes* (corn); the roosters; and the family barbecues with thirty people crammed on a front lawn abounded. The gangsters, police sirens and helicopters, nightly gunshots, murders, sixty-plus break-ins into the parish, and car washes to help pay for homeboys' funerals melded into eighty-hour workweeks, enabling us to aid minimum-wage families of six (featuring a sick momma moving in from Mexico or New Orleans). All of these remarkable, miraculous, and ordinary events mean this is home and it is good. Occasionally, some of this experience appears wrong—witness the many suburbanites who come here to worship and minister as equals to their new "inner city" sisters and brothers.

It's funny—I thought only white people were racists. I discovered that racism exists all over, still. It is really sad and disheartening. I can't tolerate racism and bigotry while trying to have the various cultures commingle together as a true community. The early Christian community dealt with bigotry from the Jewish and Gentile cultures which wished to disrupt the original disciples. Here, at the parish, we make deliberate attempts to empower, teach, and respect the beautiful qualities of each culture. We've been quite successful at it, thanks be to God. I have come to see racial and cultural integration as an opportunity to behold rather than as a problem to be solved. When I arrived—the blond-haired, blue-eyed white boy from the Westside—I immediately saw more commonalities than obstacles. The need for family, the tensions, and injustices that come from living in a white society and the need to express one's own spiritual reality (not a "Latin ritual") were forefront.

So, unlike some of my Roman Catholic peers, instead of preaching hell and brimstone, I preach heaven and acceptance. As I have said, if you want to go church and feel like you've had the life sucked right out of you, there are plenty of churches that can take care of you—but not ours. I preach what is God, more than what is sin. I preach about people's goodness, forgiveness, and tolerance—not revenge and condemnation of the sinner.

All are welcome at St. Agatha's. Who am I to deny God to anyone? Even though life is hard, we are blessed, we need to show it, and we do. That's why people travel from all over to worship and minister here. It's not because of the priest—it's because of the Spirit of the place. It's happy, welcoming, exciting, and friendly—how un-Catholic!

Of course, where there is God, there is also evil lurking nearby. Now I am not one preoccupied with "the devil," but I firmly believe that Satan, the tendency for EVIL, does certainly exist. *And now, Bush is defining for us who the "axis of evil" is? Yikes!* I have come to live with the experience of bigotry that still exists in our land. I have come to experience the sadness and indignity that is afforded good people who don't enjoy legal status. I have come to live with what others may call the "hopeless" and thank God for the hope they have given me—and the hope they give to each other. It is a privilege to serve and be served the love of God lived by those who are seen as loveless, poor, and deprived. They may not have the education, social graces, and creature comforts that we from the 'burbs take for granted. But they do know pain. They've been to the cross and are true examples of resurrection.

I know I have also been a disappointment to some. Truly, the most painful aspect of ministering here has been seeing some leave the parish because I wasn't enough for them. Still, I do give everyone a thousand chances. I rarely say no. There have been times, though, when I have had to finally lay down the law against those who act out in meanness, cruelty, and vindictiveness. I know I am not always liturgically correct. I am rarely, if ever, Roman by personality. I guess I live on the edge and welcome the adventure. I react to bigotry of any kind, and won't hold on to the politically correct "We were here first" preferential treatment. I challenge ministers who tear down and demean others because "they feel they have been given a special authority by God" to hold fast the religious tenets handed down over the years, and I don't give a hoot in hell if you're Catholic, Jewish, legal, illegal, old, young, gay, or straight—or all of the above. This is California, you know!

I am not here to be correct. I am here to live out and pursue what I have perceived as Truth. And I would like to invite you all to enjoy the same. If that Truth does not fit the specific spiritual needs of this community, then I will move on. I can only share my experience—"I was blind, but now I see." I was lost, and now I'm found. I was wounded and now I'm healed. I was abandoned and now I'm welcomed. I was rejected and now I am accepted. I was sad and now I'm joyous. I see life not death; hope not despair; dignity and not futile condemnation to depression. I see heaven, even when in hell. In short, I was on the cross of feeling misunderstood and underestimated by my peers but not by the people. Now, I am enjoying the resurrection of feeling understood and valued because I chose a new Way. I have come to discover the delightful freedom and hysterically great times that come with being on an adventure of understanding others and giving value to the hopeless. And I'm having a wonderful time at it—I ain't dying here! I receive much more than I give.

Much more.

I guess, in hindsight, this is the major reason why I enjoy living and ministering in the hood. People of the hood have justifiably felt misunderstood and underestimated. The heroes are those who have had the courage to better themselves in spite of it all while not sitting on the pity pot pissing and moaning about it. They are off the cross! They help each other carry their wood. This reality check has been a "coming to Jesus" for me. *Lord, grant that I may not so much seek to be understood as to understand.* The biggest surprise for me in all of this is that I have stayed, going on my ninth year. And though I get more hoopla and affirmation now than ever, I feel in all honesty that I have not done anything special here. All I have allowed for myself is what many people think they dare not do: be open and human. All I have done is whatever I humanly could to recognize, affirm, and enhance the delightful, surprising spirit that was given this place—the spirit experienced and witnessed among the faithful remnant who only needed to be shown their freedom. So I did. Then of course I stayed—It was immediately a win-win.

I may be dumb but I am not stupid enough to mess with the Holy Spirit!

I thank God that he has led me to these little pearls of affirmation that, in spite of my sins, everything is going to be okay. These have caused me to continue with joy and freedom. It is in being open, in allowing the Spirit and empowering the priesthoods of the laity, that a resurrection of this community and my own person has resulted. The church is full, we are no longer on welfare (archdiocesan subsidy), the racial and various other cultures are getting along, and we presently have approximately three hundred kids on the parish grounds (half upstairs in the recently re-opened middle school and the other half downstairs in our summer camp, Good in the Hood). Our parish staff is constantly growing and reevaluating itself as the parish and its needs grow, the once depressed "ghetto-looking" grounds are now cleaned up with lavish landscapes and state-of-the-art facilities, and people are coming to an "alternate" way of looking at God, church, and each other through the Catholic religion.

The generosity of some people amazes me. Though the parish gets plenty of affirmation and attention for turning itself around, when all is said and done, if it weren't for the Jean Guelpas, the Joe Galvans, the Kathleen Joneses, and the Yvonne Shoulderses, the miracle would have never come to fruition. Joe Galvan is a parishioner and everyone's favorite. "If you don't like Joe Galvan," I often say, "then you need therapy!" Joe is an Apache Navajo, longhaired, Native American man who has found home and life here. This man, also a weightlifter at Gold's Gym, Venice, is here every week purchasing and arranging the flowers in the church. A weightlifter doing flowers—who knew?! He often is here on his vacation time helping his brother and sister parishioners decorate the parish grounds when the festivals arise, and is also one of our ushers every single Sunday. To have watched this once quiet loner become a vivacious, generous pillar of our community has been so much fun to watch. His greatest gift is his person and he lends himself out most generously to the parish community. With his use of color, and creative spirit, he has enlivened in others a permission to be creative in worship, prayer, and processing of God's entire world. He is also a friend and brother. And since I am a hurricane of complications, we constantly aggravate each other. But we also know that we'd do anything for each other—it's called loyalty.

Then there's Jean Guelpa. Along the same tune as Joe, Jean is a lawyer whom I have known for most of my priesthood. She is wonderful and, like me, doesn't always believe it! If I'm Batman, she was my Robin (and vice versa) when ministering at all three of my priestly assignments. Upon my arrival here at St. Agatha's, it was Jean who got the parish office up and running. It was Jean who helped us initiate the Christmas Adopt-a-Family program, the original attempts at a youth ministry, and the many out-reaches to the poor of the community here at the parish. It was Jean who volunteered hundreds and hundreds of hours to serve the poor and imprisoned of the parish, while writing the weekly bulletin. Jean also served and continues to serve as a loyal confi-dant when I get totally frustrated by the defeatisms of my self, staff, and parish. When the parish office was downstairs and I lived upstairs, Jean was truly a welcome face in what was a depressed ministry office from what I was used to in the suburbs.

I remember so clearly the initial experience of the place my first day on the job. The constant litany of "I don't know" to sim-ple inquiries as to where something was or how something was done by my predecessor was strange. The "Oh Father, we could never do that" when I suggested new and creative ways of ministry was equally an eye-opener. The immediate challenges of being in this strange new place and inner-city environment had its sur-prises, but the true joys of the parish immediately made all these worthwhile.

Then there is Kathleen Jones, who was commonly referred to by the female elders of the parish as "Mrs. Deasy." When I had felt totally vulnerable to the criticisms and apathy of my surround-ings it was Kathleen, and her son, Ernest, who I refer to as one of my anchors, who provided me emotional rescue. Kathleen was truly a saint "with a bite." She was present, caring, and ministered to the ill and those who mourn their dead. She counted the tithing/collection every single Sunday (with her faithful disciples

Virgie and Rudy) and she was not afraid of me. Though her "sharp" honesty was not always welcome, it was always laced with genuine love and care for me as a person and the parish as a place. She referred to me as "her priest," and died on January 1, 2004. Her son called me at six thirty that morning, and I was so honored to be there with him.

Then, there's Yvonne Shoulders who quietly oversees our wonderful little church. She sets everything up for both the English and Spanish Masses, and participates in all three of our choirs. What I enjoy most about her is watching her pray. This dear woman may never make it to the cover of *Newsweek* (never say never) but she is consistent, loyal, strong, and one of the best priests with whom I have ever had the honor to serve. And of course, there are many more—lawyers, teachers, counselors, and supporters—whom I've been blessed with, who help me keep this holy, beautiful ball bouncing in the air. Without their support I never would have made this miracle shine.

It was so much easier when I first started, though. There was an excitement in the air and in my heart over the new life that the elder African American community and the larger Spanish-speaking community had prayed would return to their parish. I need to feel excited about my ministry and I hate monotony. I continue to feel excited over the growth and vitality of the place because I remember how dead people claimed the place was. And I remember how dead I believed myself to be. Most of the parish elders whom I began with have died. I miss them so much, but these people made their mark: they helped bring on the resurrections in this parish and shared the excitement about the new resurrections that were occurring! And sure, there continue to be crosses (as well as thorns, hangnails, warts, and pimples). Having said this, let me tell you about the most recent miracle we have experienced.

With a growing membership in the parish of all kinds (we've literally become a sanctuary, a fallout shelter for those who have given up on finding a Spirit-based, happy community, no matter what walk of life), there also comes with this a loss of awareness and appreciation of the history of the place—our newer members didn't experience the parish's resurrection and release from the cross. The newbies might easily presume that "this" was always here. Though many have found excitement in their going to church on Sunday experience, their excitement for the Monday through Saturday life is often unknown and not viewed with the same amazement and awe that I want. So, with the growth of resources provided from this place to the community, and the unrecognized efforts and sacrifices that come with these services, there grows a tiredness and cynicism among myself and other ministers from fighting the same old depressions, denials, and fears.

Though I love the place, there comes the constant and annoy-ing racial bigotry, especially among the Bible-quoting "holier than thous." At a recent Sunday Mass I saw an African American man deliberately ignore and reject a handshake from a white guy. There is the never-ending two-facedness of people, including myself. For example, some people will literally come up to you and kiss you on the cheek while, just minutes before, I had heard them outside my kitchen window plotting another scheme to turn me over to the Sanhedrin! The constant whining of spoiled rotten ministers that I don't love them enough and don't spend enough time with them is endless. The endless shootings, funer-als, spousal beatings, burglaries, and lootings by unsupervised children, and the resultant griping and blaming of everyone else for their problems goes on. The gossip, rumors, and decrease in parish tithing due to the economy and protests over Church scan-dals, and the stronger belief in hell rather than in heaven—man, it gets old.

It's not that I know what to do with all this mess. All I know is that even though there are good things going on all over the place, when I get tired and overextended I can only feel it's all a mess. I want more than ever to fix it all, and hate that I can't. As my best priest-friend Father Lawrence Signey says, "Ken will do anything for anybody . . . anybody . . . until you stab him in the back!" Other friends say, "When Ken starts buying Lotto tickets, you know he's about had it!" Today's numbers by the way are 9, 20, 23, 26, and 34, with meganumber 12—another $26 million that I didn't win.

Just this morning, after a long weekend of celebrating four Masses and, frankly, dreading going over to the Parish Center, I was tempted to tape the following to my office door:

YOU MAY KNOCK AND COME IN . . . BUT NO WHINING PLEASE! I AM MORE THAN AVAILABLE TO YOU . . . BUT NOT FOR WHINING.

IF YOU AREN'T GETTING ALONG WITH SOMEONE, I DON'T WANT TO HEAR ABOUT IT UNTIL YOU HAVE TRIED TO FIX THE PROBLEM YOURSELF.

BEFORE YOU PRESENT TO ME YOUR MINISTERIAL PROB-LEMS . . . BRING ME POSSIBLE SOLUTIONS ABOUT HOW TO REMEDY THE SITUATION.

IF YOU CONTINUE TO COMMUNICATE FRUSTRATIONS TO EACH OTHER THROUGH E-MAILS WHEN YOU COULD EASILY TALK TO THE PERSON DOWN THE HALL OR WALK ACROSS THE PARKING LOT . . . YOU GET WHAT YOU DESERVE.

IF YOU EXPECT A PERSON WITH NO WINGS TO FLY . . . YOU GET WHAT YOU DESERVE.

IF YOU THINK THAT NO ONE LOVES YOU AROUND HERE AND THAT NO ONE SUPPORTS YOUR MINISTRY . . . YOU ARE DEAD WRONG AND YOU SHOULD BE ASHAMED OF YOURSELF! QUIT BLAMING EVERYONE ELSE BEFORE EVEN LOOKING AT YOUR OWN BEHAVIOR.

IF YOU ARE FRUSTRATED ABOUT NOT HAVING A PERFECT WORLD . . . DON'T BLAME ME AND EACH OTHER . . . BRING IT TO GOD OR GO FIND ANOTHER WORLD!

I AM PROUD OF ALL OF YOU. I AM PROUD OF HAVING A GREAT PARISH, A GREAT LIFE, AND A GREAT DAY. DO YOU REALLY WANT TO RUIN IT FOR YOUR PEOPLE, YOURSELF, AND FOR ME?

QUIT WHINING! WE ADULTS NEED TO LEARN FROM THE BEHAVIOR OF THE CHILDREN WHO ARE ON THIS CAMPUS. THEY ARE ACTING WAY MORE MATURE THAN MOST OF US.

Funny thing is, the above is my own passive-aggressive way of whining. *Get off the cross, Deasy! Someone else needs the wood!*

But it is when I am spent, when I am just beaten up and tired, that I am more receptive to being resurrected anew—ALWAYS. When enough is enough, the Lord zaps me with a better of way of thinking and living and believing. The cross always becomes an opportunity for growth. With this growth comes the feeling of God's presence and awareness of his goodness. In other words, I feel worthwhile, dignified, and empowered with a purpose. With this growth of vision come hope, potential, and feelings of empowerment and the awareness of countless social and religious absurdities that exist in the world that I feel powerless to change.

This is called experiencing God. So, I know that when I am in the "desert" of feeling nothing that I am most susceptible to being saved. No matter how much I try to deny it, you can't go to resurrection without going to the cross. Again. When I am totally fed up with it all and am totally experiencing the "I'm done!," knowing and feeling that there is absolutely nothing left to offer or gain, the Lord zaps me with a most loving and divine kicking of my soul.

Do you want to know about the most recent? First, there is Kaye Coleman and my Jewish friends. Putting this into context, the priest abuse scandal had taken its toll on me. For all Catholics, the sadness and frustration that came with the abuse scandal (not only the actual abuse of children/adults but also the way in which the bishops appeared to have responded to this crime) was a huge wear and tear on our souls.

The victims: Who, how, and where are they today? How will they be compensated? How could they ever be compensated? The victimizers: Who are they? Why did they do what they did? What are their rights in all of this? The bishops: What did they know, and when did they know it? And after the settlements are awarded by the supposed plentiful insurance coverage, what will be done for ongoing compassionate support?

And now, for the laity: How do they see themselves, postscandal? How do they see priests now? Though the religion is shaken, how is their faith holding up?

And priests: How do we see ourselves as we attempt to handle the shame and responsibility we all share by association? How do we see tomorrow?

During this dark period in American Catholicism I, like many priests, am totally outraged and furious at the leadership of the Church and their manner of handling the victims AND the accused. Even as I write this, I find myself tempering my language and reactions to it all because, on one hand, there exist all the appearances of a "cover up" (whether it appears to be a corporate cover-up or a natural reluctance to air the dirty laundry of the family), and there is the question of "What were they thinking?" when it comes to saying one thing and being busted doing another. On the other hand, there are the personal positive/life-giving experiences that I have had with the cardinals and bishops of the accused padres which have been good, wholesome, and well-intentioned. As a result, there is that feeling of "I just can't believe it" when the clash of the negative and positive experiences comes to the forefront.

Like a parent in the bleachers, I feel totally frustrated about what the coaches with the red hats as a corporate entity are doing on the sidelines. What could they possibly do but assure that this stuff won't happen again? I have no idea of the practical financial and legal implications of owning up to the moral responsibility of restitution to the victims of abuse. Though there is not enough money in the world to fix the harm done, any monies that do go out that insurances will not cover will be taken from those services that assist the poor and the needy—thus the anger and fury at the coming unknown.

The need to be cool and calm during it all while wanting to fix this (or just wanting to be invited into the discussion of why, how, how could this happen) is a total pisser. Yet, I've had to get up in front of my congregation two times and announce, "There's been another one that I have to inform you of." (There have been three priests assigned here who have been accused of the sexual abuse of minors.)

Do you think that someone would say, "How are you, Ken?" Just a few. Ironically, it's been one of the victims whom I have been talking with who calls all the time to ask, "How are you doing with all of this?" But I have to make these dark announcements and find myself saying, "I'm sorry!"

"I have been asked to read this letter from the Vicar of Clergy's Office referring to a priest who had been assigned here in the past who is under investigation for allegedly sexually abusing a minor. If you have any information that you wish to contribute to the investigation, please call 1-800-355-2545."

Lovely. But alas, the glass is still half full.

Four things I now know:

1. The American Church has never changed (grown) so much in the past year than it has since the beginning of Vatican II in the late 1960s. *The city does not put in a stop sign until many get hurt crossing the street!*

2. That similar to the political motivations behind going into Iraq and to the current corporate scandals on Wall Street: when it comes to the rising suspicions and accusations leveled at the U.S. Conference of Bishops, we'll never know the whole story. *If you believe everything you see, read, and hear in the news, sorry, you're incredibly naive.*

3. It has been a horrific time for all concerned and, by the way, not all are concerned. *No comment.*

4. And, for me, the new blessings here have been my new Jewish friends who have come forward asking, "How are you doing in all of this, Fadda?"

Though I and the parish have been hugely blessed with a large support of my Catholic brothers and sisters when it has come to helping the poor of the neighborhood and getting this place up on its feet, only a small handful have had the courage (or sensitivity) to have simply called and inquired how I am, a current priest and man, doing with all of this. *Bejeezus! I don't even touch myself anymore. I don't want anyone dialing "1-800-Father-Touched-My-Binky!"*

Though it surely is a personal question that one may be afraid to ask any priest, it has been my Jewish friends who, not blinded by the centuries of "yellow waxy Catholic buildup," and who simply saw me as a guy who must be saddened by all of this "family scandal," who have aggressively extended care and friendship. Now, that I set up my inner disposition, I'm ready to explain how God gave me Kaye.

Instrumental to adding a positive bent and relief to this whole priest abuse mess has been Kaye Coleman, the "Irish Waitress to the Stars" (who most presume to be Jewish) at Nate 'n Al's Delicatessen in Beverly Hills, who started introducing me to her Jewish clientele. With the daily, "Geeezus! Oh my Gawd! Everyone GD morning I have to open the papers and read about some priest fondling some kid! What were these guys doing?!" this good-hearted recovering-Catholic woman who was away from the faith for centuries (Okay, a few decades) was a godsend. She is afraid of nothing and no one and calls them as she sees them. She is a prophet. She led me to discover the beauty of the Jewish people who, until they met me, thought she was Jewish also.

"Don't tell them I'm Catholic," she would joke, "it's bad on the tips!"

Truly, it was Kaye and her friends who I passionately and most lovingly refer to as "my Jews" who have been the largest communal source of laughter, release, and "we got your back" during all of this. Syd, Asher, Lois, Richard, Sam, Vickie, and a popular prime-time talk show host who meet regularly at Nate 'n Al's would be my sure solace. They would ask me questions Gentiles would never ask a priest! Of course, with Kaye, "any friend of Kaye's is a friend of mine!" Though I am not sure that her behavior is more Jewish or Irish influenced (Jews created guilt. The Irish perfected it), she really is a diamond of wholeness and genuineness. She is a waitress, as I said, and she is such a unique and caring person. She ministers while serving up sides of cream cheese and toasted bagels. She listens to everyone's problems, cares for the elderly, and volunteers at a hospice. As I have often said, when referring to the ancient and age-old Israeli-Palestinian conflict, "politicians and religious leaders cannot solve this problem. Isn't there some common hero who both sides really like we could send?"

I would send Kaye. Not only would she get them to sit down, her ability to cut through the BS is unreal and no one ever walks away offended (and does she have a sharp tongue). This is my Kay-zee. She is inflicted with cancer in her body, and though the serum that sickens her was made possible by the thousands of dollars raised by her friends, she doesn't stop being Kaye. She seemingly has been at everyone's deathbed, and now she hauls me to everyone's deathbed. I'm at Cedar Sinai these days more often than any Catholic hospital. Now, through her, I not only experience a new life-giving friend, but I've discovered my alter ego-Jewish community.

The Jews—Passovers, functions, bagels, and the loyalty along with the forwardness—the handshake with a twenty or a one hundred-dollar bill tucked inside with the whisper: "Do something for ya'self, will ya?" With my Jewish family, there is none of this timidness and awe around "Father." God, I like that. I love that! There's no bowin' and scrapin'. It is no surprise when at a Beverly Hills function where there is obviously a large amount of Jewish folk there, I'll be working the Westside of the room (Kay is working the Eastside) talking about the parish, cracking a few jokes, hearing jokes about the priest and the rabbi that I have already heard a hundred times before. It is also no surprise when an ex-Catholic-married-to-a-Jew comes up to me and confesses, "I'm an ex-Catholic, Father."

My response, "Well, I'm a current Jew!" (and a recovering Catholic). Just like my foreign-born Irish elders (i.e., the FBI) my Jewish friends are not impressed by one's title as much as their genuineness and credibility which, by the way, are not synonymous to perfection, sanctity, and the stereotypical messianic position. *In other words, you can't bullshit a bullshitter!*

I am looking forward to my bar mitzvah on my fiftieth birth-day—no bris necessary, thank you. The best Jewish gathering I've ever experienced was a Passover Seder meal in Beverly Hills. While the guests read the thirty-plus-page ritual in the dining room the bar was open and being enjoyed. *A religious ritual with cocktails? I'm game!* There is too much focus on ancient rituals. Don't get me wrong, I know all too well that these rituals were founded on important religious issues. But with the diminishing quantity of priests, the main concern is who's going to say Mass?

Mass. Mass. Mass. Everyone wants Mass. Of course, while attending to the unceasing demands for "We want Mass," and tol-erating the annoying chewing of gum, refusals to sing, reluctance to participate and observe any evidence of having a pulse during this ritual, the dear people of God have no apparent idea that the most important part of the Mass is the concluding charge to "Go in peace to love and serve the Lord AND one another"! As my vision of my own priesthood has become more one of empower-ing the ministers rather than being the Mass giver, there has come a loss of the real reason for wanting to be a priest in the first place. This minister had to become the administrator, teacher, and coach, and was no longer "one of the gang." So, as I continue to experience "hands on" ministry so I don't die, the administrating part of this deal is something I don't enjoy and can't seem to find peace in. The countless efforts balancing the age-old Irish Catholic scourge that "I am not enough" with the divine promise that "My grace will be sufficient" had become, again, quite exhausting. My urgings to love and care had not wavered. My body and emotional psyche were running on impulse power. I not only needed the strength to plant the seeds but also needed to feel the joy and satisfaction that come with watching them grow.

These empty patterns of life are common to me. My friends comment on these "down" rhythms of my passions all the time. They say, "We are concerned for you most when you get depleted."

And it is in these down times that I impatiently wait for the next miracle knowing sure well that it will come. I just hope to God I don't miss it! See? Here I go—worrying already about tomorrow while ignoring the only thing that exists—the NOW. The miracle of the NOW found me in a young person named Grover. This is a guy, a twenty-one-year-old African American, who looks like he's sixteen. This seemingly "mentally disturbed" young man was showing up at all the Masses (English and Spanish) and sitting quietly by himself. He never caused trouble though he unintentionally disturbed people with his unceasing stare. He didn't talk. He was obviously lost and needing to be found.

In the beginning, March 2003, Grover appeared to be just another mentally ill, homeless person—probably a drug-damaged youth off the streets and from some screwed-up family wherein the only kids who have the same father are the twins. To me he was just another needy person who, again, doesn't seem to be afforded the slightest chance of having a decent life; another damaged person who cannot be repaired and will just end up just letting you down anyway.

Hey, you can't save everybody, right? I mean, "The poor we will have with us always," right? When I think of all the youth, ex-cons and gangsters that I have hoped to "repair," and who have totally flaked in living up to their end of the bargain (and who have broken my heart as a result), Grover was just another one I needed to protect the community from, protect my bleeding heart from, and who will eventually disappear into the forgotten.

Ministerially, I had gotten to the point that I would bet the farm and my person, time, and talent on the prevention rather than on the repair that people like Grover needed. After ministering in jails and the hood with the homeless, gangsters, and all sorts of socially deemed "hopeless cases," I had come to believe that these dear souls needed more time, follow-up, energy, and "one-on-one" attention than I could give. Thank God that not everyone ignores the hope that motivates one to embark on a course of "repairing" someone else or I wouldn't be here today. I do not forget the good people who transformed me, this once much damaged young man, into being who I am today. Yet, my own ministerial experiences have taught that if you "nip the problem in the bud" early, there is a better chance of a positive outcome in the future.

The way I was thinking, I chose to focus more on supporting community organizations in the neighborhood (for example, don't say "get the kids off the streets" unless you have a place for them to go, such as youth centers, summer camps, and sports) rather than just taking one kid at a time and trying to work with him. I chose to focus more on empowering planning programs for education and health for parents and their children (when the kids are in Bible Class, the parents go to the Parish Hall learning about Moses, Jesus, immigration laws, and venereal disease). Though I will continue to support programs that put Band-Aids on certain problems such as food for the hungry, medicine for the sick, and a few bucks for those who need to pay their utilities, I find myself focusing more on the laws of the land that inflict hunger, illness, and poverty.

So, instead of just funding prescriptions to the poor I also have learned to support programs that deal with preventative health issues, and inform the community where one can bring their ill and what support services are at their disposal. Instead of just giving out motel vouchers to the homeless, I feel the need to also focus on affordable housing for the working poor. Instead of just helping the working poor with their utility bills, I find myself becoming more sensitive to the alarming rise of costs in Los Angeles that make it impossible for the forty-hour-a-week laborer to live with dignity and allow more time for them to be with their families. Instead of relying on elected officials and civic leadership to finance programs for the youth who are just sitting at home because Mom and Dad (if they even have those) are working eighty-hour weeks, I focus more on how we can do something ourselves—open our own doors, open our own wallets, and open our own gates.

Sounds pretty hip, huh?

Well, it is hip. For me, though, all this planning and processing has taken me away from feeling the joy that comes with the one-on-one ministering to people. Inevitably, what comes with the planning and processing of prevention programs of education and motivation is more meetings, paperwork, schmoozing, costs, managing, and hope. My relational self, though, hungers for more of the "hands-on" approach. I am much better at cooking the meal than inviting, budgeting, and planning the meal. So, with Grover's arrival came, initially, the feeling of dread and powerlessness. Though he was unknowingly scaring the people in church, I, having ministered in Santa Monica and being very comfortable around the mentally ill, kept an eye on him. Not only did I sense he wasn't about to hurt anybody, there was something that drew me to him—he was not just another problem.

Plus, I figured he'd go away; they all do eventually. They either get arrested or they die. Grover kept showing up, though. Day after day, in the morning and the evening, Grover was sitting in the front pew at daily Mass eyes locked on me. He was squeaky clean, well-groomed, and well, different. There was a simplicity and purity about the kid that was very calming, but what the heck. He'll go away soon. Then one Friday evening, he shows up at church with a much damaged eye. He was beaten up the night before. The amazing thing for me to observe, though, was whom Grover was sitting next to: an eye surgeon. I proudly watched Dr. Ron reach out to this "untouchable" and help him. *Lord, God! You rock! Thanks for walking with Grover!*

Dr. Ron prescribed some antibiotics for Grover. When I drove Grover to the pharmacy (experiencing a little hands-on ministry that I was missing) I learned more of his story. He was homeless.

He was living in an abandoned van in one of the most dangerous parts of the neighborhood. He was robbed of everything he had and beaten up at the laundromat where he daily washed his clothes and watched TV to kill time. This guy must really be nuts. Anyone with a brain isn't going to be homeless in the hood. If you're going to be homeless you go to Santa Monica! You'll get robbed, beaten, and killed if you're homeless in this part of town. As Grover and I walked through Sav-On Drugs, I found myself buying him underwear, a jacket, socks, soap, shampoo, and stuff like that. I really was enjoying myself. It felt good. I knew I was just putting a Band-Aid on the problem, but I knew I wasn't able to do much for this kid. But I had to do something for him, and for me.

But hey—he'll go away soon. They all do.

When we returned to the church there was another godsend standing around: Gilberto, a social worker, who was preparing to become a Catholic. Here is the Lord working again—sending Gilberto to us! Gilberto helped us out with some social agencies in Los Angeles—what a gift to know that Gilberto would be a resource if needed. With all these godsends of Gilberto and Dr. Ron and so many more came the affirmation that God is with me in this. There must a plan and we must be doing something right! So, with Grover, there was the "Let's see where He'll take us with this guy!" So far, I have broken every promise I had ever made to myself about getting involved with this type of situation. I had grown, though. I really wasn't as emotionally fragile as I would have been years ago and I was strengthened by knowing that I belonged to a praying community. I figured that what little I was doing for Grover was more than anyone else was giving, and it was probably the most Grover had ever had. This was looking up. Maybe he won't go away.

One Sunday evening there came a heavy rainstorm that hit Los Angeles. Grover did not show up for Mass, which was very odd. Where's Grover? He was gone. Damn, I knew it—they all go eventually. But, I didn't feel good about it. I really started to feel guilty. Here I am, living in a big old house all by myself, but, hey, there's no way he can stay here. I don't have the time to repair this guy. And, besides, no young kid is living with me in the rectory! Yet, on that very day, I had preached that "the reason there is so much hunger in the world is because we eat too much"; that "the reason there is so much homelessness in the world is because we don't open our doors and share our spare bedrooms." So all week I thought about this homeless Grover that I did not open my house to—a mentally ill kid living in a crappy part of town, in a broken-down, old van while I am in a big old house by myself all warm and safe. Bless me, Father, for I have sinned. I am a total hypocrite! I refused to give YOU shelter and genuine care because I was afraid.

Three days later, thank God, Grover showed up. He had been hiding from the rain, staying in the abandoned van that was the home he preferred to the one his mother and sister shared. He was wet and smelly. I felt relieved to see him which I thought was interesting. My heart was having a tug-of-war match with my brain. *Easy Ken!* Remember, you can't save everyone! BUT WE CAN SAVE THIS ONE! (Or at least try). But don't get in over your head, you hear me? I was convinced that Grover was sent to us to be saved and to save us. To save me? *"The reason there is so much hunger in the world is because we eat too much. The reason there is so much homelessness in the world is because we don't open our doors and share our spare bedrooms."* Grover and I immediately began searching for a cheap motel room in the hood. It wasn't easy finding one that was cheap and clean. Most "tolerable" motels did not want anything to do with Grover because of his apparent mental illness. It was alarming enough seeing the fear people have of the mentally ill, but what was more alarming were the suspicions that these motel managers had toward me. What is this white, blond, blue-eyed guy doing in this part of town with this young kid at my motel? I, trying to use some leverage to acquire a room at a good rate, asserted, "I'm the priest down the street."

Whoops, a priest with a young boy? Again, this didn't help matters. I was growing really frustrated upon learning of the lack of quality services, compassion, and patience that exist for people like Grover. Yet, a very good and wonderful friend of mine who is connected to the entertainment industry, I'll call him "T" (who would kill me if I mentioned his name here) offered a gesture of "Whatever money you need to take care of Grover let me know." Even with this financial assurance and fraternal support from "T", I am sad to say, I couldn't even find programs for this mentally ill child in a twenty-year-old body. I was finally able to land him a motel room for a few weeks which gave me time to assess the situation while, at the same time, having to run my own inner-city parish. On one hand, I was feeling quite alive and challenged. I was feeling good. At the same time, though, I was also feeling powerless, useless, and . . . *oh my God, what did I get myself into here?!*

Marco, my secretary at the time, was a tremendous help. Having gained some trust and information from Grover, I learned that he had been under a doctor's care—he showed me his Los Angeles County Mental Health card. I had asked Marco to call his doctor to make an appointment so we could finally find out what this kid's story is. You can't imagine the shock when Marco called me and told me, "The police are coming to pick up Grover. He is AWOL from his mental health program! You've got to come back and keep him here until the police come!" I was relieved to at least learn something about his medical history and, specifically, what his problem was—Grover was a diagnosed "paranoid schizophrenic" and was off his meds—and that the matter was about to be resolved by the police coming to take him away, but I still felt devastated. I was turning him over to the authorities, and had to keep him at bay until the cops arrived. *Oh man, was I a Judas or what?* The thought of having him handcuffed and carried away was killing me.

The sting was set and the police came into the conference room where Grover and I were watching the movie *Door to Door,* a story about a mentally challenged but successful businessman. When the police arrived not only was Grover surprised but the look of "You betrayed me" was evident. Grover was not a happy camper and I chose to leave the room while the police worked their magic. *And it was magic!* They were totally cool with Grover. They spent an hour working with him on his level and I was most impressed. They even allowed him one last smoke and, acting on my request, only slapped the handcuffs on him as he slipped into the police car's passenger rear seat. Grover was admitted into the mental health unit of Robert Kennedy Hospital in Los Angeles. I visited him as often as I could. Grover was placed back on his meds and was beginning to get his head adjusted. Amazingly, one of the nurses in the unit was a parishioner of St. Agatha's! *Godsend!* I knew she would take extra care of Grover.

Lord, you are a rascal! You are really with us on this, aren't you? As long as we hang together on this, Lord, I'll allow you to use me! JUST DON'T AGGRAVATE ME! *Please?* One day when I was visiting Grover during the unit's recreation hour there must have been three or four patients who came up to him looking for some type of help—everything from lighting cigarettes and dialing the phone to just listening to their complaining. These poor people were very ill and very medicated. But it was really cool to see even the nurses and the patients cognizant of the goodness of Grover. "You like helping these people, Grover"? I asked.

"Yup."

"Why?!"

"Because you do, Fadda Ken," came his simple response.

Okay, God. Now you're killin' me! ENOUGH ALREADY, LORD! You got me, okay? About three weeks later, Grover gets discharged and shows up at the parish office. Grover had been sprung and was back home living with his momma, brother, and little sister.

As the week progressed Grover would come to the office and just hang out. He was so happy to be out of the hospital and back in the safety of the parish. Up until now, we had never seen him smile; we had never heard him say much and, yet, he would try so hard to relate!

To this day, Grover enjoys hanging out here. As each day goes by it is equally amazing watching the parish community and staff grow in love with this guy. They were seeing something happen before their very eyes that we hear about and preach about but never experience in such an obvious way—it's called conversion. This totally hopeless, homeless, and hapless man was being resurrected before our very eyes and all it took was a little attention and persistence.

My business manager, Tom, and new secretary, Sandra, were very protective and supportive of him. Miraculously, at a staff meeting, my parish personnel lobbied together and made the suggestion, "Why doesn't Grover live here, above the offices upstairs (a former convent)?" Today he is living in one of the bedrooms on top of the Pastoral Center, is attending night adult school to get his high school diploma, and is performing chores during the day. Now, he has become a miraculous sign of hope beyond despair. Not only was Grover a walking miracle, he was bringing out the best, the God, in everyone else. Grover experienced a miracle in the same way that this parish converted my own soul. Often people will say, "The Lord surely sent you to us, Father Ken, to save the parish!" I, in turn, have become quick to respond, "Well, to tell you the truth, the Lord sent you to save me!"

All I can tell you is that from being a driver and passenger in this journey called life, experience has shown me that when anyone is instrumental in giving hope and life to another person, the power of the hope-giver is so ignited that he or she can't help but want to do more. Yet, of course, this is where our freedom of will creeps in. Yes, we have choice. We have a choice to continue to respond and participate in this newly discovered power/experience of God from within or, rather, spend our time on other things. When we pray for miracles we pray for something to come at us from the "God-Beyond"! Yet, when I experienced Grover, I realized that when we pray for miracles we should pray to the "God-Within Us." This is my new emphasis in my mission, I believe.

Among many things, I feel driven to help people discover that real happiness comes from sharing what they already have. But what is needed, first and foremost, is to help people recognize how they've been blessed, I mean really blessed. In so doing, we discover together a Truth inherent in their walk. So, while my dear Church leadership will continue to focus on everyone else's behavior and continue to point out what is sin and who are the sinners, I shall help to point out who and where is God, and that we are all able to approach the frontier of grace in our present moments and not just after we're dead. This is the Holy Spirit, Holy Ghost, or whomever you want to refer to Him or Her. So after many years of therapy, spiritual direction, failures, successes, loves, enemies, awards, and betrayals: Thank you, God. Thank you for the grace and slices of heaven that you have sent me along the road to my own recovery, renewal, and freedom. So many times I wanted to say, "Screw it! And Screw You!" Today though I am feeling good. I still combat feelings of inadequacy, doubt, and fear. But, I am grateful to God to proclaim, I am less angry and more understanding of self and others.

I am no longer feeling or acting dirty. I am not feeling sorry for myself anymore. I have been able to be grateful for all the crud of my past and use it to help others transcend their own crud. With all the mistakes I have made and the guilt that has come with these mistakes, I am not feeling sorry about being me anymore (i.e., ashamed), though I am still banking on a lot of further growth. I am so blessed to have come to my own truth, and remain a priest—TODAY.

Tomorrow doesn't exist.

Yes, there will be other crosses that will find me. I know that if I chose to stay nailed on the cross it is due only to my own lack of faith in my own resurrections that I have been awarded—a lack of faith in the resurrections that I have been allowed to recognize and experience—and a lack of faith in the resurrection that I pray for the generosity to share. I have only touched the tip of the iceberg with my confessions here.

And I am not presuming that we are all on the Titanic.

"Tell them what they already know but don't express," Robert Frost is known to have said.

"Show them what they already have," I conclude.

Okay. Got it?

And so now, ladies and gentlemen, with no further ado—

This is all I know:

I believe in the message and power of the historical Jesus of Nazareth and the Holy Spirit of Christ in the present. Though I get frustrated and exhausted with being a Professional Catholic, just as one vents while trying to understand his lovers, I believe in the mission and can't deny the experiences that it has given me. I know I have often strayed from the course, but am comforted to know that it's not how you start, it's how you finish. If I've made a judgment about another's faults and inadequacies, it is only a judgment—not a conviction or condemnation.

It takes one to know one!

For those of you who still need to see miracles, they're right in front of you.

Please don't wait until you're forty-nine to begin seeing them, and don't gripe that you're not included, when in fact, you have never shown up. For those of you who doubt: Welcome to the club. It's a good thing. It's called being human. For those of you who feel unloved by the Church: Welcome to God's world.

Bruce, in *Bruce Almighty*, when questioning God about freedom of will said: "Why can't I get her to love me?" God replied, "If you can answer that one for me that would be great." Remember, you've got the power, and no one can stop you from using it. Though faith is often presented graphically as rainbows, happy faces, and sunshine—it takes guts! *"You know what your problem is? You keep looking up!"*

It takes the cross. Just remember that the cross is only temporary. The resurrection is now and forever. Amen.

And for those who still need to see the priest as ANSWER-MAN (the *Mr. Goodwrench* of God) ponder on these commonly asked questions that need not a fix but simply some thought:

Why is there so much hunger and starvation in the world?
Because we eat too much.

Why is there cancer in the world?
Because the guy who God gave the ability to cure it is reupholstering cars because he couldn't get out of the hood and attain a decent education.

Why is there war in the world?
Because people make weapons and bombs.

Why are there homeless in the world?
Because we don't share our homes with them.

What does God will of us?
To be ALL we were created to be.

What is the ultimate promise of God?
The best is yet to come.

When is the promise of God going to be fulfilled?
Now. Yesterday and tomorrow don't exist.

What is the most effective way to live?
Affectively.

Why did God allow me to live today?
So the Lord could love you through it (and love others through you).

Why do people die?
Who wants to live forever?

If Church sacraments are "encounters of Christ" in the present, what is the greatest sacrament?
The Now.

How many sacraments are there?
The Church teaches that there are seven. The Holy Spirit teaches that if there are one billion Christians, there is the potential for one billion Christ's sacraments.

Who are the best priests you have ever met?
The laity.

Who have been the most Christlike people you've experienced?
My Jewish friends.

In what churches have you felt God's presence the most?
Hospitals, prisons, the hood, Nate 'n Al's Delicatessen

What holy places have you experienced as disappointing?
The Holy Land, Vatican City, parish rectories.

Where is this "New Jerusalem" to be found?
First, in your own heart.
Secondly, in your homes.
Thirdly, in the poor (if not in your own poverty).
Fourthly, in your enemy.

Where is the loveliest altar you've ever seen?
Your dining tables (if you have one).

What is the greatest Eucharist you've ever been to?
Dinner at your house, especially when you can't afford a dining-room table.

Who are the hardest working pastors in the world?
Moms and dads.

What do you think is the major ministry in a capitalistic society?
To make the marketplace a holy place.

What are the greatest miracles you've ever experienced?
Allen and Kathy Lund; Matt, Sue, Clay, and Brynne Young; Kathleen Jones; Ruby Aklamake; Shirley Jackson; Jean Guelpa; Joe Galvan; Brother Tom Shadyac; Kelsey Grammer; Lou Marino; Ashley Merryman; Ana and Herminio Zuniga; Joe and Lori Sikorra; Grover Thornton Jr.; Mike Armbruster and Andy Chi; Wilkie Au; Dr. Tim Burke; Johnathon Schaeck; Lyn Parker; Lady Marion; Jack and Patt Shea . . . plus thousands of others.

Generally speaking, who are the greatest miracle workers you've ever seen?
The poor helping the poor.

What is the most obvious consequence of sin that you've ever experienced?
American politics, exclusivity in religions, reality TV.

What is the most common sin you seem to encounter?
Ambition: people trying to be God. We're all guilty of that one!

Who is the biggest sinner you've ever known?
Since I only know about myself, that would have to be me, I guess.

What is the thing that everyone seems to want and can't get enough of?
Trying to be God.

Why does God not answer everyone's prayers?
I don't know. He's God! Ask Him!

What is the greatest obstacle to true happiness?
Individualism (i.e., lack of concern for the common good).

What is the ultimate goal of ministry?
To point out what and where God is—and what YOU are.

What is the apparent goal of religion?
To point out what is not *God. (The only way we know to get to heaven is to keep out of hell which we know all too clearly.)*

What is the one message that God wants us to hear?
You are beloved. I believe in you.

What is the greatest question you have for Christians, today?
If living a Christian life were illegal, would there be enough evidence to convict us? (And going to church doesn't count).

What is the one message that people don't want to hear?
You are beloved. I believe in you.

Why do religions instill the fear of God in people?
Because it is the motivation that works the most. (Get off your butt, we need the pew!)

What is the greatest ministry you've ever experienced?
Marriage.

What is the biggest problem with empowering people to minister?
Getting them to show up, and not on Sunday!

What is God's greatest gift to us?
Freedom of the will.

Why do people choose not to love God, self, and others?
Freedom of the will.

Where do I go if I am not being empowered at my local church?
Somewhere else. Going to church is not as important as being church.

Why do bad things happen to good people?
So bad people can someday see how good they can be.

Where is the cheapest retreat house you've ever been to?
Your backyard.

What if I don't have a backyard?
Climb into bed and pull the sheets over your head. (It works for me!)

Where is the cheapest retreat house away from home that you've ever been to?
Any Motel 6.

What spiritual book are you reading now?
The Enduring Heart, *by Wilkie Au. (I've read it eight times.)*

Why are there so few priests today?
We can look so passionless!

What are the best movies showing the saving power of God?
Beauty and the Beast, Elephant Man, On Golden Pond, American Beauty, Shoes of the Fisherman, Bruce Almighty, *and* Jungle Book.

What are the worse movies showing the saving power of God?
The Ten Commandments, The Bible.

Why do priests wear black?
It makes us look thin.

Why are cathedrals so big?
It's a male thing. Do the math:
Big Hands + Big Feet + No Sugar = Big Cathedrals!

What's smaller than a teeny weenie flea?
A flea's teeny weenie.

And yes, finally,

Why is the Church having so many problems?
Men run it.

Allow me to explain.

The day when Adam bit the apple and subsequently screwed everything up, he went for a walk by himself, now walking with his "off the rack" fig leaf. God appeared to Adam and said, "Adam, we're not having a good day, are we?"

"No we're not," said Adam. Adam continued. "Hey God!"

"Yes, Adam," He replied.

"Why did you make Eve so beautiful?"

"So you'd like her, Adam."

"Why did you give Eve such beautiful eyes?"

"So you'd like her, Adam."

"Why did you give her such luscious lips?"

"So you'd like her, Adam."

"Why did you give her such nice breasts?"

"So you'd like her, Adam."

"Hey God!" Adam persisted. "In light of the bad day we're having, why did you make Eve so damn stupid?"

God responded:

"So she'd like you, Adam!"

Buckets of Love,
Ken